Useful Gaming Web Sites

Information sites

Blues News	www.bluesnews.com
GameSpy	www.gamespy.com
Gaming Events	www.gamingevents.com
GameSpot	www.gamespot.com
Planets Web sites	Examples include www.planetquake.com, www.planettribes.com, and so on.

Game Vendor Sites

Microsoft	www.microsoft.com/games
Activision	www.activision.com
Electronic Arts	www.ea.com
Sierra	www.sierra.com
id Software	www.idsoftware.com
Interplay	www.interplay.com

Player Linking Sites

MPlayer	www.mplayer.com
Heat.net	www.heat.net
MSN Gaming Zone	www.zone.com
Def-Con Online	www.def-con.net
Kali Inc.	www.kali.net/

Cheats and Hints

PC Game World	www.pcgameworld.com/cheats/
GameZone	www.gamezone.com/hints/hints.asp
Chapter Cheats	www.chapter.cheatguide.com
Cheat Index	www.cheatindex.com/index2.html
Cheater's Guild	www.cheater-guild.com/index.asp

Hardware Information and Review Sites

Tom's Hardware Guide	www.tomshardware.com
Sharky Extreme	www.sharkyextreme.com
Thresh's Firing Squad	www.firingsquad.com

cut here

Hardware Vendors

3DFX	www.3dfx.com
NVidia	www.nvidia.com
Creative Labs	www.creativelabs.com
Aureal	www.a3d.com
Matrox	www.matrox.com

Driver Software Downloads

3D Files	3dfiles.com
WinDrivers.com	www.WinDrivers.com
DriverHQ	www.driverhq.com
WinFiles.com	www.winfiles.com
DriverZone	www.driverzone.com

LAN Party Sites

LAN Party	www.lanparty.com
The LAN Party Coalition	www.lanpartycoalition.com
The LAN Party Ring	www.bangg.org/lanring
LanWar	www.lanwar.com
Quake Con	www.quakecon.com
Battle Connection	www.battlecon.com

Other Useful Sites

Yahoo Clubs	clubs.yahoo.com
ICQ	www.mirabilis.com
AIM	www.aol.com/aim
Hotmail free email	www.hotmail.com

One last tip...

Are you feeling lucky? There's a good chance you can find your game in part of the "Planet" Web site ring. Try typing http://www.planet*yourgamename*.com/, and where *yourgamename* is insert the name of the game you're interested in. For example, Planet Quake is at www.planetquake.com.

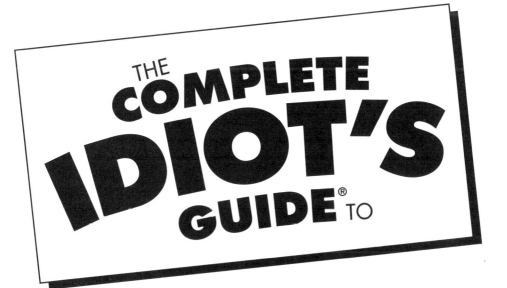

THE COMPLETE IDIOT'S GUIDE® TO

Playing Games Online

Loyd Case

A Division of Macmillan USA
201 West 103rd Street, Indianapolis, Indiana 46290

The Complete Idiot's Guide to Playing Games Online

Copyright © 2000 by Que Corporation

International Standard Book Number: 0-7897-2223-2

Library of Congress Catalog Card Number: 99-64764

Printed in the United States of America

First Printing: July 2000

02 01 00   4 3 2 1

Trademarks

Warning and Disclaimer

Associate Publisher
Greg Wiegand

Acquisitions Editor
Stephanie J. McComb

Development Editor
Gregory Harris

Technical Editor
John Ray

Managing Editor
Thomas F. Hayes

Project Editor
Leah Kirkpatrick

Copy Editor
Kay Hoskin

Indexer
Greg Pearson

Proofreader
Benjamin Berg

Illustrator
Judd Winick

Team Coordinator
Sharry Gregory

Interior Designer
Nathan Clement

Cover Designer
Michael Freeland

Production
Steve Geiselman

Contents at a Glance

Contents

ix

Introduction

To Start It All Off...

If you're reading this right now, you're one of two types of people. Either you're a computer gamer or you want to be a computer gamer. In either case, I hope you'll find this book incredibly useful. If you're new to the computer gaming world, what you find in this book will help you get acquainted with nearly all aspects of multi-player gaming; over the Internet, over a LAN, or even by attending a LAN Party. We're going to cover how to get connected, what hardware is best, what games are dominating the computer gaming world, how to meet other gamers, going to LAN Parties, creating or linking up with a clan or tribe, and much more. If any of these terms are throwing you for a loop, don't worry. By the end of this book, you'll know exactly what each term means.

If you're a veteran gamer, this book will also be useful to you. It will be your concise and complete (well, as complete as I can make it) catalog of valuable information that you usually spend an hour or so on Infoseek or AltaVista searching for. Inside you'll find information on the best LAN Parties, the toughest clans and tribes, the Web addresses for all the major game vendors, tips on gaming hardware and software utilities, and more. Don't let the title *Complete Idiot's Guide* fool you. There's stuff here for newbies and veterans alike.

Throughout this book you'll also find comments from dozens of gamers about gaming strategies, the best Web sites to check out, the best LAN Parties to attend, how to tweak your computer to run its best, and more. Let's face it. I may be a gamer but I don't know all there is to gaming. I do (unfortunately) have to get offline and go to work in the morning. And admittedly, there are other people out there who are (cough) better than me at a few games. You'll get to read their own words and learn from their insight. If you're a veteran gamer, you might just recognize the names of the people spouting these words of wisdom as an arch nemesis or a fellow clan member.

The online multiplayer world exploded with the debut of a little game that set the scene on its ear. It was called Doom. It's rare that you can point to a single, definitive event that directs the evolution of an industry like you can with the release of Doom by id Software. You can't look back and say, "Oh yeah, WordStar. Now *there* was the father of all word processors." That just won't happen. But Doom's release in December of 1993 was the starting point of all contemporary online gaming. And by starting the gaming revolution you might also make a point that Doom helped get computer technology going at its incredibly accelerated pace. No other aspect of computing drives technology to new heights like gaming.

Doom started online gaming before the Internet was in full swing. This meant that although Doom had the ability to allow people to connect with other people and play head to head, their options were fairly limited to do so. You either dialed up with your modem to another gamer, which only allowed you to play one on one, or you packed up the old computer and hefted it over to a friend's house where all of your friends were congregating for a Saturday of network mayhem. In that sense, online meant LAN connectivity and not the Internet.

Shortly thereafter came the IPX wizard Jay Cotton, who wrote a little application called Kali that allowed games like Doom to link up over the Internet. Back then, when the Internet was far less congested than it is now, it was actually possible to dial up with a 9,600 baud modem and successfully play a four-player game of Doom with your buddies over the Internet. That ability enabled people from all over the world to begin playing against each other. Until then, most gaming companies paid little attention to creating multiplayer games. Once id Software set the example, everyone got on the bandwagon and an explosion of multiplayer games found life on the market.

Though Kali is still around today, its functionality has been made slightly obsolete due to the fact that most multiplayer games released today have a native ability to connect up with other gamers playing the same game. Once we get talking about that we'll be bouncing around terms like IPX, TCP/IP, frame type, address, and so on. All these terms refer to how a game actually connects with another copy of the same game on another machine whether that be over a local area network or the Internet.

Today, multiplayer gaming is a *huge* industry with dozens of companies releasing more than 100 games each year. Evolved around those games are followings of loyal players who spend their evenings and weekends linking up with each other to commit electronic carnage. The gaming community is one that spans thousands of Web sites and encompasses hundreds of thousands of people who call themselves gamers. And, the numbers are growing each week. The enthusiasm has grown to such a degree that the masses have spilled out of the Internet and are starting to creep into hotel conference rooms, university auditoriums, and almost any place with enough power to support dozens if not hundreds of gamers for a weekend of LAN Party action. Anywhere you see a dimly lit room with network cables strung between boxes of flashing amber and green diodes you can bet that the place is filled with computer gamers.

That's the whole reason for this book. If you're new to the world of online gaming read on and ye shall find enlightenment. If you're a veteran of the realm, ye shall find familiar names and places and have with you a resource to make your travels quick and easy.

How to Use This Book

We're going to cover a wide range of topics throughout the course of this book. When it's all over, you should be able to consider yourself well versed in all topics relating to online gaming.

This book is organized into five sections. The sections are laid out in such an order that if you're not already a gaming guru, you'll be able to easily follow along with the topics covered. It's a big gaming world out there and it's easy to get lost without a proper guide.

The first section, *The Basics*, covers the basics of online gaming such as the hardware you need, the Web sites to bookmark, how to meet people, and so on. The second section, *The Big Fight*, is the bulk of the book and covers what you want to know about all the major shooter games and real-time strategy games currently on the market. The third section, *Becoming Someone Else*, continues the discussion of specific games but looks at the niche of role-playing games, which has become a major subgenre of the gaming world. The forth section, *Simulations Galore and the Oldies*, covers simulation-based games such as sports games, flight sims, and card games. The final section, *The Gaming Community*, covers the world of gaming: the places to be, attending LAN Parties, the utilities necessary to get around, and much more.

Part 1—The Basics

This section covers the preliminary things you need to know to be an informed gamer. New gamers will benefit from the information in this section concerning such things as the best areas on the Internet for gaming info, how to optimize your connection, how to build a better gaming machine, and introducing you to the major game makers.

Chapter 1—"The Multiplayer Gaming World." This chapter will familiarize you with the concepts of online gaming. Here you'll learn what kind of people are gamers and just why they stay up late at night trying to get the last kill. You'll also learn about the terms and lingo used by gamers. This section will also introduce you to the major game vendors and just what goodies they produce.

Chapter 2—"Your Connection to Other Gamers." This chapter delves into the oh so murky region of just how to connect. The term *connect* can mean different things to different people. This chapter will look at connecting via the Internet, a LAN, or even person to person through a serial connection.

Chapter 3—"The Gaming Hardware You Need." Ah… The bane of my existence. This chapter will examine gaming hardware. I also affectionately subtitle this chapter "Why I'm always in debt." Video cards, memory, motherboards, CPUs, sound cards, joysticks, and much more will be looked at here.

Chapter 4—"The Online World of the Internet." Here we're going to look at the places on the Internet that make the gaming world alive with people. Gaming Web sites such as the GameSpy Network, MPlayer, Won.Net, and others will be looked at. I'll also cover Web sites dedicated to clan organization and talk about how you can best set up a Web site dedicated to your gaming clan.

Part 2—The Big Fight

Once we have all the preliminary stuff out of the way, it's time to get down and dirty and talk about the best of bash fest and the hottest and heaviest RTS (real-time strategy) games on the market. This section will look at individual games and it will also give tips and technique hints on how to best play each game. You'll hear from me and other gamers about the games covered here. First-Person Shooters like Half-Life, Quake, Unreal, and Tribes will be covered and RTS games like Age of Empires, Tiberian Sun, Dark Reign, and Home World will be looked at as well.

Don't think this section is going to be just warm and fuzzy comments about all the games covered. I think some of these games stink and I'm not shy about saying so. Each game will have easy to view stats on things, such as how complicated it is, whether it supports 3D acceleration, how reliable its multiplayer engine is over the Internet, and so on.

Chapter 5—"First-Person Shooters." Annie git yer gun and let's go out to the shootin' range! This chapter will look at all the bloodiest shooters like Quake, Half-Life, Tribes, Shogo, Dark Forces, Rainbow 6, Alien Versus Predator and many others.

Chapter 6—"Real-Time Strategy Games." All right General, it's time to look at the big board. This chapter will cover all the best RTS games like Battle Zone, Age of Empires, Tiberian Sun, Total Annihilation, Dark Reign, and many others.

Chapter 7—"Mech Games." Although a small niche in the gaming world, Mech games like Star Siege, Mech Warrior, and Heavy Gear have a loyal following and are pretty entertaining multiplayer games. This chapter will look at these games.

Part 3—Becoming Someone Else

Let's face it. Most of us techno-geeks double as role-playing gamers. The gaming vendors have picked up on this and have created games that allow us to become someone (or something) else. Games like the incredibly popular Diablo (which is still selling for the customary $39.95 at my local CompUSA more than two years after its initial release), Darkstone, Baldur's Gate, Might and Magic, and so on, are all based on the concept that you're going to be playing a character in a story. Unlike most other multiplayer games, these games are more entertaining when you play cooperatively with other players rather than against them.

This section will also look at persistent universe games like EverQuest, Ultima Online, Asheron's Call, and others. These games are played completely online via a service you have to drop a few bucks on each month but they open the door to worlds populated by thousands of others gamers and offer a much more complete experience.

Chapter 8—"Personal Role-Playing Games." This chapter will look at multiplayer games that can be played independently on your home computer and don't require an additional service. These games include Diablo, Baldur's Gate, Darkstone, Might and Magic, Dungeon Keeper, and others.

Chapter 9—"Persistent Universe Role-Playing Games." This chapter will look at online services that provide a role playing experience via the Internet. These games include EverQuest, Asheron's Call, and Ultima Online. These games cannot be played unless you are on the Internet.

Part 4—Simulations Galore and the Oldie

If sports are your gig, this section will let you know which games are the best when it comes to multiplayer gaming. This chapter will also look at flight sims, tank sims, and all other popular military-type simulation-based games. And, because it doesn't really fit anywhere else, we're going to also look at some of the gaming classics in this section like Doom, Duke Nukem 3D, Command and Conquer, and one of my personal oldie favorites, Redneck Rampage.

Chapter 10—"Online Sports Gaming." So real you'll almost blow out your knee (but it'll probably be after trying to get up after being in front of your computer for six hours straight). We'll look at football sims, baseball sims, racing sims, and fishing sims (a niche that your humble author admits to being hooked on—hahahaha. Whoops, time to increase the Prozac again.)

Chapter 11—"Online Simulation Games." There's nothing like trying your hand at taking an Apache AH64 into combat to see if you've got what it takes (which apparently I don't). This chapter will look at the best military oriented sims on the market. Games like Jane's Longbow, Microsoft Flight Simulator, and Air Warrior will be covered along with many others.

Chapter 12—"Online Card Gaming Sites." Strangely enough, online card gaming is a big deal on the Internet (hahaha, I guess I shouldn't have taken that extra Prozac with vodka). Gaming sites like Microsoft's Gaming Zone and Yahoo are always filled will gamers playing things like Hearts and Spades through all hours of the day and night. This chapter will look at this genre of multiplayer gaming.

Chapter 13—"Oldies but Goodies." Ah for the good old days of DOS and Doom. This chapter will cover the games that began this multiplayer revolution. Don't let their age fool you. They're still viable games and are a hoot to play.

Part 5—The Gaming Community

After you read all about the games that are out there, you need to know about the community of players that plays them. This section will introduce you to areas of the Internet that cater to the gaming community. It will also introduce you to the idea of LAN Parties and actually taking your computer to someplace where other gamers are gathering. We'll also look at important software utilities such as Kali, GameSpy, Roger Wilco, and others that help gamers get connected.

Chapter 14—"Other Important Online Sites." This section will cover important Internet sites that gamers need to know about. Sites like where to get the most recent hardware drivers, where to find other gamers to talk to and get advice from, where to find game updates or reviews of games, and much more. There are thousands of voices talking about online gaming. This chapter will help you locate the best ones.

Chapter 15—"Online Competition." If you want to test your skills against other players, there are plenty of ways to do that. This chapter will look at Internet sites dedicated to ranked gamers or organizing competitions between players. We'll look at the idea of a *ladder* and how you can start your climb to the top.

Chapter 16—"The Phenomenon of LAN Parties." Online gaming has spilled out of the Internet and into garages and hotel conference rooms. This chapter will look at the relatively new development of LAN Parties and what people do when they get together for a weekend of gaming fun. Just as *Star Trek* conventions exploded in the early '70s, computer gaming conventions are poised to do the same thing.

Chapter 17—"Online Gaming Utilities." This chapter will look at the tools of the trade. Utilities like Kali, GameSpy, Roger Wilco, AOL Instant Messenger, ICQ, and others that help gamers get connected and talk to one another.

At the end of the book, you'll find a few appendixes dedicated to such topics as The Future of Online Gaming, Cheaters: How to Spot Them and Avoid Them, Gaming-Related Publications, and Macs in the Online Gaming World.

Conventions Used in This Book

Throughout this book, you'll run into reoccurring items. These are sidebar callouts that point to items of special interest. These include:

Tech Tip

Tech Tip—A sidebar that points out special information relating to a technical matter. This could be something like how to improve a game's performance, how to do something special on the Internet, and so on.

Lingo

Lingo—A sidebar that points out a definition, a term, or phrase related to online gaming.

Note

Note—A sidebar that points out general special information. This might also contain a warning or a tip about a game or utility.

Gamer Comment

Gamer Comment—A sidebar by someone in the gaming community about nearly any topic. These will be the most common sidebars in the book. This book contains dozens of comments from real gamers. These might be advice, a personal story, or a criticism of some kind.

Tell Us What You Think!

As the reader of this book, *you* are our most important critic and commentator. We value your opinion and want to know what we're doing right, what we could do better, what areas you'd like to see us publish in, and any other words of wisdom you're willing to pass our way.

As associate publisher for Que, I welcome your comments. You can fax, email, or write me directly to let me know what you did or didn't like about this book—as well as what we can do to make our books stronger.

Please note that I cannot help you with technical problems related to the topic of this book, and that due to the high volume of mail I receive, I might not be able to reply to every message.

When you write, please be sure to include this book's title and author as well as your name and phone or fax number. I will carefully review your comments and share them with the author and editors who worked on the book.

Fax: 317-581-4666

Email: consumer@mcp.com

Mail: Greg Wiegand
          Que
          201 West 103rd Street
          Indianapolis, IN 46290 USA

Part 1

The Basics

Let's get things rolling. In Part 1, we're going to look at the basics of online gaming. We're going to look at the people in the gaming world, their connections to each other, the hardware they use, and the places they frequent. We're going to look at what the term online *means. Many people consider online to just mean the Internet but in gaming terms, online can mean quite a bit more.*

If you're serious about gaming, performance matters—a lot. This is true of almost all game genres. So we'll walk you through some of the hardware performance issues you'll need to know . It's hard to keep up with the hardware of the gaming world. It changes at lightning speed it seems. I have always said that computer gaming is the main force that drives computer upgrades. In Part 1 you'll learn why this statement is true.

And finally, we'll examine in depth the places on the Internet that unify the gaming world and drive its development forward. So many new online gaming sites are popping up on the Internet every day that it's hard to keep track of them all. I'll show you the ones that I think will be around for a while and which are the best to bookmark.

Sit back and read on, intrepid gamer!

Chapter 1

The Multiplayer Gaming World

In This Chapter

➤ What type of a place is the gaming world?

➤ Who are online gamers?

➤ Gaming lingo you should know

➤ The software companies making games and utilities

Just what kind of world is the gaming world? Well, it's a big place that's getting bigger every day. People of all shapes, sizes, ages, and ambitions roam its electronic hallways. You'll find 10-year old kids whomping the tar out of veteran gamers that have been in the realm for years (much like me). There are people driving old clunkers down the road with nothing more than an old Pentium 90 under the hood and there are people ripping up the asphalt with Athlon 1 GHz systems. Some gamers do little more than come home from work or school and sit down in front of their computer for hours on end and bash pixels until they can't stay awake any longer. Some just play now and then when they get together with their friends. Most are somewhere in the middle.

The online gaming world really isn't that old when you look at it in depth. Doom was released at the end of 1993. That's only about six years ago. Obviously there were other forms of online gaming long before then. Before Doom, online gaming really took the form of MUDs (MultiUser Dungeons) on the Internet and BBS (Bulletin Board System) games like Tradewars, Land of Devastation, Solar Realms Elite, and others. MUDs are online chat role-playing games and old BBS doors are usually some kind of text-based game where only one person at a time could play. Still, for their low-end eye-candy appeal, MUDs and doors caused tons of gamers to dial into the Internet or their local BBSs and blaze the trail for the future of multiplayer gaming.

I take a pretty liberal view of the term *"online gaming"*. To me, online gaming is any form of gaming that connects players together. That can be over a LAN, over a serial connection, over a direct modem connection, over the Internet, over an office network RAS connection (if you can keep the network admins from catching on), or between two tin cans glued to your CPU with a string stretched between them (yeah, that's at 300 baud but it does have data compression enabled). Obviously most people think of the Internet when the phrase "online gaming" comes up in conversation. But, as you'll see throughout this book, online gaming is really any form of multi-player gaming. The society that has evolved around multiplayer gaming has begun to significantly extend beyond the shores of the Internet and into things like this book, living rooms packed with friends, and hotel conference rooms stuffed with a couple hundred people for weekends of fun.

In this chapter, I'm going to try and set the stage for you. I'm going to get you familiar with the people, places, lingo, and game makers in the online world. Somewhere in there you're going to find your place. If you're already familiar with the realm you might just recognize some of the things discussed here.

The Internet World

The Internet has been around for a while now, even longer than online gaming, although you'll find some folks now who primarily only use the Internet as just a gaming conduit. The Internet allows people from all over the planet to link up with each other to chat, send email, check out gaming Web sites, and even game together. It's the veins that carry the blood of the online gamer, but it also carries the bits and bytes of millions of non-gamers too. It's both a blessing and a curse depending on how clogged your connection may be—and believe me, I'm usually more cursed than blessed.

Gamers on the Internet tend to be a little more technically savvy than the average Internet user. They know how to make the connections necessary to game through and they know the best places to frequent to find out the latest information. They tend to stay online longer and put more pressure on the Internet pathways than your average Internet user. Let's face it. Online games today are getting more and more bandwidth hungry. It's getting tough to make your average modem connection to the Internet work for gaming purposes. Luckily the options for high-speed connections are growing both in scope and availability. ISDN, DSL, and cable modems are all becoming viable options for a good percentage of gamers. Don't know what these acronyms mean? Don't worry. In Chapter 2, "Your Connection to Other Gamers," I'll give you all the information you need to know about your pipe to the Internet.

All throughout the Internet, you'll find gaming stops. You'll find software companies, commercially run gaming sites, player run gaming sites, gaming servers running specific games for people to connect to, LAN Party sites, clan sites, and more. Some ISPs (Internet service providers) are even branching out their services and are offering dedicated gaming servers for players to connect to as part of their overall service package for customers. Gaming has really taken hold and become a viable business opportunity for a lot of people.

In the early days of multiplayer gaming, most games used a connection protocol known as IPX. This was the most commonly used networking protocol before the Internet became the force that it is today. A protocol is just a way that two devices talk to each other, much like two humans do when they first meet. There's a handshake, a "hello" and a sequence of spoken words that alternately pass back and forth between the people communicating, and then a goodbye. Mixed in there is the language that is spoken, body language, vocal inflection, and so on. Networking protocols are very similar. Both ends have to speak the same language, know how to receive information from the other side, and know how to end the session.

TCP/IP started out in the academic world where it was developed and put to use in the fledgling new world of the Internet (and no, Al Gore did not invent the Internet). In the 1970s mostly just universities and government agencies were part of the Internet. You might be asking how do all these places on the Internet physically link up with each other? It's all well and good to talk about protocols but what does that protocol travel over?

The Internet is an ethereal concept. It doesn't refer to a unified set of wires or cables connecting every point on the network. The physical side of the Internet actually exists in several different ways. There are several major hubs or routing points on the Internet. Most of these routing points are in the United States and are linked to each other via extremely high capacity lines. These lines are provided by the government and by commercial companies that were contracted to help develop the Internet. This set of core lines and routing points is known as the "backbone" of the Internet and is maintained by several large communication companies such as MCI and Sprint. In the early days of the Internet (mid 70s through the 80s) new networks were allowed to join directly with the backbone. In 1995 new networks were no longer permitted to join directly with the backbone and people and companies had to begin buying their connectivity from existing hosts. This began the *ISP (Internet service provider)* revolution and hundreds of companies began reselling connectivity.

Communication companies such as AT&T, MCI, and Sprint are in the business of installing new communication lines and linking people and places together. It's on their lines that the Internet has grown. These lines are known as *leased lines* and can range in capacity from 1.5Mbps per second to 45Mbps per second and beyond. Companies lease these lines from one of these major communication providers and the lines are connected between two points. For example, if "The Really Big Bank, Inc." wanted to lease a line and get on the Internet, they would need to do two things; contact someone who could lease them the physical line and then contact someone who could sell them the connectivity to the Internet. Now, most of the major communication companies can provide both, if necessary, but they can also just provide the line and let companies get their Internet connectivity from someone else. In those latter cases, the line that is leased by The Really Big Bank, Inc. would be routed between the bank and the ISP they have chosen. All sorts of good stuff like network addresses, domain names, routing tables, and such get thrown into that mix but the general connectivity concept is pretty straightforward. Buy your line, pay someone to give you access to the Internet, and there you go.

Now, obviously your average home user doesn't have to buy a line and get permanently hooked up to be on the Internet. The other major form of connectivity comes as a standard analog or modem connection to someone who is on the Internet. These dial in points are known as *ISPs* or *providers* who sell dial-up accounts for those home users who want Internet access. ISPs are a dime a dozen these days. You can't swing a dead cat without hitting one it seems. There are local providers, national providers, mom-and-pop shops, and more. Being an ISP is a big competitive business these days, mostly due to the ease of setting it up and getting going. In Chapter 2 we'll discuss how to choose the right provider for gaming and how to tell if they have the performance you need to game successfully.

So, we have the Internet and people are jumping on and off all the time. The Internet is continuing to grow at a rapid pace, which is causing some serious congestion problems. Providers are keen on making as much money as they can which generally results in them overselling their capacity. A lot of people are really excited about the new forms of high-speed connectivity that are becoming available in many areas but it worries me a lot. If you have 20 people connecting to an ISP at 56kbps, that's a maximum theoretical data pull of about 1.12Mbps. Your average small time ISP with a single T1 line (a leased line with a capacity of 1.5Mbps) can easily handle this level of a load. But, if those 20 people have the capacity to pull data from the ISP at 128kbps (the speed of a dual channel ISDN connection) that overall data pull becomes 2.56Mbps which would exceed the capacity of the ISP. That creates lag and that's something I'll define later in this chapter. Time will tell if the Internet structure is able to handle the increased end user connectivity speeds that are becoming available in many areas. But, if you increase the end user speeds you have to increase the ISP speed back to the backbone.

That's a general overview of the Internet and its situation today. As a gamer, you should be aware of the issues that are involved in selecting a good ISP. If you get your service from an overloaded ISP, your online gaming experience is not going to be a pleasant one.

The LAN World

While the Internet was developing rapidly in the '80s, so was the world of private networks. The hardware was becoming reasonably priced and ease of use was becoming greater. The practicality of networks also grew. Businesses began to realize that they could benefit from interoffice email and the ability to transfer data between employees. By the start of the '90s, nearly all major companies connected their employees together with interoffice networks.

The IPX protocol was the language spoken over these private network lines. All hail Novell! In the '80s, Novell was the leader in private networking solutions although there were other companies like LANtastic and Banyan that also made their presence known. Because of Novell's dominance in the market and their reliance on IPX as the de facto network protocol used on private networks, it makes sense that the connectivity of early multiplayer games would be based on IPX protocol so that they could be played over IPX-based networks. Early on, little thought was given to gaming over the Internet. The two pieces of the puzzle, gaming and the Internet, hadn't been tested to see if they fit together.

As we got into the mid '90s, private networking wasn't just something that companies did to connect their employees together. The price of network hardware had fallen and with the introduction of Windows 95 in August of 1995, it literally became a no-brainer to link two computers together if you had the right hardware. By default, if Windows 95 found networking hardware it would install all the necessary components needed to connect to another computer via the IPX protocol. Of course it snuck in the Microsoft client alongside the Novell client but that generally didn't cause problems at least for gamers. So, for 40 bucks for a network card and 100 bucks for mini-hub, you could get connected to your buddy's computer in a few minutes. In fact, you could get connected to a lot of your buddies depending on how many ports your mini-hub had. Ah what to do, what to do….

I know! Let's play Doom and kill each other! Everybody over at my place next Saturday and bring your computer!

I know a lot of gamers who began just like this. Doom was released at the end of 1993, well before Windows 95 was released. That means that any home networking you wanted to do would have to be done through DOS, which was a little intimidating for many people. That's why Doom's release at the end of 1993 didn't really spark a major multiplayer revolution. It was just too tough for many people to set up their home machines to connect with another system.

Windows 95 changed all that and made it easy for novices to hook up. By the time Windows 95 made it onto the scene, Id had already released Doom II, the sequel to Doom. Another factor that drove multiplayer gaming were the online flight sim squadrons. These were driven by game titles like Falcon 3.0, which had leading edge support for multiplayer, cooperative dynamic campaigns. Many groups of diehard gamers would get together every weekend and hook up their computers for some rocket launching or mega-missile fun. Wives were miffed and many hours of sleep were lost. It was the start of the LAN party revolution though it would take a few more years before it would grow beyond the confines of living rooms and garages.

Another major environment that fueled the network gaming craze was found on college campuses. Many college students enjoy the luxury of having network connections in their dorm rooms. If they don't have network connections available in their dorm rooms, students can often be found working in computer labs on college campuses that are interconnected with networking hardware. And of course, nothing except schoolwork ever goes on in a college computer lab. Uh huh. Sure.

College campuses were perhaps one of the few places you could find people playing Doom or Descent against each other on a large scale before the introduction of Windows 95. Everyone else had to do it the hard way and lug their computer over to a friend's house or worse yet, have their house invaded by all their friends and their computers and have their circuit breaker panel abused by the excessive power load. Much to the consternation of lab administrators, lab machines quickly found themselves loaded to the max with Doom and Descent and network bandwidth clogged with gaming traffic.

Whether you were a college student sneaking in a game of Doom in the nearest computer lab, an employee staying late to whack your buddies in a game of Descent over the company network, or you hefted your system over to a friend's house for a Saturday of gaming fun, it was clear that the mid-90s was the start of a permanent trend in computer gaming. Just a few years later, the first thing many people look for when shopping for a new computer game is whether or not the box says "Multiplayer Ready". Game manufacturers know this and almost every game that is made today is designed to connect to another copy of itself over the Internet, a LAN, a serial cable, or head-to-head with a straight modem connection.

Who Are Online Gamers?

Who are online gamers? That's a pretty wide open question. It used to be that just your hardcore geeks were the ones willing to risk the white water world of setting up a LAN connection or an Internet connection to game over. In the early days, it was quite a chore to get two machines to talk to each other in the right way so that they could game together. Heck, I still go to LAN Parties and see people with their computer cases pulled off and a look of frustration on their mugs.

But, anymore, almost anyone can rub two sticks together and make an IPX or TCP/IP connection. Windows 95 and 98 have opened up a whole new world to novice computer users. I know that the Mac-heads and Linux-goons out there always rail against Windows but I have both a Mac and Linux machine sitting in my den at home and I'm fairly decent with both. But when push comes to shove, I generally reach for the Windows 98 machine to do what I need to. Perhaps that will change in a few years but right now, Windows gets the nod for ease of use.

So, just who are these people? Heck, who are you? Where do you fit in with this diverse crowd? Are you a newbie or are you a veteran? Do you have a Ferrari or a Volkswagen? Do you eat macaroni and cheese five times a week so you can save up enough money to buy the next hottest title? Let's just see where you fit in.

The Kids

I'm not just talking about the child prodigies who were born with a slide rule in one hand and a Nintendo controller in the other. As much as you might think, the gaming world is not overly packed with kids. No one that I know of has really done a study on what percentage of online gamers fall into what age bracket but I would guess that kids under the age of 16 make up around 20% to 30% of the online gaming population. I'd really like to get a gander at some demographics studies that some of the big gaming companies have done to see how right I am.

Most younger gamers find their time dedicated to one of the popular console systems available. Console Systems are devices such as Nintendo 64, Sega Saturn, Sony Playstation, Sega Dreamcast, and so on. These are the gaming systems that hook up to the TV. For a couple hundred bucks for the console and a couple hundred for a decent TV, a kid can have a great gaming system. That may be $400 for something to play games on but it's a lot better than $2,000 for a complete computer system. Dang those parents for thinking with their checkbooks. But, things are looking up. Even the major console gaming system manufacturers are acknowledging the power of online gaming. The latest contender to the console system fight, the Sega Dreamcast system, comes with a built-in 56k modem and the ability to connect up to the Internet. Pretty soon little Johnny is going to be asking for his own phone line just like his sister.

That brings me to another big point. Online gamers are primarily male. It comes from the fact that most online games are by nature confrontational games and most females aren't really interested in that type of fun. It's that age-old difference thing coming into play. But, as you'll see in a little while, as some women mature a little, they develop a very manlike quality of wanting to whomp you good.

Most of the time it's very easy to spot younger online gamers. Their chat text may be a little slower than normal and the tone of their conversation is usually a little more abusive than an adult. That's not always the case. I have encountered many 13-year-olds that conduct themselves with a lot more civility than most adult gamers.

The Gamers at Work

I work as a support professional in Information Management for the company I'm employed by. Granted, the number of online gamers in my profession is statistically higher than in any other profession out there. In fact, we're pushing 90%. Let's face it. If you're a computer geek working in Information Management, most of your co-workers are going to be gamers. I go to many LAN Parties and almost all of them are run by people who work as technical support professionals with each other at the same company. It's sort of like a club.

The Gamers in College

Now we come to the bulk of the online gaming world: the college student. Mom and dad have bought him a computer to better his education and take to school. He's going to write reports and essays. He's going to use it to do research on the Internet. He's even going to use it to email mom and dad and thank them for buying him all the neat hardware. But, mom and dad are still wondering why their son asked for something called a "Voodoo 3000" video card and a "Sound Blaster Alive" audio card when the parental units bought the computer. Oh well, the salesman seemed to know what they were asking for so they tacked it on to the bill.

Now their son sits up all night hooked up to the dorm's direct T1 line to the Internet and games until the wee hours of the morning. While he's at class, he sets his new education tool to decode hundreds of megabytes of binary files from selected newsgroups of high educational value.

Male college students are the single largest gaming group in the online gaming world. I would conservatively estimate that 40% to 50% of online gamers are currently in college and many of them enjoy the status of being LPBs (Low Ping Bastards) because of high-speed connections to the Internet provided by the college they attend. Most of these gamers tend to be the best gamers because of a) their LPB status and b) their excessive "study time". Ahhh, for the life of a student.

It's in college that online gamers begin to develop the extended relationships with other gamers that lead to *clans* or *tribes* which are groups of gamers who game together as a unit in semi-serious competition settings. These groups of gamers tend to remain gamers from years to come after graduating and even sometimes for life (of course we haven't quite come that far in the gaming evolution but we will see if we're all still gaming in 50 years).

The Rest of Us

Who does that leave? That leaves the rest of us. Those people too old to be in high school or college and too young to retire our electronic gloves and be put out to pasture for stud duty. We have a little disposable income at our discretion because we do have full-time jobs and we also can stay up as late as we want as long as we're prepared to take the consequences (a firm chastising from the boss for another late arrival or worse yet, a brow beating from the wife for not coming to bed before 2 a.m.).

I'm a single guy in a married world. I work with a group of great people in the IM department of our company. We're all gamers to some degree—either casual or hardcore or somewhere in between. We tend to have lunch with each other a lot and the conversation of gaming pops up quite frequently. Whenever someone throws out a suggestion like "Hey, let's get online tonight and do some Tribes," inevitably there will be a chorus of replies of, "Oh, I don't know if I can make it tonight. I'll have to clear it with the wife first." I get no end of pleasure out of seeing my married friends hem and haw over being able to game. It's worse than they ever had it in high school or college. Hehehehe.

Another faction of gamers that is gaining numbers is the relatively small faction of female gamers. A lot of people tend to forget that women do sometimes jump online and want to work out some built up tension. Nothing better than getting online with your other female buddies and bashing some male heads. I have a good friend whose wife has an obsession with the game Carmageddon, one of the bloodiest, pedestrian killingest games there ever has been. It makes me nervous sometimes to think about it.

Although women gamers are still few and far between, they are making their presence known on the Internet. Later in Chapter 4, "The Online World of the Internet," we'll look at some of the Web sites dedicated to female-only gaming groups and how you can get more information about these folks. I'll admit I've had my clock cleaned by a few women at LAN Parties before. There's nothing inherently better about male gamers. Online gaming can be the great equalizer of the sexes.

Online Lingo You Should Know

If you're not much of a gamer yet, you may have a tough time understanding some of the jargon pitched around the newsgroups, message boards, or chat rooms on the Internet. The language that most gamers speak can be comprised of a lot of acronyms, slang terms, abbreviations, and new phrases that most people don't encounter very often in every day life. This List section in Table 1.1 will help familiarize you with some of those terms.

Table 1.1   Common Terms and Phrases of Online Gaming

Term/Phrase	Definition
Bandwidth	A measure of how much communication data can be carried by a connection method. This is usually measured in bits per second. High bandwidth = good. Low bandwidth = Hijack gets killed a lot.
Bot or AI player	A computer-controlled entity in a game. Most players like to warm up on a ro[Bot] or an [A]rtificially [I]ntelligent player and then move on to a real human opponent.
Camper	A gamer who tends to remain in one location waiting for goodies to reappear so that he or she can load up, or for opponents to reappear so they can take a cheap back shot. Camping is not looked at very kindly by die-hard gamers. It's akin to cheating.
Chat Abbreviations	Too numerous to list them all, some common chat abbreviations you might see online are: **BTW** (by the way), **IMHO** (in my humble opinion), **:-)** (a smiley—and expression of approval), **WTF** (what the heck—an expression of surprise, and no, the F doesn't really stand for heck), **OMG** (Oh my God), **NP** (No Problem), **LOL** (Laughing out Loud), and **BRB** (Be right back).
Chipset	Usually a reference to the brain of your video card although it can refer to chips on a motherboard, sound card, or nearly any other piece of computer hardware. The two most popular chipsets for video cards suited for gaming are made by NVidia (the TNT chipset series) and 3Dfx (the Voodoo chipset series). These two manufacturers are duking it out to see who can make the fastest chipset and gamers are reaping the benefits.

continues

11

Table 1.1 Continued

Term/Phrase	Definition
Clan	A group of gamers who game on the same side. You typically encounter clans in First-Person Shooter games like Tribes, Half-Life, Quake, Unreal, and so on. Clans are usually organized and each member will have a dedicated role to play (such as Defense, Offense, Repair, and so forth). Many clans have built their own Web sites dedicated to their gaming efforts.
Console Game	Game systems like Sega Dreamcast or Sony Playstation. An all-in-one gaming unit. Not really the topic of this book but something you should know about and the term used to describe it.
DirectX	An API layer within Windows that permits gaming applications to communicate directly with video and sound hardware in the computer without having to go through the Windows overhead. This permits games to increase performance to an acceptable level under Windows. The APIs consist of DirectDraw (2D and final display of 3D), Direct3D (3D pipeline), DirectSound (standard and positional 3D audio), DirectInput (game controllers), and DirectPlay (networking).
FPS	First-Person Shooter—A game like Quake, Half-Life, Tribes, Unreal, and so on. A game in which your point of view is "first-person" as though you were looking through the eyes (or cockpit) of the person (or vehicle) you are playing.
	FPS also stands for Frames Per Second. This acronym refers to the speed at which your video card can redraw the screen when gaming. Lower FPS will result in a poor display and a bad gaming experience.
Frag	To kill another player.
Frame rate	A speed measurement of how fast your video hardware can redraw a screen of information. Frame rates of 15 to 25 frames per second (FPS) are acceptable for average gaming to most people. Frame rates from 26 to 35 are considered good. The human eye has a hard time seeing any smoothness improvement over 30 FPS. Current video technology (as of the writing of this book) has put frame rates around 60 to 80 FPS for gaming. This may sound like overkill but frame rates this high allow games to begin drawing more complex video images. The more complex or dazzling the video output, the slower the frame rate. But, if you have room to take the FPS hit due to the more complex video display, you'll have a better gaming experience.

Term/Phrase	Definition
GLIDE	A method of communicating video instructions to your video card. This is also known as an API or Application Programming Interface and allows software to tell your video card what to draw. This programming interface was developed by the company 3Dfx and is commonly used on video hardware powered by the Voodoo chipset.
Lag	When data arrives late to a computer due to some delay in the connection. Lag is the enemy of all gamers. Different ISPs will suffer different amounts of lag depending on how congested their service is. Peak Internet times (5:00 p.m. until around 9:00 p.m.) will have the greatest amount of lag and are usually not good gaming times for most people.
LAN Party	A physical gathering of gamers who bring their computers to a central location for a day or weekend of LAN-based gaming. This might be someone's house, garage, or even a hotel conference room. LAN Parties are growing quickly in popularity. If you don't have a large one in your area currently, you probably will soon. Some are commercially run events but most are simply run by avid gamers with too much cash on their hands.
LPB	Low Ping Bastard. A gamer that has the great fortune of having a high-speed connection that gives him or her an advantage over slower players. Ping times of around 150 to 250 are considered excellent for gamers connected via a 56k modem link. Ping times of 250 to 400 are considered high but playable. Ping times over 400 will lead to lag. ISDN connected players should see a ping time around 60 to 150. Players with permanent T1 or better connections to the Internet will see ping times of under 60 and sometimes much better (in the teens usually).
Millisecond	1/1000th of a second. The unit of measure most common when gauging Internet/LAN connectivity. Low is better when gauging connectivity speed—just like golf.
Mod	A modification to an existing game. Many companies and talented gamers make changes to the way a game behaves. These changes, called Mods, are often available on the Internet. Most games released today can be modified legally (within certain limits). Game manufacturers build this feature in so that the game will have a longer life in the gaming market.
OpenGL	Similar to GLIDE in nature, OpenGL is a method of communicating video instructions to your video hardware. The video hardware must be OpenGL compatible to be able to natively take advantage of OpenGL compatible games.

continues

Table 1.1   Continued

Term/Phrase	Definition
Ping	The action of sending a small data packet to a computer over a connection (LAN or Internet) and measuring the time it takes for the other machine to respond. The time returned is in milliseconds and is the roundtrip time the packet took to go out and come back. Ping is a utility available on most operating systems. In Windows, just jump out to a DOS prompt and type `Ping xxx.xxx.xxx.xxx` Where xxx.xxx.xxx.xxx is the address of the computer you want to send a ping packet to. Four packets will be sent and the roundtrip time each took will be displayed.
RTS	Real-Time Strategy—A game like Red Alert, Total Annihilation, Star Craft, Dark Reign, and so on. A game that is played out in map overview type setting when the gamer is not within the game. The play of these games happens in real-time and the more quickly a gamer can marshal his or her forces, the better he or she will do.
Sim	Short for simulation. A Sim is any game that attempts to mimic the real world. Sports games, military jet or helicopter games, fishing games, and so on are all considered sims.
Spawn/Respawn	The action of items or players appearing inside of a game. If an item respawns that means it reappears for someone else to pick up. Weapons, ammo, items, health, and so on all respawn quite frequently in most multiplayer games. When players enter the game either for the first time or again after a death, they are said to have spawned in the game.
TBS	Turn Based Strategy—A game like Alexander the Great or Civilization. Much like an RTS except that each player takes his or her turn much like in a board game such as Monopoly or Risk.
Tribe	A tribe is the same thing as a clan. The term tribe became popular with the release of the game Starsiege: Tribes by Sierra. Starsiege: Tribes was one of the first games designed exclusively to promote team play with multi-faceted player roles.

As you can see, gamers can speak a pretty unique language. Throughout this book you'll encounter these terms very frequently so it's best that you become familiar with them or bend the corner of the page over now so you can come back later. By the end of this book, if you don't already speak game-ese, you will be able to speak it like a native.

Gaming Software Companies

There are a lot of companies making games; some good, some bad. Some are newcomers to the business, trying to make a name for themselves while others are old timers who have seemingly been around since the first IBM XT machine was released in the '80s. This list will give you an idea of who is out there and just exactly what software of which games they make.

It's hard sometimes to tell who makes what because of the nature of the business. A gaming software company may be fairly small but creates a great game. Because they're small, they work with another larger gaming company to market their software. The end result is usually that the larger company that markets the game has nothing to do with it but appears to be the maker of the game because their name is stuck all over it. Table 1.2 shows some examples of this.

Table 1.2   Gaming Software Companies

Company/Web Site	What They Make
Activision www.activision.com	Activision is a solid, long-time player in the gaming software market. They have made such outstanding games as Mech Warrior II, Battlezone, Interstate '76, Dark Reign, and many, many more. Activision has also served as the marketing/distribution arm for many Id games like Quake 2 and Castle Wolfenstein. Activision will be around for years to come and then continue to pump out excellent titles. Watch for Battlezone II and Dark Reign II coming soon (hopefully by the time you read this book).
Blizzard Entertainment www.blizzard.com	Blizzard has three main claims to fame.Warcraft, Starcraft,and Diablo. Warcraft and Starcraft are popular RTS games. Warcraft is based in a fantasy environment and Starcraft on a science-fiction environment. Diablo is one of those trend-setting games that the rest of the gaming market struggles to catch up to. Diablo is a game that created its own category. A fantasy-based game of adventure and fighting, it looks like an RTS game since it has an over-the-top type interface but it plays more like a computer role-playing game. Diablo II, while it has been delayed many times has everyone (me included) waiting excitedly for a peek.

continues

Table 1.2   Continued

Company/Web Site	What They Make
Cave Dog www.cavedog.com	While they don't have as complete a line of multiplayer games as larger companies like Activision, Cave Dog has made a very popular game called Total Annihilation. This is an RTS game that has given Cave Dog some acknowledgement in the gaming world and has lead to a series of add-ons for the game. Be looking for more good RTS games from Cave Dog in the future.
Delphine www.delphinesoft.com	Delphine has made a splash in the gaming world with racing sims like Moto Racer 2 and fantasy role playing games like Darkstone. If it wasn't for the release of Darkstone to tide me over until the release of Diablo II, I think I would have gone into withdrawal. Darkstone is obviously a direct imitation of Diablo by Blizzard Entertainment, but for those of us who need our fix, it was a welcome sight. The fact that it's a great game in its own right and has enough new features like better 3D graphics and a rotatable environment makes it all the better. Rumor has it that Diablo II's chronic release delays are due in part to the success of Delphine's Darkstone. Perhaps Blizzard needed to improve the original concept of Diablo II to better compete with Darkstone?
Dynamix www.dynamix.com	Dynamix is owned now by Sierra Online and the unionappears to be a good one. Dynamix has been in the gaming software business for many years and is the creating force behind the incredibly popular StarSiege series of games. Tribes has given Dynamix a lofty position in the gaming world as being one of the few games designed to promote team play by having more tasks than just shoot and kill. They also made the game David Wolf: Secret Agent years ago in the late '80s. Boys, I just wanted to tell you one thing, you forgot the "e" at the end of my last name. Where's my royalty check?
Electronic Arts www.ea.com	Electronic Arts is like a huge juggernaut rolling down a hill, scooping up smaller gaming software companies. Companies like Janes, Westwood, Maxis, Origins, and Bullfrog have all become members of the EA family of gaming companies. It appears though that EA is allowing these subsidiaries to remain independent and produce titles as they wish (although EA has flexed some unwanted muscle in the past). EA itself is the maker of many good sports sims such as Madden 99 and Madden 2000.

Company/Web Site	What They Make
Epic Games www.epicgames.com	Epic is the maker of many fine single-player games such as pinball games, but their foray into the multiplayer gaming world was done with Unreal. Unreal has proven to be a visually amazing game with graphics like no other game on the market today. Unfortunately people weren't very impressed with Unreal's game play, especially in the multiplayer arena. Epic hopes to change all that with Unreal Tournament, a version of Unreal better suited for multiplayer gaming and one that is impressing people quite a bit, at least in its demo form, which can be downloaded as of the writing of this book. Watch for Epic to push Unreal back into the spotlight.
GameSpy www.gamespy.com	GameSpy is a fairly new player in the gaming world but its presence has been large to say the least. GameSpy is a gaming tool designed to help players locate games to play on the Internet. GameSpy can give players a concise list of what games are currently being played and also provide a great deal of information about each game, too. Things like how many players are in the game, how long it has been running, is it free to join, and more can be determined with GameSpy. GameSpy is also the sponsor of the Planet series of Web sites. These Web sites are dedicated to specific games like Quake, Unreal, Half-Life, Shogo, and others. You can find these sites at www.planet<game>.com. For example, the Quake planet is found at www.planetquake.com.
Id Software www.idsoftware.com	Ah, the mother of all multiplayer gaming. Id is the maker of the Doom and Quake series of games. Id has always stuck to what it knows best: First-Person Shooters. For all its presence in the gaming world, Id is actually quite small and relies on Activision to do a large portion of its marketing and distribution. Id pioneered the concept of shareware games by releasing Doom as a shareware title. The first few levels were free but you had to buy the rest of the game. They even include multiplayer connectivity in the shareware release of their games. They're kind of like a drug pusher. The first few samples are free and after that, you're hooked.

continues

Table 1.2   Continued

Company/Web Site	What They Make
Interplay www.interplay.com	Interplay's release of Descent shortly after Id's release of Doom helped bring about the multiplayer revolution. Descent had one major advantage over Doom. That was the ability to asynchronously join a game. This meant that you didn't have to be present at the start of the game to get in. You could join any time if there was a spot open. This made Descent a major player in the gaming arena. Today, the Descent series of games continues. Interplay has also produced other titles like Kingpin, Redneck Rampage, Carmageddon, Baldur's Gate, and many others. Interplay also takes a very generous approach to supporting LAN Parties and other gaming events.
Kali www.kali.net	Kali isn't really a game software maker. Kali is a gaming tool that allows older IPX only games to be played multiplayer-wise over the Internet. While most games these days have native TCP/IP connectivity built into them, Kali is still a tool to be noted. It has been around since the early days and can still be used to track newer TCP/IP games.
Lucas Arts www.lucasarts.com	Okay, so they make a lot of games based on the *Star Wars* movies but many people find Lucas Arts games incredibly fun to play. Games like X-Wing vs. TIE Fighter and Dark Force are games that have a solid following even though they're not quite as popular as some other titles within the same genre. Even though it's not a multiplayer game, the game Grim Fandango by Lucas Arts is an outstanding example of a graphical adventure game and deserves all the 9 and 10 scores it has gotten in reviews since its release. Can you tell I'm a big Grim Fandango fan?
Microprose www.microprose.com	Microprose has become the caretaker of the Mech Warrior line of Mech games. Mech Warrior 3 was produced by Microprose and while it wasn't very well received, due to its lack of innovation over its predecessor Mech Warrior II by Activision, its improved graphics and better physics do make it worth noting. Another popular title by Microprose is Mech Commander, a RTS-type game that many people find enjoyable.

Company/Web Site	What They Make
Microsoft www.microsoft.com	While you might not think of them as major players in the game market, Microsoft has made and/or marketed many game titles that have been well accepted by the gaming world. The Microsoft Flight Simulator has done well as a sim game and Microsoft's Age of Empires series, a good adaptation of the RTS genre of gaming, has done very well. Don't ignore them just because they are Microsoft. Give Age of Empires II a try and you'll be impressed, I'm sure.
Sierra Online www.sierra.com	Sierra grew to be the powerhouse it is now based largely on the incredibly popular King's Quest series of adventure games. Although this series was/is not a multiplayer game, it is played by millions of people around the world. Today, Sierra makes or markets games like Half-Life, Homeworld, StarSiege, StarSiege: Tribes, and Red Baron. Half-Life and Tribes catapulted Sierra firmly into the multiplayer arena. Much of this success has to go to Dynamix, a newly acquired subsidiary of Sierra and the actual makers of the StarSiege line of games.
Westwood Studios www.westwood.com	Another big player in the gaming world, Westwood is the maker of such games as Command and Conquer, Red Alert, and Tiberian Sun. Westwood pioneered the genre of the RTS game with its release of Command and Conquer. This game has lead to a series of popular RTS games by Westwood. Electronic Arts has recently purchased Westwood. While Tiberian Sun was a disappointment to many gamers expecting something exciting and new after such a long dry spell from Westwood, we still have hope that Westwood will release something that will once again put them at the top of the RTS pile.

Obviously there are many other companies making software, utilities or Web sites dedicated to gaming. To list them all here would be impossible. Throughout this book you'll read about the specifics of what these companies make and you'll find out which ones are best for you. If you spend any time paying attention to the events in the gaming world, the names of these companies will continue to pop up time and time again.

The Least You Need to Know

➤ Online gaming can take place over the Internet, over a LAN, over a modem-to-modem connection, or between two computers connected via a serial cable. Online doesn't just mean the Internet.

➤ Gamers come in all shapes and sizes, metaphorically speaking. A gamer can be a high school student, a college student someone at work, a neighbor, or nearly anyone.

➤ Gamers use dozens of strange words and terms to refer to the business of gaming. Learning the lingo is key to communicating with other gamers.

➤ Dozens of major companies are in the business of making games for online gaming. Some have been around for a long time; others are fairly new to the business of gaming.

Chapter 2

Your Connection to Other Gamers

In This Chapter

➤ Essential hardware for going online

➤ Connecting via the Internet

➤ Dialing another computer direct with your modem

➤ Plugging in with a null modem or cable connection

➤ Gaming across a local area network (LAN)

So you think that you want to play computer games with other, live humans? You've been playing against the computer and you think that playing against other players would be fun. You're right, it is fun. But, you're asking yourself, "What will I need for my computer so I can play against other gamers?" I have the answer for you in this chapter.

The Hardware You'll Need

To play against another player, you will need to be able to connect to their machine in some way. There are several ways to go from here. There are expensive and complex connectivity paths as well as simple and cheap options for getting connected. There are also fast connections and slow connections. In the next sections, I will present various connectivity technologies and describe some of the options for you.

A Modem

Modems are the most common way for getting your computer connected to the Internet. They are simple to use, easy to set up, and you don't need any special advanced degree to operate one.

Note

How to Tell a Fast Modem, Other Than by the Racing Stripes

In looking at a modem speed of 56K, you might ask what the K stands for in the 56K. *K* refers to 1000; thus 56K would truly read 56,000bps (bits per second).

In today's market, modems have reached the maximum speed based on the technology of the analog phone. The top speed modem today is the 56K modem, sometimes called the V90. The V90 refers to the way the modem talks to other modems, but the 56K refers to its speed. Even this is a little deceiving. When you use a 56K modem to dial a friend, you might get a connection of a whopping 28K. When you get this speed from your modem, it doesn't mean that your modem is broken. To get the full 56K speed from your modem, you must dial into a special modem that can send only at 56kbps. ISPs (Internet service providers) have these special modems. So you will get data sent to you at 56kbps, but your modem will send at a lower rate.

My opinion for looking for a modem is to find one that is in your price range, is compatible with your system, and will work with your ISP. There are several.

Gamer Comment

Quote from Anonymous

"I get a 49,333 connect most of the time and that yields me about 5.5kbps per second on my transfers when I'm downloading. However, during peak times, that rate can fall to 3.5kbps per second even if I get a 49,333 connection."

An ISDN Connection

ISDN is much different from 56kbps modems for a couple of reasons. First, ISDN uses digital communications instead of analog. Which means that noise and interference influence it much less. With an analog line, noise and static can reduce the connect rate or even prevent you from getting connected at all.

With consumer ISDN you have two lines. These lines are called B Channels. Each B Channel can operate at 64kbps. Hey, look, you are already faster than the modem. But wait, there's more. The 64kbps goes both directions, and then you can combine the two channels to have a 128kbps connection. This combination is called *multilink*. There are ways to use this technique with modems, too, but I'm not going to cover multilinking modems. Just know that it is possible.

One of the drawbacks with ISDN is that you must have the phone company install the ISDN to your house. And the hardware required can get expensive and difficult to setup. There are internal ISDN modem cards and there are external units that can connect to an Ethernet network. If you go this route, shop around for the equipment and be sure that your ISP can handle a multilink ISDN connection. Your ISP might even have preferred equipment or recommendations.

Quote from FMKid (A.K.A. Bill Heizer)

"NetGear from Baynetworks is the best for connecting to the Internet with ISDN. I can have one out of the box and running in 15 minutes."

When looking for a device to connect to ISDN, you have several options. Baynetworks carries three types: modems or adapter cards (for inside the computer), terminal adapters or network bridges (which connect to an Ethernet network and can have analog phone ports), and USB devices (which can connect to any USB-ready laptop or desktop).

DSL

DSL means Digital Subscriber Line. There are two types of DSL, Symmetric and Asymmetric. Symmetric DSL (SDSL) means that communications speed to and from your location is the same both directions, whereas asymmetric DSL (ADSL) communications speed is different in each direction.

The advantage of the DSL is that the data rate starts at 128Kbps and can go up to 7Mbps plus. The available speed of the DSL is dependent on the distance from your location to the DSL switch. It can be a little more expensive than ISDN, depending on the service costs in your local area. The nice thing about DSL is, like ISDN, it needs only a single phone line going into your house and the signal is all digital.

The timing of this chapter was amazing. I just signed up for DSL service from Rhythms and can tell you its popularity is increasing in my area. The cost for 24-hours a day, 7-days a week 256K service is under $140 per month and that includes the hardware and the line to the house. Not too shabby if you can afford it.

Cable Modems

Cable modems have gained amazing popularity recently. Cable modems share a 30Mbps connection to the Internet. The problem is that you are sharing that speed with everyone else on your cable modem neighborhood. Cable modems can have

Quote from ElfKing (A.K.A. John Kaufeld)

"In my experience cable modems are great when they work. I've been able to get 450K during the day and 95K at night."

amazing speeds, but sometimes your old modem might be faster if everyone in your neighborhood is using their cable connection.

There has to be availability in your area in order to get a cable modem. Even though they have such favorable benefits, not all areas have this wonderful technology. Some cable companies have a couple of years to go before they have updated the infrastructure (the cabling in the street) to handle the cable modem technology. The cost is comparable to any other ISP, but you have a 24-hour a day connection to the Internet and the hardware is included in the price also.

Satellite Links

In some locations, a satellite link might be the only high-speed connection to the Internet that you might feasibly be able to get. The download rate for the satellite link is great, around 400Kbps, but it uses a regular modem to upload. Your communication will be lopsided. This is not a bad thing if all you want to do is download or receive information, but if you want to play games online, you might not have the best time.

The Internet

The Internet used to be the hangout of the geeks and computer jocks. Now everyone wants to be a part of this cyberspace. It has become the breeding grounds for all sorts of new businesses with e-commerce, the location for newspapers, and other bits of information. The Internet can also be the perfect battleground for computer games.

Using/Choosing an ISP

Choosing an Internet service provider (ISP) can be a challenge. You need to think about what you want to do on the Internet. Oh, I forgot. You want to play games over the Internet. Some of the things you want to consider might be

➤ What are the monthly fees for the service?

➤ What are the upfront costs?

➤ Are there any hardware costs?

➤ Is there any special software needed to access the ISP's system?

➤ How many clients does the ISP currently have?

➤ Is the ISP local?

➤ Do they have a local phone number?

➤ How effective is their support?

I prefer a local provider for playing games online because I am competing with fewer people for their phone lines and I can usually get more information about the ISP's system. Picking the most popular or largest ISP might not be the best choice for your needs. Sometimes a smaller, local provider can provide better service for your needs than a larger national ISP can provide. Also, if all you and your gaming buddies are using the same ISP, the online game traffic doesn't have to go outside the ISP's network. This helps with game performance.

AOL/MSN

A couple of the more popular ISPs are America OnLine (AOL) and Microsoft Network (MSN). There are several other popular ISPs, but you will get the idea from these examples.

These popular ISPs can have many people using their system. Many people can equal slow access. Slow access means slow game play. Slow game play equals frustration and aggravation. I know that you don't want any of that. If you already have an ISP, you can check the performance of the ISP and your connection to the ISP.

Connection Performance

The bottom line for playing games on the Internet is the performance. Many games are very forgiving of performance. Some games will match the speed of the game to the speed of the slowest player. That way everyone has the same handicap. Other games do not seem to take into account the connection speed or even the computer speed. In those cases, he whose machine rocks wins. So you want to take advantage of every opportunity you can to have a fighting chance at competing online. You can upgrade and buy the newest and fastest computer system, but when you are playing over the Internet against other players, your fancy computer system will do nothing for you, if you run into the dreaded lag (which doesn't stand for anything).

Defining Lag

Lag is the delay you experience when the connection performance in a game is so slow that it makes playing the game nearly impossible. Another term for lag is *latency*. Let me share with you a situation where my connection caused much frustration—to the point of not wanting to play online.

A group of my friends and I had set a time to meet online to play a little first-person StarSeige Tribes. We all were on even ground as we all were using modems to join the game. In the past, we had used a server to host the games, but that night the server wasn't working. One of the players volunteered to host the game instead and we all started to play a mission. There were some occasional refresh delays, but generally the game was playing smoothly. Once I began to encounter someone and engage them in battle, the refresh delays became longer. Eventually I couldn't maneuver to get out of the line of fire and when I would pull the trigger to fire back, the enemy had moved out of my sights. His bullets hit and mine seemed to miss.

I know what you are thinking. You're thinking that I stink at that game. Well, you might be right, but I'm not so bad that I can't hold my own against the group that was playing that night.

Here is a case in which my computer was fine to handle the game and the graphics. The problem was that my connection to the host computer was too slow. There was more information to send between computers than the connection was able to handle. The person who was hosting, naturally, had no problems. I have played with the same group of people on a LAN (Local Area Network), instead of using modems, and the lag wasn't noticeable.

Using ping*,* tracert*, and* winipcfg

There are ways to measure the lag of an Internet connection or even a direct LAN connection. You can get some ideas from these measurements on how a connection speed will affect your game play performance. These tools are readily available in Windows, but are not listed among the installed applications.

These applications are ping, tracert and winipcfg. ping and tracert are DOS applications and are best run in a command shell, while winipcfg is a Windows application. Let's go over these applications one by one.

Ping.exe—Ping is the application that tests the presence of another machine and displays the communication delay between the machines. Both machines must use IP addresses and both machines must be connected to the Internet or a LAN. To ping a machine, first start a DOS session.

1. Click the **Start** button and click **Run**.
2. Type command.com in the space and click **OK**.

From the command line, type ping, a space, then the IP address (or a valid domain name) of the computer you want to check the response time for. You should see a screen that looks like the one in Figure 2.1. (See winipcfg for details on obtaining an IP address.)

Figure 2.1

The Ping *command is a simple way to measure the speed of a network connection.*

By looking at the time value in the figure, you can see one of the tries was very long. However, the overall average was fair for game play. When looking at the time from the results of the ping, lower numbers are always better, but not always possible.

Sometimes a segment of the path of the communication might be the cause of excessive delay. To find that segment, you can use the program called `tracert.exe` that will trace the route of your connections to the other machines.

The Time To Live (TTL) value of an IP packet is the number of hops allowed for the packet to reach a recipient, then the packet will be discarded. This only happens in really bad lag situations. Playable `ping` time ranges can be in the 200ms to 300ms range. You might be able to tolerate higher ping time ranges, but I find this range works for me. Remember, the smaller the number the faster the connection.

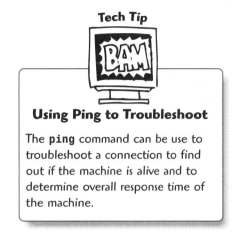

Tech Tip

Using Ping to Troubleshoot

The **ping** command can be use to troubleshoot a connection to find out if the machine is alive and to determine overall response time of the machine.

Tracert.exe—This program traces the route between two machines and lists any machine and their response between the source computer and the destination computer.

1. To see the responses for the machines on the route to the destination machine, start the command shell by clicking the **Start** button and clicking on **Run**.

2. Type `command.com` on the line and click **OK**.

3. Type `tracert.exe`, then a space and the IP address (or a valid domain name) of the destination machine, then hit the **Enter** key. The result appears as shown in Figure 2.2.

```
C:\WINNT\System32\command.com                                    _ □ ×
Microsoft(R) Windows NT DOS
(C)Copyright Microsoft Corp 1990-1996.

C:\>tracert.exe www.mcp.com

Tracing route to www.mcp.com [198.70.146.70]
over a maximum of 30 hops:

  1   <10 ms    <10 ms    <10 ms  router.rhino-tech.com [209.131.202.129]
  2    47 ms     62 ms     47 ms  tci.iei.net [209.131.216.211]
  3    47 ms     63 ms     46 ms  rtr1.iei.net [209.131.216.221]
  4    47 ms     46 ms     47 ms  IEI-atm-our17.onecall.net [216.37.31.17]
  5    47 ms     47 ms     62 ms  IndyX-Enoch.OneCall.Net [216.37.1.5]
  6    62 ms     47 ms     63 ms  NChicago1-core1.nap.net [207.227.0.173]
  7    93 ms     94 ms     78 ms  NChicago1-core0.nap.net [207.112.247.153]
  8    78 ms     78 ms     78 ms  chi-f0.iquest.net [206.54.225.250]
  9   219 ms    516 ms    297 ms  204.180.50.9
 10    79 ms     93 ms     94 ms  iq-ind-core1.iquest.net [206.53.249.1]
 11   250 ms     94 ms    109 ms  www.mcp.com [198.70.146.70]

Trace complete.

C:\>
```

Figure 2.2

Tracing machine routes is easy with `tracert.exe`.

In Figure 2.2, you can see each machine and the connection time for each machine. The first column is the number of hops to the destination. The next three columns are the time of three ping tries to that point in the route. The last column is the machine name and IP address of each point on the way to the destination.

I realize that I must be taking some of the mystery out of the Internet. As soon as you begin to grasp some of these concepts, you too will be the neighborhood geek. But the question still remains, "How do I know what my IP address is?" After all, you never have had to enter an IP address at any time when connecting to the Net. In most cases the IP address and other information needed by your computer to communicate on the Internet was given to your machine at the time you dial and connect to your ISP and might change each time you connect. To get this information, use a program called `winipcfg.exe`.

Winipcfg.exe—This Windows program gives you the details of the IP settings for your computer.

1. To open `winipcfg`, click the **Start** button on the taskbar and click **Run**.

2. Enter `winipcfg.exe` in the test field and click **OK**. The resulting screen will look like the one in Figure 2.3.

3. Click the down arrow on the right side of the first line and select the adapter you want the information on.

4. (Optional) Click the **More Info** button to display all the settings for the selected adapter.

Figure 2.3

The `Winipcfg` *display window provides details of the IP settings on your computer.*

The most important information that you will need when checking on lag is your own IP address. The PPP Adapter is the dialup adapter. Most games don't display the IP address, so using `Winipcfg` can give you that information. Setting a shortcut to the application on your desktop can come in handy if you game a lot online.

Modem to Modem

Eventually, when I start playing a game that has a multiplay aspect to the game, I like playing with someone. I enjoy the challenge and the variability that a real human adds to the game. Most of the games today have the multiplay function to them and often they will have connection options available. One of these options is using a modem to play head to head with someone.

One-on-One Gaming

One-on-one game play is fun and can help tune your strategies and hone your skills. All you need to play head to head is a modem and a phone line on each end. Most times the game will even allow for you to start a phone list; if not all you need to do is enter the phone number. To play head to head, one person will start the game and host the session, while the other will call the hosting party from within the game and start the play once the two computers have completed the connection.

One-on-one gaming isn't rocket science, but can sometimes take a couple of tries. The performance of the game play can vary, depending on the modem speed.

56kbps Doesn't Mean 56kbps Unless You Are Dialing an ISP

When playing one on one and using 56kbps modems, you might find that your connection speed isn't 56kbps. You might find that your true connection speed is somewhere around 33.6kbps because of how the 56kbps modem works.

Here is a little lesson on how modems get their speed: With conventional modems, analog-to-analog communication, the modem transmits an analog signal from your house to the phone company. The telephone company converts the analog signal to a digital signal, sends the signal to the destination, and then converts the digital signal to an analog signal for the destination modem to receive. This process only allows 33.6kbps to be the maximum speed between two analog modems.

Along came the 56kbps modem. This speed is achieved by converting the analog signal only once. For the 56kbps modem to even come close to the 56kbps speed, you have to connect to a digital modem that your ISP would be using. These digital modems are able to send the signal at 56kbps. Your modem is not capable of this because the connection to your modem, the phone line, is analog. Your modem will transmit at 33.6kbps and receive at 56kbps (assuming your ISP provides digital 56kbps).

Note

Modems Don't Always Reach Top Speed

If you have had a 33.6kbps modem in the past, but you were never able to get a connection speed of close to 33.6kbps, then it is likely that you will not get the full speed with a 56kbps modem.

Gamer Comment

Quote from an Anonymous Online Gamer

"I like using an external modem, like one from US Robotics. That way I can see the lights flashing and know if I'm waiting on a transfer or if my computer is locked up."

Null Modem

If you plan on playing against someone when the computers are in the same room, the modem would not be the best choice. You can get around the overhead of the modems with a simple cable called a *null modem* or *Data Link cable*. This cable connects to the serial ports of the two computers and communicates directly through the cable.

Windows comes with software that lets you establish the connection; to use it, click the **Start** menu, choose **Programs**, choose **Accessories** (and **Communications** for Windows 98), and then click **Direct Cable Connection**. If the last doesn't appear, you need to rerun the Windows installation program and install it.

One-on-One Gaming

Because the overhead of the modes is no longer an issue, the performance has increased because the speed is limited by the speed of the serial ports on the computer.

Depending on the chipset for the serial port, the communication rate can reach 115,200bps. This speed is faster than you would be able to get from a modem.

Tech Tip

Any COM Port in a Storm

The serial port on a computer is referred to as a *communication port* known as COM1 or COM2. Your computer should have at least one communication port.

Where to Get a Null Modem Cable

When shopping for a null modem cable, be sure not to get a regular modem cable. This will not work. It must be a null modem cable. These cable have a transmit pin from one end tied to the receive pin on the other end. You can find these cables at electronic parts stores or you can mail order them from a cable catalog such as DATA Warehouse (www.warehouse.com and search on null modem). Your local Radio Shack might also have these cables.

Note

Be Sure to Get the Correct Null Modem Cable

When buying a null modem cable, be sure to get the correct gender for both ends to connect to your computer. In most cases, but not all, the computer has a DB9 male connector.

LAN

Gaming on a Local Area Network (LAN) is the best possible choice, in my opinion. It offers the most flexibility for games and most all games make provisions for a LAN connection. Besides, I find that it is so much more enjoyable to see the people that I play against. A LAN connection also allows for more than two people to play against each other.

A new trend among First Person Shooters is a team aspect. You can also team play with some of the Real Time Strategy games. A team of one just doesn't work very well. You can't use a modem to dial in to more than one computer and a null cable only allows for one computer to connect as well. The only choice left is for a LAN.

If I use a LAN to play games, does that mean that I am approaching being a geek? Not really. To be a real geek, one has to have several computers and have them all connected to a LAN. I fall into that classification. I have several computers connected to my LAN. I even have a computer connected to the LAN for my wife so she can print and check her email.

Getting a LAN Card

How do I go about setting up my computer for a LAN? The first thing you will need is a LAN card. These cards go into your computer and will allow the computer to communicate with the other computers on the LAN. I am sure choosing a LAN card can be more fun than you will want to have.

There are several brands and models of LAN cards, also called Ethernet cards or Network Interface Cards (NIC), available on the market today. These cards come with many features and come in a wide price range. There are name brands and off brands. Is there a difference? Some say yes. I usually play safe and stay away from the no-name brands of Ethernet cards. Yes, you can get one for next to nothing, but that is what you might end up with in the end. Adaptec, 3Com, Intel, Kingston, Diamond, D-Link, Linksys, SMC, and AMD are all common brands of Ethernet cards.

Things to look for when choosing an Ethernet card are

➤ Does the card match the slot, ISA or PCI, I have open in my computer?

➤ Does the manufacturer of the card have a Web site where I can get updated drivers?

➤ What types of connections will the people I play with use?

➤ What types of connections does the card support? RJ45? AUI? Coax? Combination of connections?

➤ If you are choosing an Ethernet card with the RJ45 connector, can the card use 10BaseT and/or 100BaseT?

Tech Tip

A Field Guide for Identifying Network Cables

RJ45 looks like an oversized phone plug. AUI looks like a DB15 connector. Coax (BNC) is a round connector and will protrude from the card about 1/2 inch or more.

With regard to the last couple points, almost across the board, the connection of choice will be RJ45. This has become the standard for businesses as well as for gamers. Although you will find exceptions from time to time—that's why it is a good question to ask. Coax can also be found because you can chain several computers together with only some connectors and cable.

10BaseT Versus 100BaseT

Why has the RJ45 connector become the standard? This same connector type also upgrades to the 100BaseT standard. You guessed it, 100BaseT communicates at

100Mbps. The cable used for this standard is called twisted pair because it uses two twisted pairs of wire. When picking a cable for your networking, you should use a CAT5 cable because it is able to work with both of the communication standards, 10BaseT and 100BaseT.

Which standard should you use when you are playing games? That's hard to say. At this point, I would say that 10BaseT is sufficient for your game play and it is the most common. The additional equipment you need for multiple players would be a hub.

Hubs Versus Switches

Hubs come with their share of choices also—depending on the Ethernet card you chose. Hubs come in either 10BaseT or 100BaseT. If you want to remain flexible, because you are unsure who will have what ability when playing, you might want to look at a switchable hub that will automatically change the communication type based on what plugs into the port on the hub.

Something you might come across while looking for equipment is an Ethernet switch. The difference between a switch and a hub is that with the hub all computers communicating on the hub have to listen to see if anyone is talking to them. With the switch, the switch makes some of the decisions about who is talking to whom. To help explain the differences, refer to Figure 2.4 during the following discussion.

Figure 2.4

Hub and switched net-works are distinct.

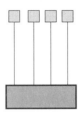 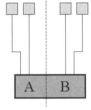

Hub Network   Switched Network

On a hub network, all the computers (the small boxes) can directly talk to each other, but on a switched network, some of the computers are separated from each other. If a computer on side A wants to speak to a computer on side B, the switch opens a path between the two computers so they can talk. However, if the two computers on side A want to talk, the switch does not get involved. What is so important about this technology? If you had a large number of computers on a network and they all talked at once, the traffic would be high. But if some of the computers were on switches, then the switch would control and separate the traffic somewhat.

Cabling

Cabling can be just as important as choosing the Ethernet card. Some people make their own cables, but when it comes to having trouble getting your computer to connect to the network, I like to eliminate all unknowns whenever I can. You can purchase your cable and have the assurance that the cable was factory made. You can get CAT5 RJ45 cable in various lengths from local computer stores or online.

Crossover Cable for One-on-One Twisted Pair

Now you have read all about Ethernet and understand all about it, but you just want to play against one person and still have the option to play on a network. How can you connect two computers together without a network? The answer is a crossover cable for the Ethernet. This allows two computers to connect to each other without using a hub. You can pick a little device called a cross-over coupler (less than $10) which you can add to a regular Ethernet cable and thereby allow two computers to connect.

TCP/IP

In order for games to communicate on an Ethernet, there has to be a communication protocol available. A protocol is the standard communication format that is established to allow data to be transmitted between computers. There are two primary protocols that games will use. The first protocol is called Transmission Control Protocol/Internet Protocol (TCP/IP). This is the protocol, as you can guess from the name, which is used on the Internet.

Basically, the TCP/IP protocol requires that each computer on the network or Internet must have a number associated with it. This number identifies the computer as unique on the network.

I am not telling you all this so that you can become a networking expert, but so that you will have some idea of how this protocol works. When you are dialing and connecting to your service provider, they will give your computer a number automatically. When you go to play a networked game and use the TCP/IP protocol, you will need to give all the computers that are going to play together a number. This number has four parts with a period (.) separating the sets of numbers. This number or IP address looks like this: 192.0.10.123.

Static IP Addressing

You will need to set an IP address for your computer. If you don't have one set then let me instruct you on how this can be done.

1. Click the **Start** button and go to Settings, then click **Control Panel**.
2. From the Control Panel, double-click the **Network** icon.
3. Now you should see a configuration panel for the network as shown in Figure 2.5. The large display box, which shows the network adapters, should also show the protocols installed. Look for the TCP/IP protocol that is installed. (If one is not installed, click the **Add** button and follow the wizard to add the Microsoft TCP/IP protocol.)
4. Double-click the TCP/IP protocol for the Network Interface Card you are using. This should open a new display window.

Figure 2.5

The Network Configuration dialog box lets you establish TCP/IP settings.

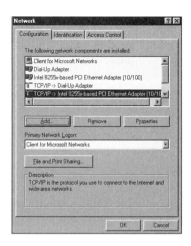

Note

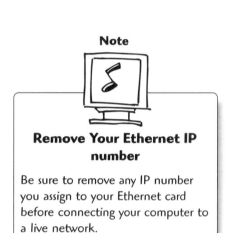

Remove Your Ethernet IP number

Be sure to remove any IP number you assign to your Ethernet card before connecting your computer to a live network.

5. Check the box for Specify an IP Address and enter a number—in this case, use **192.168.0.0**; it's reserved for non-Internet use and won't cause any problems. (You can use any numbers between 0 and 255.) For other computers on your network, change the last of the four numbers from 0 to a number between 1 and 16 (usually incremented by one).

6. You can set the Subnet Mask to the one shown in Figure 2.6, as long as all other computers on your game network have the same first three numbers.

7. Click **OK** to commit the changes and close the windows.

Figure 2.6

Establish the Subnet Mask settings in the TCP/IP Properties dialog box.

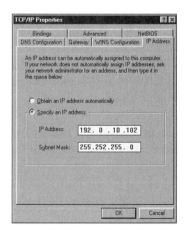

Following this procedure will help to get your computer set up to play an IP game on a network. If you were intending to play the same game over the Internet, you would use the program `Winipcfg.exe` that I mentioned earlier to determine your IP address, which you acquired when you connected to your Internet service provider.

By default, Windows 98 will auto-assign a bogus IP address within a subnet if you have the protocol set to automatically get an address but it can't find a DHCP server. A DHCP server will automatically hand out IP addresses upon request, like when you dial up to your ISP.

IPX

Another network protocol used by games, though commonly older games, is the Internetwork Packet Exchange (IPX). This networking protocol is used by the Novell NetWare operating systems. Many of the earlier games use this protocol when playing networked games.

This protocol is much simpler to use with a game because you have one person to host the game and everyone else joins. With some exceptions, IPX game play will only work on a LAN because of the Internet and because of the protocol incompatibilities. To use IPX on the Internet you need to use third-party software that will take the IPX information and wrap it in an IP datagram. This is a form of tunneling.

Frame Types

Setup for IPX isn't nearly as involved as for the IP addresses. The only real variable and setting to worry about is the Frame Type. This setting can be found in the network properties. Follow along and I will show you where and how to modify this setting. You might find some of this information familiar.

1. First, click the **Start** button, move the mouse to Settings and click **Control Panel**.
2. You will see the window that looks like the figure below. Double-click the **IPX/SPX compatible Protocol** which is bound to the network adapter for your computer. You can see an example in Figure 2.7.
3. Now you should see the IPX/SPX-compatible Protocol Properties window. Click the center tab labeled **Advanced**. You will see a list of properties, one of which will be Frame Type.
4. Select **Frame Type** by clicking on it in the list.
5. You will notice that the contents of the box on the right side of the window changed. It most likely displays Auto, but if you click the drop-down arrow to the right of the box, you will see all the types available, as shown in Figure 2.8.

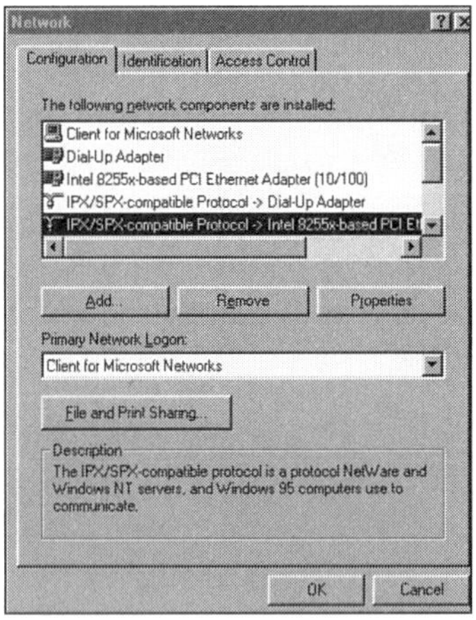

Figure 2.7

You can also change IPX settings in the Network Properties dialog box.

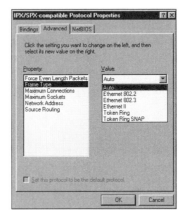

Figure 2.8

The IPX/SPX-compatible Protocol Properties dialog box includes a list of all possible frame types for your computer.

6. Select a frame type and be sure that everyone that you are playing with uses the same frame type. (Use one of the Ethernet choices.)

In my gaming experience, Ethernet 802.3 frame type has worked very well. There have been times we had to change to Ethernet 802.2 to get the game to work consistently. If there are problems you will notice problematic connections or game play for individuals during a game.

Performance on a LAN

Now that you have chosen how you want to play your games with others and maybe you've tried to play a game or two, you are starting to get the full online gaming experience. There is nothing like the thrill of victory when playing against live people. As you start playing more and more on the connection of choice, you will start to recognize for yourself that the faster the connection the more fun there is going to be.

Whenever we can, my friends and I bring our computers together in one place to play on a LAN. Since this can be a lot of work for a couple of hours of play, we'll resort to the dialup connections. If you haven't guessed by now, I like the LAN connection to play games.

Sometimes even using a LAN can have its drawbacks. It can take a couple of hours to get everything set up to play on a LAN because each computer needs to be set up nearly the same and the fact is that everyone has some settings that are different. The more people that get together can also factor into the prep time. We have had as many as 20 people show up at someone's house to play online games. Once you have seen the light and packed your computer to a friend's house (Careful not to drop it on the way. Broken computers tend to put a damper on things.) and have everything setup and working, you never turn back.

Most large-scale LAN parties, with attendance of 100+ gamers, use 10BaseT switches for game connections but have a 100BaseT segment for game servers. The two segments are linked with a speed switchable hub. If that many gamers were on conventional hubs, the traffic would make gaming impossible.

To determine the speed of your network, use the tools that I mentioned earlier in this chapter. `Ping` is an excellent tool. I use it all the time to determine if a computer is live on the network or to locate an unresponsive or slow machine. `Tracert` works well too, when I want to confirm the speed of the network. `Winipcfg.exe` is nice to quickly verify that I set up the IP address correctly.

Hopefully I have disspelled some of the mysteries of connecting computers and you're ready to give it a try. The bottom line to online gaming is to get connected and have a ball!

The Least You Need to Know

➤ There are many different types (modem, ISDN, DSL, cable, and satellite) of connections available to access the Internet.

➤ You should check your connection to the Internet and your Internet service provider to ensure the fastest possible gameplay.

➤ You can also use null modem, direct connection, and LAN connectivity to play other gamers.

Chapter 3

Gaming Hardware You Need

In This Chapter

➤ See how computers or hardware have a huge impact on your ability to run games

➤ Learn about the core components of your computer—the motherboard, processor, and memory

➤ Check out how improvements in video technology have enabled gorgeous game landscapes

➤ Get a handle on the latest in joystick technology

Computer games tend to drive consumer-oriented computer technology. My experience was typical: I was happy with my computer until I started getting into computer gaming. The computer speed was fine, but my graphics were awful. After I upgraded my graphics card, I had to upgrade the processor, which meant I had to upgrade the motherboard and memory. After it was all said and done, I had completely replaced my computer with a new one, one part at a time.

I don't know about you, but I can't afford to upgrade all the time. The best thing to do is to choose what and when you upgrade. The games that you prefer to play will help in deciding what you will want to upgrade. In fact, one thing that sets computer gamers apart is that many buy or build machines optimized for playing certain games.

There are seven key components to your gaming system. The final component, connectivity, I just covered in Chapter 2. I'll discuss these remaining six components in this chapter.

➤ Video Hardware
➤ Memory
➤ CPU
➤ Motherboard
➤ Sound card
➤ Controllers

Each component has a different effect on gaming. Look through each of the areas and determine for yourself which and what you want to upgrade or include in your system. If you read through this chapter and are still unsure what you need for your system, then I'd direct you to one of the many review sites on the Internet. One of the sites is Tom's Hardware Guide (www.tomshardware.com).

Tech Tip

Buy the computer you need for your purposes

When looking to upgrade your existing system or purchase a new system, consider first what you are going to use it for. Games? Work? Both? The longer I've been in this business, the more I am a believer that you should buy a computer based on what the computer is going to be doing, rather than based on what is cool at the time. But if you intend on gaming, go for what is cool—with caution. Chances are the hot game PC has the juice to play today's hot games and probably even tomorrow's.

Video Hardware

Video hardware is one of the key components to enjoying the games. I have upgraded the video cards more than any other component in my computer system. The video card affects the aesthetics of the game. Some of the older games will be no different in how they look, but the newer games...wow! In the newer games, you will see smooth shapes and special effects that the game programmers included for the higher end graphic cards.

If you have a computer, it's going to have a graphic card. The real question is whether you need a new video card. All graphic cards can display in two dimensions, or 2D. Most of the newer games render graphics in three dimensions, or 3D. A 3D accelerator card will enhance the performance of many games; others won't run without one. If you like your current video card, you can get add-on cards that will process and display the special 3D information and pass through the normal 2D graphics to the monitor. The goal of all graphics cards is realism. The more realistic you can make the image, the better gamers like it and want it.

Voodoo and Voodoo2 and Voodoo3

There are several generations of the Voodoo cards. With each generation there was improvement on how the card handles the graphic input. The Voodoo was the first on the market with a 3D-accelerator card to enhance the graphic effects. Then along came the Voodoo2 card that allowed you to use two in the same machine. This is an expensive solution, but the hardcore gamers went for it to get the results they were looking for. You can see the various Voodoo cards at their Web site, shown in Figure 3.1.

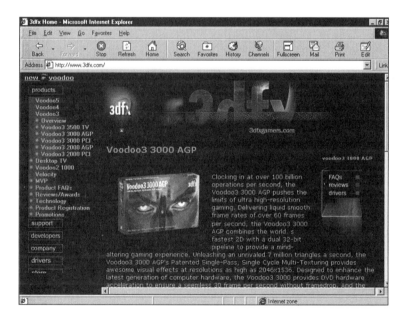

Figure 3.1

The Voodoo3 Web page can be found at www.3dfx.com.

When the Voodoo3 hit the market, it promised to outperform all others. But it was hard to beat two Voodoo2 cards linked together while Voodoo3 cards can't be linked. Though the Voodoo3 card helped keep 3dfx as the leader in the video market, the margin of improvement was thin.

TNT and TNT2

When the TNT chipset hit the market, the Voodoo2 cards were still the hot item. Video cards with the TNT chipsets did not perform as many people had hoped. But once the TNT2 was released, its improvements became evident to make it stand out in the video market. The RIVA TNT2 operates 10% to 17% faster than the TNT, suports AGP 4x, and has a digital flat-panel interface. It easily beat the Voodoo3 cards in performance, as the company's Web site, shown in Figure 3.2, boasts.

Figure 3.2

RIVA TNT's Web page is found at www.americas. creative.com/graphics/ tnt2-ultra/.

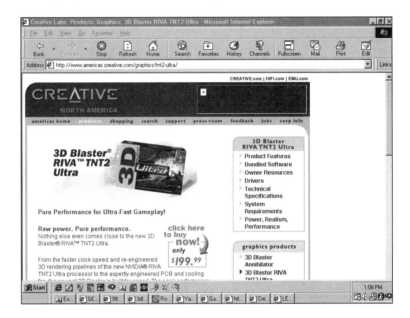

Other Chipsets

Because this graphic processing area is so new to the computer industry, there have been other attempts at producing chipsets. Most of the video card manufactures have taken a beating compared to the CPU manufacturers. The graphic chipsets can be and are as complex and costly to make as some of the processors. But the returns are much less. Several of the video card manufacturers have experienced losses.

DirectX, OpenGL, GLIDE

This is the software component for the games. Some games only allow for certain graphic types. It really does no good to have the top of the line, supercharged, 3D-accelerated graphics card if the software wasn't programmed for it.

OpenGL is primarily used in First-Person Shooter games such as Quake, Half Life and Unreal. DirectX was developed by Microsoft and is used in most of the flight simulator and racing games. GLIDE is yet another graphic format and stands for Graphics Language for Interactive and Dynamic Environments.

Note

DirectX for Games

DirectX is a Microsoft product, free to download from their Web site. Several games require DirectX or a certain version number of DirectX to be installed in order for the game to work. Use your Web browser and enter `www.microsoft.com/directx/homeuser/downloads/default.asp` to download the latest version of DirectX.

The Rest of Your Computer

Although the video card is the most esthetic component to your computer, the rest of your system needs to be competitive. It would not do any good if you have the fastest graphics card in your computer, but you were still using an old 486 processor and had 8MB of RAM.

Note

Safety First!

Whenever you are working on your own computer, be sure to follow the safety precautions found in your computer owner's manual. You should also follow the instructions for any of the components you are adding to you system. If you don't feel comfortable working on your own system, there are many service centers where you can take your computer to have changes made to your system.

To optimize your computer, you need to match each component with the others for the best performance of your system. To do this, you need to look at your computer components and compare them to what you want to do and what you are willing to live with. Some people like to be on the cutting edge of technology, while others like to be safe and use proven technology. In fact, some people like to be on what they call the "bleeding edge" of technology—a little ahead of the cutting edge. The disadvantage is if that particular technology doesn't work out or doesn't become a standard, you might need to replace the hardware for future games.

I prefer to be somewhere in between the cutting edge and proven technology. But let's face it, when it comes to computer hardware, it never stays the same. What is standard today will change a few months from now.

Memory

Let's take a look at memory. This technology is always changing. It started with literal chips, then moved to modules, and then 30-pin boards that you could add to your system board. Now there are several variations and varieties of memory types that go with specific system boards. Each system board has specific requirements for the memory that is needed. You'll need to consult your system's manual for the specifications on the memory that you need.

The bottom line is that the system board sets the requirements for the memory that is installed. If you are looking at a new computer, my advice is to get all the memory you think that you will need at he time of purchase, because adding it later might prove difficult.

Since most games run under one of the Windows environments, most of these games require a minimum of 32MB of RAM. These same games prefer 64MB of RAM to perform their best. Spending that little extra in the beginning will save you frustration in the end.

CPU

The CPU is the key component of your computer system. You have many choices available today to pick from for the CPU. There are Pentiums, Pentium IIs, Pentium IIIs, and Celerons of the Intel family, and from the AMD family there are the K-6, K-7, and Athlon. The speeds of these processors can range from 300 to 750 Megahertz. You can look at Table 3.1 to get a better comparison.

Table 3.1—Processor Speeds

Processor	Available Speeds					
Intel Processors						
Celeron	400	433	466	500		
Pentium II	333	400	450			
Pentium III	450	500	550	600	650	700

Processor	Available Speeds					
AMD Processors						
K6-2	350	380	400	450	500	533
K6-3	400					
Athlon	500	550	600	650	700	750

If you are looking for a bargain, the reports show that the Celeron processor outperforms the Pentium II processors for gaming. However, I've found that this is not always the case. You might find that the AMD processor has the performance and the price to meet to your liking.

If you are up for a challenge and don't mind the risk of blowing a component, you can try something called *over-clocking the processor*. This action is not for the faint of heart, as it can cause damage to you computer and require replacement. I don't advocate over-clocking, as it can decrease the life of your computer. Basically, to over-clock the processor, you adjust the settings on the system board to increase the effective speed of the processor. Doing this will increase the operating temperature of the computer, and you might need to add cooling fans to the computer to keep the temperature down. Many Web pages can give more details on over-clocking, if you're really interested.

Just as an example of the risk over-clocking poses, consider a story in a Web page I came across. Some hardcore gamers took an old 25Mhz 486 processor and over-clocked the processor to more than 125Mhz—five times its original speed. They then played Quake, which would have been impossible at the original speed, for seven minutes before the processor crashed—just to see if it could be done.

Overall, when looking for a processor, use a processor that meets or exceeds the requirements of the applications and games you plan to use. The optimum requirements today will be the minimum requirements tomorrow. Maybe not literally, but you get the idea.

Motherboard

Motherboards are the glue to your system. They are the single most critical component to your system. All devices in your computer interact through the motherboard. Motherboards, also known as mainboards or system boards, can also be the hardest component to pick out. If you are buying a preconfigured system, such as an HP or Compaq, you won't have much to worry about, because this component has already been picked out for you. But if you happen to have the ability to custom make or have your system custom-made, you will want to carefully choose your motherboard.

When I am selecting the components to a new system that I am putting together for myself, I start with the processor that I want to use, then choose the motherboard to optimize and enhance the processor that I just chose. I have to do some research to find out what all the new techno-talk is all about, then I can start to set some feature priorities.

I choose the processor first because each processor type has a different connection or socket type to the system board. This narrows the number of boards available. The second variable is the chipset. The chipset controls the flow of information between the components of the computer system. There are a number of manufacturers that make chipsets as well as motherboards. The trick is getting the right combination to optimize your system.

The diagram in Figure 3.3 is a good example of how a motherboard interacts as a system. This diagram appears at Tom's Hardware (`www.tomshardware.com`), where you can find out about some of the new computer technology as it's being released. (Guess I'm letting you in on my little secret. I'm really not that smart—I just know how to read.)

Figure 3.3

Here's a functional diagram of a motherboard, found at Tom's Hardware Web site.

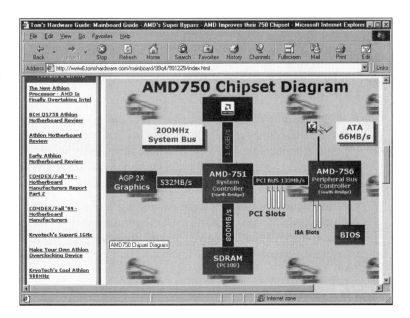

After you have picked out the processor and the chipset, you are down to only a few boards. Then all you have left is to choose if you want integrated sound, video, network, or SCSI controller—that is, to have those components built into the motherboard as opposed to installed later into card slots. I would recommend not having integrated components on the motherboard if you want to customize a computer. However, if I had to pick something to be integrated, it would be the network card. All the others I would install separately.

Sound Card

Here is an area that often takes a back seat on computers. Granted, visual effects of the graphic components are impressive and have progressed by leaps and bounds. Sound technology has also made many improvements. Three-dimensional sound is now the big thing, with speakers and a subwoofer. I will confess that the sound is impressive. However, most computers, while they have a sound card as a standard component, don't feature the best or latest technology.

The whole game experience is to give you the illusion that you are in the middle of the experience. If you want the best in sound, you might need to upgrade your sound card and perhaps your speakers. For the ultimate in interactive experience, there's even something called a game chair (www.imeron.com/products/products_LX.html) that has speakers built in for an increased illusion—and vibration when you take a hit or perform a rough landing.

Controllers

Every game needs some type of input device, and each player has his or her preference on what that input device is: Whatever that person thinks will give them an edge in the game they are going to play. The edge can make the difference when playing games against another player or the computer (which doesn't have to worry about pushing buttons to do what it wants).

Some games only need a keyboard and a mouse—which should be your minimum controller configuration—while other games are best played with a joystick. In addition, game pads resembling the controllers for console-type games are available for computers. Everyone must choose for themselves the best input device for the game they are going to play. Some games might even need multiple input devices for optimum performance—for example, Mech Warrior and some flight simulators that use both joystick and throttle controllers.

The feel of the controller is also important to consider. If I don't like the feel of a controller, I won't be as comfortable to use it, and therefore won't play as well. I spent several months looking for a joystick to use.

For those gamers that go all out on their equipment, there are force-feedback controllers. These are joysticks that will respond to what is happening in the game by vibrating or by increasing the stick resistance. Let's say that you are flying a jet and are pulling the jet out of a nosedive. In real life, there would be major G-forces pulling at you, so the force-feedback joystick will resist your pull at the stick or shake in rough weather. This feedback gives those games a whole new feel of reality.

Picking out the right game controller doesn't have to be a simple selection if you don't want it to be. You can spend a lot of money for one too.

Mice and Trackballs

When it comes to the basics, if you have your computer, you're going to have a keyboard and some type of pointing device. When it comes to desktop work, I prefer a trackball. But the trackball isn't always the best game control device. Sometimes I prefer a mouse to the trackball because it can give me better maneuverability in some of the First Person Shooter (FPS) games. However, I do like the trackball for Real Time Stratagy (RTS) games because it gives me better control.

Joysticks and Wheels

The joystick is probably what most people think of when you talk about game controllers. My first joystick was a Kraft and had two buttons. It worked great because most of the games didn't have much complexity to their controls. Today, however, I have a much more complex joystick with a myriad of customizable control buttons.

Let me briefly mention wheel controllers. Yes, you guessed it—wheel controllers are used for racing games and can have foot pedals and steering wheel buttons. These wheels can also have force-feedback features, which react based on the road conditions.

There are two classes of joysticks. There are the digital joysticks that first hit the market only a few short years ago. Then there are the old analog joysticks. "What is the difference?" you ask.

Analog

An analog joystick uses a range of control values to measure movement to be processed by the computer. The analog components measure how much you move forward and back and side to side, and measure input from any other controls that are variable, such as slides and dials. Push buttons can be interpreted either as analog or as digital, because they are either on or off.

Digital

With a digital joystick, the movement of the joystick and any variable controls starts out as a digital signal. Being a digital device, you also have more customizing flexibility. You can adjust the sensitivity and tweak the controls to fit your playing style.

Throttles

Throttles are the extras—the added controls that you might find useful for some of the games. Mech Warrior is a great example of a game that can use a throttle control. The throttles let you use your left hand to adjust the speed of your battle machine, while your right hand controls direction and weapons. Although you can use a keyboard for these controls, you might find it handy to have everything literally at your fingertips.

Joystick Vendors

There are a number of game controller manufacturers, and many of them have great products. This can make it very hard to choose between them. There are a number of Web sites that can help you evaluate and compare the features. Some of the features will have no rating, such as how the controller fits in your hand. But you can get an idea of the performance of the joystick. FPgaming (`www.fpgaming.com`), shown in Figure 3.4, is one site where you can find some comparisons. Another site is GameCenter, at `www.gamecenter.com/Hardware/Controllers/`. You can search for other sites also. In addition, many game-oriented magazines regularly publish reviews of the latest hardware.

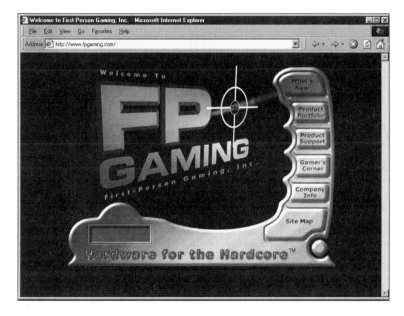

Figure 3.4

The FPgaming Web site is one review site for controllers.

In the following sections, I've listed some of the top game controller vendors. Each one has a Web site that you can visit and preview some of what they have to offer.

CH Products

You can find a variety of controllers at the CH Products site (`www.chproducts.com/index.html`), shown in Figure 3.5. They carry products for both the PC and Macintosh that come in both digital and analog versions and various price ranges, including controllers that use USB.

49

Figure 3.5

CH Products offers a wide variety of controllers.

Act Labs

Act Labs (www.actlab.com) covers the range of computer and arcade controllers. They offer racing systems, guns, game pads, flight sticks, and arcade sticks. With each new generation of controllers is added a higher degree of realism. You can see their Web site in Figure 3.6.

Figure 3.6

Act Labs makes more controllers than you can shake a stick at.

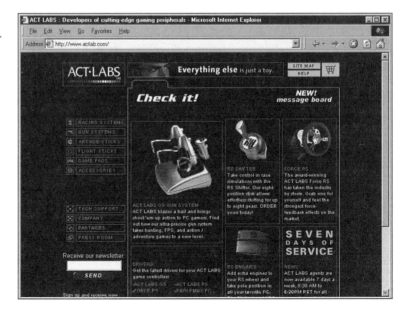

Microsoft

In spite of the fact that Microsoft (www.microsoft.com/insider/sidewinder/default.htm) is known for their software they also produce several game controllers. One, called Dual Strike, uses an innovative design, as you can see in Figure 3.7. They seem to have been able to combine mouse, keyboard, and joystick all into one controller. In addition, their SideWinder line includes several force-feedback models.

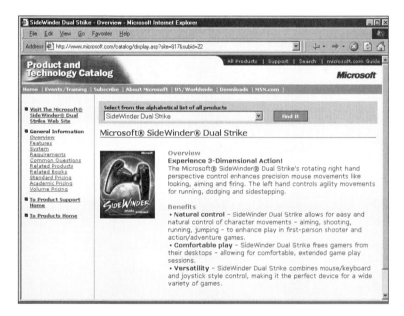

Figure 3.7

Microsoft produces game controllers as well as software.

Thrustmaster

When I hear the name of Thrustmaster (www.thrustmaster.com), I think of solid and reliable. Thrustmaster has been around a while and looks like they will continue to be around for a while longer. They have just released their line of new racing wheels, as you can see from their Web site, shown in Figure 3.8.

Logitech

Logitech (www.logitech.com/us/products/) is not just a mouse and keyboard company. Their line of WingMan game controllers are top of the line. Their controllers combine new technology and ergonomics, as noted in their Web site, shown in Figure 3.9.

Figure 3.8

Thrustmaster's Web page includes information on repairing their older controllers to extend their life.

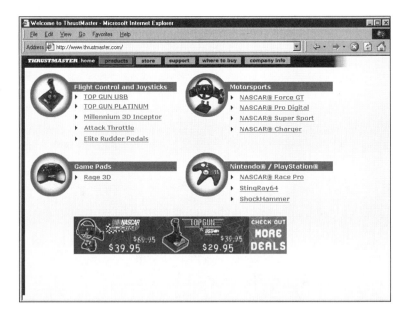

Figure 3.9

Most commonly known for their mice, Logitech also offers game controllers.

Gravis

Gravis (www.gravis.com/products/) holds its own when it comes to game controllers. They have a range of controllers to fit anyone's needs. I have a friend that will not play a game with another controller. He will only use his Gravis controller. You can see Gravis's Web site in Figure 3.10.

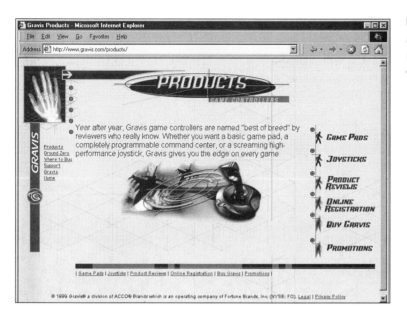

Figure 3.10

Gravis is keeping up with the new controller technology.

Mad Catz

Mad Catz (www.madcatz.com) is a game controller company. They have an innovative use of technology in their controllers. They have controllers for other systems and not just PC games, as you can see in the Web site shown in Figure 3.11.

Figure 3.11

The Mad Catz Web site is loaded with as much technology as their controllers.

Saitek

You might find, as I did, that Saitek (`www.saitekusa.com/home.html`) has pulled out the stops and broke the mold when they made their Cyborg game controllers. These controllers are not only customizable for the games, but for the hand as well. The Cyborg works with the right or left hand, as you can see in Figure 3.12. You choose and adjust it yourself.

Figure 3.12

Advanced designs and engineering of controllers is a Saitek hallmark.

Optimizing Your Existing Hardware

This section is a little different, because everyone has different hardware and therefore will have different adjustments that they can make to their personal PC. I am going to try to cover all the areas that you can optimize on your computer. I will try to cover four areas that I feel can be easily adjusted to improve your performance when gaming, thus help you to win.

Graphics

One of the areas is obviously the graphics. If you have gone all out and loaded your computer with video cards that have 3D graphic capability, you can make some adjustments. Those of you that didn't, well, follow along and you will find that you can make adjustments as well. In fact it might be even more important for you.

One of the biggest performance problems that I run across is graphic refresh. If the refresh rate is too slow, I won't be able to see everything that is happening in the game because the computer skips several screen refreshes. Normally when I see that happening, it's because my connection to the other computers is really slow. However, when the connection is fast and I still have that problem, I have had to adjust the video settings to improve the refresh of the screen. In most cases the game has had the control of the screen and control of the method of the video processing. I have even had to turn off the special video features because the computer could not handle the graphic processing.

Another way to increase the refresh rate is to increase it. Wow. What a novel idea. You might or might not have the ability to adjust your monitor refresh rate. To make that adjustment under Windows, go to the Control Panel and double click the Display icon. Here is where you are somewhat on your own because everyone has different video adapters. For me, I had to click the **Advanced** button and select the **Monitor Refresh** tab shown in Figure 3.13.

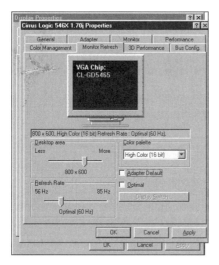

Figure 3.13

An example of finding the refresh rate setting in Windows 98.

Another adjustment to improve the refresh rate is screen size. The smaller the screen, the less the computer has to process. That means that a 340×480 screen will work better than an 800×600 screen size. In this case, bigger isn't always better.

Other Modifications

There are two related areas that I will spend some time on before playing any game competitively. Those two areas are the pointing device (mouse or joystick) and the keyboard. The reason is I will pick the mouse or the joystick for the responsiveness in a game. If I choose the mouse, I will adjust the sensitivity up or down for better control in the game. You can find the controls for the mouse in the Control Panel— Mouse icon.

The other component is the keyboard mapping. I do this by remapping the keyboard to what I am familiar with and what is comfortable for me. You will find many different opinions on this, but here is an example of what I do in FPS games. I prefer to use a mouse for target tracking. I will then remap the keyboard for motion and special game functions to keys in close proximity to increase efficiency during the game. The location of the keys are up to you, but I can tell you that keys "A", "S", and "D" are the left, forward, and right keys respectfully. I use the "X" key for reverse and will map the remaining keys in the area for the special functions. You might feel more comfortable doing something different, but the bottom line is that you need to feel comfortable.

This might be common sense, but I feel it is worth mentioning. Your overall performance depends on the resources available. When you are playing games on a Windows machine, the more applications you have open at the time of game play, the less resources will be available for your game and for Windows.

The Least You Need to Know

➤ A computer's components, or hardware, have a huge impact on its ability to run games, especially newer ones.

➤ The core components of your computer—the motherboard, processor, and memory—work together to run your software.

➤ Video technology affects games' display and is always improving.

➤ Joysticks and other controllers provide ease of play and, sometimes, even a winning edge.

Chapter 4

The Online World of the Internet

In This Chapter

➤ What types of gaming Web sites are on the Internet?

➤ Using the Internet as a connection vehicle for games

➤ Communication utilities used by gamers

➤ Popular player linking services on the Internet

➤ Popular gaming information Web sites

➤ Popular proprietary game Web sites

➤ Popular hardware review Web sites

➤ Popular LAN Party related Web sites

There are a lot of places on the Internet dedicated to gaming. It's one of the biggest genres of Web sites that you might run across. With the Internet weaving its way into nearly every home and computer system on the planet, many people are using it to make connections with other people like themselves, and that includes millions of computer game enthusiasts. It's not just a place for online shopping.

With this desire for making connections with others in mind, there are several types of gaming Web sites that you might run across. You might run across gaming Web sites dedicated to

➤ Information sites like Blues News (www.bluesnews.com); GameSpy (www.gamespy.com); VoodooExtreme (www.voodooextreme.com); GoneGold (www.gonegold.com); Gaming Events (www.gamingevents.com); GameSpot (www.gamespot.com); the Planets Web sites like www.planetquake.com, www.planettribes.com, and so on.

➤ Game vendor sites like Activision (www.activision.com), Sierra (www.sierra.com), Id (www.idsoftware.com), Interplay (www.interplay.com), and so on.

➤ Player linking sites like MPlayer (www.mplayer.com), Heat.net (www.heat.net), MSN Gaming Zone (www.zone.com), Def-Con Online (www.def-con.net), and so on.

➤ Hardware information and review sites like Tom's Hardware Page (www.tomshardware.com), Sharky Extreme (www.sharkyextreme.com), Thresh's Firing Squad (www.firingsquad.com), and Web sites from specific hardware vendors like 3DFX (www.3dfx.com), NVidia (www.nvidia.com), Creative Labs (www.creativelabs.com), and so on.

➤ LAN Party sites like LAN Party (www.lanparty.com), The LAN Party Coalition (www.lanpartycoalition.com), The LAN Party Ring (www.bangg.org/lanring), and Web sites dedicated to specific LAN Parties like LanWar (www.lanwar.com), Quake Con (www.quakecon.com), Battle Connection (www.battlecon.com), and so on.

➤ Clan sites sponsored by gamers themselves. *Clans* are groups of gamers who game together as a cohesive unit in team-oriented matches. Locating these sites is pretty easy. Just go to your favorite search engine and search on the words "Multiplayer Clan Computer Gaming". Most of the sites will be sponsored by gamers who primarily play First-Person Shooters but you'll find that all forms of multiplayer gaming have gaming groups associated with them.

➤ Sites that offer useful things to gamers such as chat services, message board services, and so on. These are sites like Yahoo Clubs (clubs.yahoo.com), ICQ (www.mirabilis.com), AIM (www.aol.com/aim), free email sites like Hotmail and Yahoo (www.hotmail.com and mail.yahoo.com respectively), and so on.

➤ Download sites, where the latest demos and patches can be downloaded. These include 3DFiles (www.3dfiles.com), CDROM.com (www.cdrom.com) and a number of the gaming sites, such as GameSpot and GameCenter.

The toughest part of gaming online is finding someone else to connect to. Many game makers are creating their own list service that can help players find one another and there are utilities like GameSpy that are designed exclusively to help players find out which games are being played and at what address.

What follows in this chapter is a survey of many of the popular Web sites associated with online gaming. It's by no means a complete list. Most people have a list of their favorite sites that they have bookmarked and which they return to on a weekly or daily basis. Maybe you'll find some sites in here you weren't aware of.

The Internet as a Connection Vehicle

There's nothing that says you can't use the Internet just to link up to your buddy in Seattle to play a satisfying game of Age of Empires II. You don't need to concern yourself with all the various gaming hoo-ha that can be found on the Internet if you don't want to. All you need is a phone line, an Internet service provider, an address to hook up to, and some good luck as far as connection performance goes. Now you're all set to play.

Now, most people only have one phone line, and that's fine for the majority of the world. But, if you're a gamer, it behooves you to make the investment and get another phone line, if for no other reason than to keep peace in the family. If you get involved in a game, you could be online for several hours at a time. Tying up your only phone line for hours on end tends to make the wife (and/or kids) rather miffed.

In addition, having only one phone line makes it difficult to inform the person (or persons) you are playing of your address or find out their addresses unless you are all using some chat client line ICQ or AIM to communicate with after everyone has connected. Some games have built-in chat interfaces that do not require you to know the addresses of those you want to connect to but these in-game chat clients are often difficult to use.

If you game with a private set of friends rather than out in the public venue against strangers, using the Internet as your connection method is a simple thing to do as long as everyone can easily communicate with one another before trying to connect within the game of choice. This can be done via a second phone line or it can be done with some chat client that does not rely on people knowing the specific address to connect to to see other chatters. ICQ and AOL's Instant Messenger are two examples of very popular chat clients that make it a snap to communicate with other people over the Internet without needing to know the addresses of any of the people involved.

ICQ by Mirabilis (`www.mirabilis.com`)

ICQ is a powerful chat client that has taken the Internet by storm. It offers an easy and convenient way of communicating with people on the Internet without needing to know the address of the people you are chatting with. The ICQ client can be downloaded from the Mirabilis Web site and quickly installed on nearly any PC or Mac. Over the last year, ICQ has evolved into something more than just a chatting utility. The original nature of the ICQ chat client was just an easy and intuitive way of chatting with other people on the Internet. Mirabilis has grown ICQ into something like a networking utility to communicate with people in many ways like message boards, personal home pages, special interest forums, Web, email and alpha paging services, voice chatting features and more.

59

Gamer Comment

Stinger (a.k.a. Paul Morris)

"ICQ is the only chat software you need to install on your machine. Well, that and maybe a good IRC client. Any good gamer uses ICQ to talk to his clan–mates."

If you are looking for a full-featured way of communicating with your buddies over the Internet, today's ICQ, shown in Figure 4.1, might be just what you need. However, some people are finding it to be a little overdone for their liking. Many companies fall into the trap of wanting their software to be too much and it grows into something that many people find too complex and confusing. I have a feeling that ICQ might be bordering on that edge right now.

The thing that has given ICQ such a strong place in the chat software arena is its capability to perform real-time chatting and not just line-by-line IRC style chatting. Chat text appears as it is typed, one character at a time rather that showing up only after a chat participant hits Enter. As you can see in the screenshot, the ICQ interface is very easy to follow.

Figure 4.1

The ICQ chat client lets you see when your friends are online.

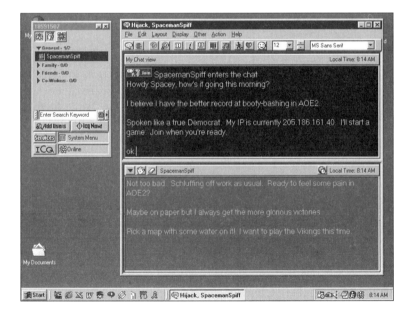

While the Mirabilis Web site might be a little confusing, their chat software is excellent for communication between gamers. If you're not already familiar with ICQ, you'll find that most gamers have an ICQ number and can easily be reached via this chat interface. Unfortunately ICQ is prone to connectivity problems since it is so heavily used. There might be times when you see people suddenly drop out of a chat session or are unable to connect at all. But, these problems will hopefully be less frequent as ICQ is perfected.

AOL's Instant Messenger (www.aol.com/aim)

Okay, so it's from AOL and not many Internet gamers are AOL users. But, you don't have to be an AOL user in order to use AIM (AOL Instant Messenger), shown in Figure 4.2. AIM can be downloaded from the AOL Web site and installed on any computer. Users can register screen names free of charge and use the chat software without any fees. AIM has a more traditional line-by-line interface than ICQ but it's a great chat client that is used by millions of people (AOL users and non-AOL users alike).

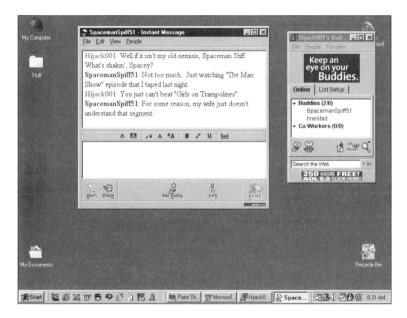

Figure 4.2

The AOL Instant Messenger is a popular chat client.

AIM users can communicate with other AIM client users as well as communicate with AOL users since the full AOL client has a built-in AIM component also. Strangely enough, the external standalone AIM client that non-AOL'ers can download and install has more features (such as group chatting and user-to-user file transfer capabilities) than the internal AIM component of the full AOL client.

The AIM client is simple to use and maintaining your contact list of buddy gamers is a breeze. The chat client plays a sound chime whenever someone sends a block of text to the chat window so you don't have to be looking at your screen to know you have something new to read. It does support group chats and have a Warn feature that allows users to begin to squelch annoying people. My gaming group (and co-workers too) tend to use AIM more than any other chat client.

Yahoo Clubs (clubs.yahoo.com)

Yahoo Clubs is a feature of the Yahoo Web site that can quickly give a group of gaming buddies a place to congregate and leave messages. Anyone can create a Yahoo

61

club, which is the perfect place for gaming groups, as you can see in Figure 4.3. Yahoo clubs offer many features that are rarely found on Web sites run by your average gamer. Clubs have features like bulletin postings, message boards, a chat interface, calendar postings and more. It has all the features that a gaming group needs to organize their online activities.

Figure 4.3

The Battle Connection Yahoo Club links you to other online games.

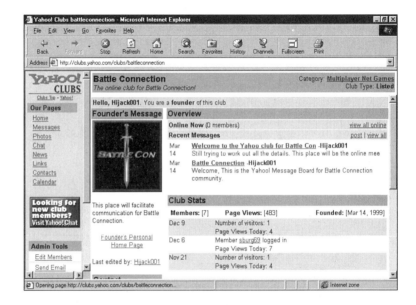

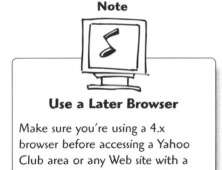

Note

Use a Later Browser

Make sure you're using a 4.x browser before accessing a Yahoo Club area or any Web site with a chat feature. Most of these features are now Java based and only work with a 4.x or higher browser.

I really like Yahoo clubs for gaming groups and always advise people to create a club for their own group. Yeah, you do have to sign up for a free Yahoo account and yes, there are strategically placed banner ads in a few places but it is completely free of charge and does have all the features most people want to use. Many gamers run their own Web site and try to replicate many of the features that you see on a Yahoo club, but it is often complicated if not impossible to do them all because of site limitations and so forth.

The chat interface is very clean and easy to use, as you can see in Figure 4.4. When a new user accesses the chat feature for the first time the Yahoo site will download a small chat plugin to their browser. That's all that's needed for chatting. It's quite a bit easier than having to manually download a chat client and install it and then configure it. The chat interface is traditional IRC style but it does have many customizable features and the latest version allows for voice chatting if you have the right hardware (sound card and a microphone).

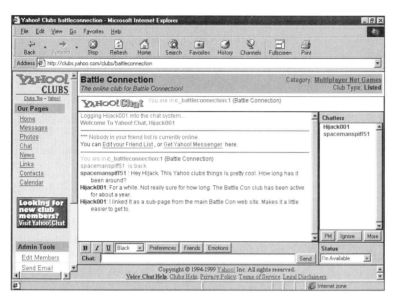

Figure 4.4

The Yahoo Clubs chat interface lets you brag about your kill score and get advice from other gamers.

If you're looking for a place for your gaming group to call home, don't bother with getting a free Web page from Geocities or Angelfire. Yahoo clubs is by far the better choice for gamers.

Player Linking Services

There are several large companies on the Internet today that are trying to succeed by providing gaming services over the Internet. Thousands of people are taking advantage of these services to link them up with other gamers. One of the main advantages these services have over player-run organized gaming is a customer commitment philosophy. Services like Heat.net, MPlayer, The Zone, and Def-Con make their money by providing a quality environment for their customers. Player-run organizations and sites have less incentive to provide a complete range of services since they usually don't charge anything. So, you have to make the call on what type of environment is best for you. If you have a little extra scratch in your back pocket and would like to game in an environment that is professionally administered or offers competition services, a gaming service might be right for you. On the other hand, if you're just a casual part-time gamer who wants to game purely for fun and doesn't get too perturbed when things go wrong, social gaming over the Internet on your own might be what you're looking for. Many gaming services have both a paid membership level and a free membership level. Free memberships allow casual gamers to utilize the service without any long-term commitment but usually limits some of the choices available through the service. These limitations typically come in the form of being unable to participate in official online tournaments that affect member rankings or being unable to redeem gaming points for prizes that paying members can.

Drakar (a.k.a. Bill M. Chamberlin)

"Choosing an ISP that remains consistently good is the hardest part of gaming. The minute an ISP grows past its capacity, it's time to move on. My main email account is a free Hotmail account so that my friends don't have to keep changing my entry in their address book when I change to a new ISP."

What about gaming services, like Heat.net and the Microsoft Gaming Zone? These services act as matchmaking services, allowing you to find human opponents to play. They're typically very good at that. But they are not service providers—you still need an ISP to log on to the net. They do typically have fast servers and really large data pipes to the net, so game connections can be better than connecting directly with other players—but that isn't always the case.

Online gaming services do provide a community environment and typically a client software component that allows players to launch games and connect to other players who also use the service. Some services even offer proprietary games that can be played straight through the service's Web site. These are usually Java-based card games or board games and are usually very fun. Most gaming services also provide a ranking system that allows members of the service to gauge themselves against other members. Some services even offer prizes and rewards to the best gamers of the month or have some other kind of prize system that allows members to get rewards for their gaming efforts.

Many gaming services are working with game publishers to incorporate their service directly into games. This allows games to operate on the gaming service more completely and sometimes does offer more stability for online play.

MPlayer (www.mplayer.com)

MPlayer is one of the most popular gaming services available today. Many games do not have direct MPlayer support and can operate online by running through the MPlayer gaming servers on the Internet. Online games can operate in one of two ways; peer-to-peer or server based. Peer-to-peer connections require that all players connect to another player in the game. Depending on that one player's connection to the Internet, game performance might be good or bad. By going through a dedicated server, bottlenecks are many times eliminated. Services like MPlayer provide such features in the games that support direct MPlayer connectivity since all players connect to the service rather than to one player over the Internet.

MPlayer reportedly has millions of gamers signed up through its service, although I have a feeling that a large percentage of this count comes from folks who have signed up once, checked out the service, and decided against it. MPlayer is a totally free service; you can see its interface in Figure 4.5. The service makes its money by banner ads and promotional activities. Unfortunately the intrusiveness of the ads on MPlayer can sometimes be rather irritating. I was stunned recently to see a pop-up window appear over the top of my chat session and a "Sing along with Andy Kaufman" session start all without my clicking anything ad related. But, free is free and people gotta make a buck somehow.

Figure 4.5

The MPlayer interface is your access to this free service.

MPlayer does have a client piece that can be downloaded from the MPlayer site. This client piece integrates nicely with their Web site and it really isn't a standalone EXE that you run when you want to connect through the MPlayer service. Most things are done via the MPlayer Web site and the client piece starts up automatically when necessary. The screen shot shows the Direct Play lobby. The Direct Play lobby is the area that you'll be placed in if you want to play a game that doesn't have built-in MPlayer support. For these games you'll still be doing peer-to-peer connections but MPlayer does offer you an environment through which you can meet other players.

All in all, MPlayer isn't too bad a service, especially since it's free. In most games that you buy today, you'll find a promo card for the MPlayer service. It's worth it to check it out, especially if the game you want to play has direct MPlayer support.

Heat.net (www.heat.net)

Heat.net is the main competitor to MPlayer. Like MPlayer, Heat.net offers a free membership level but it also offers Premium memberships for a monthly cost. Heat.net goes quite a bit farther than MPlayer does as far as what types of membership services are available. Whereas MPlayer mainly offers game connectivity services, Heat.net offers a wider range of player services like personal Web pages, online shopping, wagering with credit units called Degrees, and other such things.

Heat.net is a subsidiary of Segasoft. It is professionally run and has a bit less ad intrusion than MPlayer does (although it does still have some). The site is quite good at being a point of information about things happening in the online gaming world. Heat.net does keep up on all current events and their home page is always populated with good gaming information. Although, you'll see a lot of news items there that are really ads for their own services. Premium membership offers access to all features of the Heat.net service and costs $5.95/month, $15.99/3 months, $29.99/6 months, and $49.99/12 months.

There is a client piece of software, shown in Figure 4.6, that does need to be downloaded if you want to play through the Heat.net service. Like MPlayer, in order for a game to take full advantage of the Heat.net service, the game has to have built-in connectivity to the Heat.net gaming servers. And, like the MPlayer interface, most things are done through the Heat.net Web site and the client piece is started automatically when needed. The Heat.net client piece can also tunnel IPX communications just like Kali and Kahn can. This means that with the Heat.net client piece, you can play IPX only network games over the Internet. The Heat.net client will "tunnel" the IPX packets over the Internet, which is a TCP/IP environment.

Figure 4.6

You need this free Heat.net client software to use the service.

Heat.net provides more than just connectivity between commercially released games like Battle Zone and Quake. It also has many proprietary games that members can participate in. These games are action/role-playing games and are a far cry from the proprietary card games you might find on other similar sites.

Heat.net members also get the benefit of having a central location from which to download game updates, patches, and add-ons that might be available. Updates and patches are always being released for games and locating them can sometimes be difficult. If you are a Heat.net member, you'll also be informed when a new patch is available for the games you frequently play.

Another novel feature that the Heat.net service provides is something called Degrees. Degrees are sort of like online money within the Heat.net community. When you compete against other players you can bet Degrees against them and if you win, you collect the swag. With Degrees you can buy things from the Heat.net store like retail games, t-shirts, and so on or cash them in for discounts on larger items for sale in the Heat.net store. Cashing in or spending Degrees is only available to paying Heat.net members. Free membership users can only use them as bragging points.

All in all, Heat.net is a fairly decent online gaming service although connectivity problems do exist. I have had trouble downloading the Heat.net client for several weeks but that might just be me (it usually is). Heat.net is worth a look at least as far as its free membership level goes.

MSN Gaming Zone (www.zone.com)

The Zone is Microsoft's foray into the online gaming world. Like MPlayer and Heat.net, it has a client piece to assist in connecting retail games, as you can see in Figure 4.7, and it has a slew of free proprietary card and board-type online games. It also has several premium games that require a subscription fee before playing. The most notable one currently is Asheron's Call. Premium game prices on the Zone range from about $10 a month to $50 for a six-month subscription per game. Each game must be subscribed to and one fee does not cover all premium games.

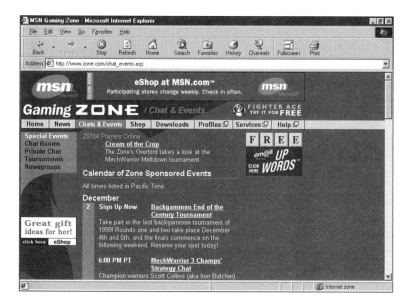

Figure 4.7

The MSN Gaming Zone Web Site is your one stop for information about connecting to Microsoft online games.

The Zone does provide a gathering ground for gamers. It provides a chat interface and a schedule of official events that members can participate in. It doesn't have quite the range of member services as Heat.net but it does have a much cleaner interface and is considerably less confusing.

The client piece for connecting retail games doesn't actually provide the connectivity for the game. It's like a front end that allows a player to notify the Zone populace that a game is available and then manages who signs up to play. It also tracks player latency before the game starts so you can get a good idea of how good each player's connection to the Internet is. This means that all games must have native TCP/IP connectivity since the Zone client does not do IPX tunneling like the Heat.net client can for older IPX-only games. Imagine the Zone client piece as being an advanced communication aid that can launch your games and manage who plays before the game starts.

The Premium games on the Zone are very popular. Asheron's Call typically has 3,000+ players playing at any given time. And other Premium games like Hercules and Xena and Tanarus do very well also.

Like other similar sites, the Zone does have a fair bit of spam floating around its pages but it's not too overwhelming and it does usually relate to Microsoft matters so at least it all looks the same. It does have a news section to keep its members up to date on events and items of importance in the gaming world but this section is obviously not high on Microsoft's list of things to maintain on the site.

Def-Con (`www.def-con.net`)

Ahhhh...Although Def-Con is a newcomer to the gaming service arena, it definitely has a pleasant look, as you can see in Figure 4.8, primarily because it has few if any banner ads plastered all over its Web site, like its large competitors. We can only hope that should Def-Con grow to a like size as MPlayer or Heat.net that it won't succumb to the same spam fate.

Def-Con is a bit more focused on supporting retail games than any other services. In fact, it doesn't have any proprietary games. It's just a linking service between existing retail games like Quake, Tribes, and similar games. Def-Con does have a set of servers that act as communication hosts between players and that help facilitate a smooth game. There is a Def-Con client piece that members need to download and install. This client piece is a front-end shell for launching supported games and provides an up front linking method of joining players. Players link up in the Def-Con software prior to starting the game to be played and then Def-Con launches it and tosses all players in.

An integrated ranking system is built into the Def-Con client that allows players to keep track of wins and losses. Part of the Def-Con system is to install an ODBC component on your machine that allows the Def-Con client to communicate win/loss data back to the main Def-Con tracking server.

Currently, Def-Con is offering $19.95 to the first 2,000 signups. There is no information posted to their site about what the fee will be after the 2,000th signup.

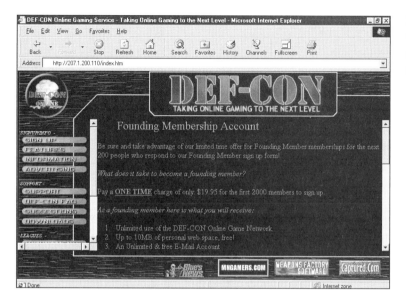

Figure 4.8

The Def-Con Web Site is an attractive gaming service.

Gaming Information Web Sites

There are a bunch of excellent gaming Web sites available for players to choose from. There are also some fairly mundane gaming sites on the Internet too. Many offer great hints, tips, and insight by experienced gamers on all aspects of gaming while others only seem to be able to regurgitate press-release information already spit out on game vendor Web sites. What most gamers find useful in an information site is whether or not it provides real world gaming information rather than corporate speak. Wading through all the gaming Web sites that are available to find the ones that give real information is a little tough to do. Here is a list of sites you might run across on the Internet and my take on each of them.

Blues News (www.bluesnews.com)

Blues News is an excellent site to bookmark to stay informed about what's happening in the First-Peron Shooter world. They have a lot of player-generated reviews on such games and they do have hooks into many companies that allow them to get stories and news items out first.

Quake and Unreal are the two most commonly covered items of interest on Blues News and they always have the most recent demos and patches available on the site. If you're looking for a place to bookmark in order to follow the latest happenings in Quake, Unreal, Tribes, or nearly any other FPS game, Blues News is for you.

daNger (a.k.a. Dan Jelks)

"Blues News is the only place you need to hit on a daily basis if you're a Q3 or UT player. Blue gets all the best information from all the right people and posts it first."

Sometimes the news items do get a little excessive (IMHO). The site typically posts a dozen or more news items on their main page daily. Wading through all that info is a little ponderous at times but it is usually useful or at least entertaining material.

Another gaming item that Blues News is well known for is its list of LAN Parties from around the US and rest of the world, shown in Figure 4.9. If you are organizing a LAN Party and would like to get the word out about it, posting it on Blues News is one of the best places to do it.

Figure 4.9

The Blues News LAN Party list lets you know where gamers gather.

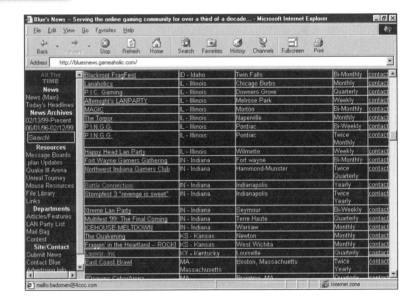

Insider news items, easy to download FPS demos and patches, and LAN Party listings make Blues News a great site to bookmark. However, there are also features like gaming articles and a message board area that allow gamers to interact with each other rather than just reading news items posted by the Blues News staff. All things considered, Blues News should be at the top of your favorites list if you are into First-Person Shooters.

GameSpot (www.gamespot.com)

Even although GameSpot is a corporately run gaming Web site, it's surprisingly player oriented. A subsidiary of ZDNet, GameSpot has nearly all of the features that Blues

News has but has a wider gaming genre coverage than Blues. GameSpot doesn't focus only on First-Person Shooters. Everything gets a fair shake at GameSpot, which is very refreshing, since First-Person Shooters tend to get the majority of the attention in the gaming world.

GameSpot has professionally written gaming articles, forums (message-board areas), reviews, hints, insider information about upcoming games, and an extensive downloads area for obtaining up-to-date patches, demos, and add-ins. You can see the site in Figure 4.10. The only major missing component is a LAN Party listing area for people to post notices about upcoming LAN Parties.

Figure 4.10

The GameSpot Web Site contains news, reviews, and demos of computer games old and new.

Another unfortunate aspect of the GameSpot Web site is that it's fairly heavily spammed with banner ads in all areas of the site. I find all the ads slightly annoying but I can forgive that transgression because the GameSpot site is very well organized and much easier to follow than most other gaming information sites. That and their expansive collection of gaming tips and complete walk-throughs are real treats. Don't call that 900 number hint line for whatever game you might be stuck in before you check out the GameSpot hint database. I'm pretty sure you'll find what you need in there. It got me past a few tough spots in Grim Fandango.

GameSpy (www.gamespy.com)

Most noted for their online game tracking system by the same name, GameSpy is a site that provides a nexus point that links all its child Web sites, which are focused toward specific areas of gaming and even toward specific games (such as RPGPlanet or PlanetTribes). You can see the site in Figure 4.11. While each of the child sites contains news and reviews of the games or gaming themes they are focused toward, the main GameSpy site offers a more universal flavor of the information it presents.

Figure 4.11

The GameSpy web site provides much information and lets you download its game tracking software.

The Green Knight (a.k.a. Jimmy Lutton)

"GameSpy is linking the entire gaming world! Hey, it's only 20 bucks and you get it for life! No monthly fees, no paying for upgrades. No nothing. It let's you know what is going on and where to connect to join the action."

Most gamers are very familiar with the GameSpy family of Web sites (the Planet series of sites). For as popular as they are, the GameSpy parent site and the child sites are fairly clear of banner ads and focus clearly on gaming for the sake of fun. This is almost certainly why they are so well received by gamers. Each of the Planet sites shares a common design without being identical to each other. Each supplies important info about the game or theme it focuses on as well as message board areas for players to communicate through. FilePlanet, another member of the GameSpy family of Web sites is one of the largest and most up to date file download centers available for gamers to use to download gaming related files.

GameSpy has caused such a splash in the gaming world that I decided to cover them in greater depth in their own chapter (Chapter 14). Chapter 17 will cover how to use the GameSpy gaming utility as well as several other utilities like Kali and Roger Wilco. The GameSpy connection utility is a one time charge utility that threatens to make obsolete most of the online player linking services like MPlayer and Heat because it performs the same basic functions but doesn't require players to sign up for any monthly service.

Electric Games (www.electricgames.com)

Electric Games is another good site to bookmark if you're looking to stay informed about items in the gaming world. Electric Games is a much more information-oriented Web site without user features like message boards, user-submitted articles, or LAN Parties listings. But, it does have some valuable information posted about all sorts of things in the gaming world and is one of the few sites that covers events in the Macintosh gaming arena.

Electric Games offers up-to-date downloads of demos and patches as well as offering Windows 9x themes based on many games that are available these days. It's also an excellent source of links to other sites on the Internet that are related to gaming: sites like gaming magazine Web sites, game vendor Web sites, hardware company Web sites, and other important links in the gaming world. Their links section is well organized by game so you can quickly locate a Web site related to the game(s) you most enjoy playing. You'll also find a links page listing hint and cheat Web sites that you can visit.

The site does have banner ads on it but not nearly as prominently as GameSpot, which is very refreshing to see. Check them out and you might find them a good place to bookmark.

Other Information Sites Worth Noting

While it's impossible to list all gaming related Web sites here, I did want to give a list of some other sites that gamers might find useful but might not be aware of currently (see Table 4.1).

Table 4.1   Gaming Information Web Sites

Site	Address	Items of Interest
Games Mania	www.gamesmania.com	A good multilingual site that features news, preview, and hardware tech tidbits about events in the gaming world.
GamePro World	www.gameproworld.com	An excellent site for information on both the PC and console gaming industry. Offers reviews, hardware tips, hints and more.

continues

Table 4.1 Continued

Site	Address	Items of Interest
MN Gamers	www.mngamers.com	Although a regional site run by gamers in Minnesota, this site is well organized and supplies well written articles and reviews of items in the gaming world by real gamers. Offers LAN Party postings, message boards, and gaming clan organization features.
PC Gaming	www.pcgaming.com	A small but well run site supplying player generated gaming information and news. Offers patches and demo downloads.
Threshes' Firing Squad	www.firingsquad.com	An excellent site packed full of valuable gaming reviews, hardware reviews, downloads, message boards and articles of interest about gaming.
Gamers.com	www.gamers.com	A spin-off site from Threshes' Firing Squad, this site offers a lot of gamer services like free email accounts, home pages, and some proprietary games that can be played through the Web site. It also offers good information on PC, Mac, and console gaming points of interest.

Proprietary Gaming Web Sites

If you're just looking to have a little quick fun on the Internet there are many good Web sites that offer proprietary games such as card games, board games or action/adventure games that you can play for free or for a small fee. You don't just have to play commercial games online. In fact, thousands of people use these types of Web sites everyday. Some sites are even designed as organized casino-type sites where online betting is carried out.

Table 4.2 shows a list of Web sites that offer various types of online gaming fun.

Table 4.2   Proprietary Game Web Sites

Web Site	Games/Theme
2AM Games www.2am.com	Strategy games like Chain of Command, Alliance and Defense, and others. Also traditional games like Poker, Chess, and Backgammon. Service is free but banner ads are displayed in the games. A client piece must be downloaded in order to play.
Game Storm www.gamestorm.com	Game Storm is the site for one of the most popular proprietary games on the Web, Air Warrior III. This site also features many common games like Hearts, Spades, Bridge, Poker, and many others. Game Storm also features several other popular action games. The simpler games can be played free of charge but the "Extreme Games" like Air Warrior cost $9.95 per month. This fee does allow access to all "Extreme Games." A client piece must be downloaded.
iEntertainment Network www.iencentral.com Also available by connecting to The Games Arena www.thegamesarena.com	iEntertainment offers a wide range of flight simulator games like Warbirds and Dawn of Aces as well as roleplaying games like The Eternal City. iEntertainment offers many more games like these also. The site is a pleasant change from the other proprietary game sites that typically offer primarily card games. The iEntertainment games set requires a client piece as well as the gaming modules for their big titles like Warbird. Some of the download can be quite hefty but Warbirds does come in a Macintosh flavor as well. Many of the simpler games are Java only and require no manual download prior to playing the game. The costs for this gaming service can range from $9.95, $19.95, or $29.95 a month for premium services (allows access to Warbirds and the other large titles). Alongside these flat month's rates are hourly charges of $1.99, $1.75, or $1.50 an hour respectively for each of the previously noted monthly changing plans.
iGames www.igames.com	iGames is a simple Web site that supports a proprietary gaming client piece of primarily card games. This is a free service although iGames has started to ask for voluntary yearly contributions of $25. This contribution allows you to override the prohibition of joining full chat rooms and it eliminates the banner ads that non-paying users are forced to see. If you enjoy playing cards online, give iGames a look.

continues

Table 4.2   Continued

Web Site	Games/Theme
Multi-Player Online Gaming www.mpog.com	This site is a little confusing to the novice online gamers. It's tough to know what this site is all about. It has some gaming information related to online retail games and it also offers free access to its proprietary games like Europa and World at Ruins (a.k.a. War). These games are Java/HTML based games and don't do well at holding most people's attention. The site needs a serious over-haul to clarify the nature of the theme.
Pogo www.pogo.com (Formerly TEN.NET)	Pogo offers a good selection of card, board, word, trivia, and casino type online games. Pogo is a free service and there is no client piece required to be downloaded. Plug-ins will be automatically sent to client machines when a player selects a game to play. Pogo offers cash rewards in several of its casino type games if money is your ultimate goal. Formerly the Total Entertainment Network and a service that offered retail game connectivity ser-vices, Pogo now focuses on its current theme of proprietary online games and cash rewards to play-ers.
Won www.won.net	Won offers a large selection of card, board, and game show type games. It also offers some higher end RPG and strategy games too. The service is free and most of the games do not require players to manually download anything prior to playing the game. Plug-ins will be downloaded at play time. The Won service also offers some file down-load features for popular retail games like Half-Life, Tribes, and so on. Users of Won can customize a free Web page for themselves if they would like.
Yahoo Games games.yahoo.com	Yahoo games is a simple yet very popular set of Java based games (mostly card and board games) that anyone can play for free. Players do need to have a Yahoo account but this is a free ser-vice of Yahoo and does offer access to other Yahoo features like clubs and email.

As you can see there is a wide range of available proprietary online games. Many are free but some do cost money. The ones that charge a fee are worth a look if you are into community gaming. Be careful because you might find yourself becoming addicted to many of these games even though they might seem simple at first.

<unknown> (a.k.a. Brad Colwell)

"Sometimes you just want to kick back and play a game of Hearts. I usually use the Zone. Their card games are pretty decent."

Hardware Review Web Sites

Near and dear to all gamers' hearts is the hardware that runs the magnificent games that they play. No other aspect of computing is changing more rapidly than the hardware related to online gaming. Video card technology and CPU technology are being driven forward by the incredibly fast growth rate of computer gaming. The multimedia demands that game designers ask of the hardware that runs their games is massive and hardware vendors are doing their best to keep up. Actually, they're doing a pretty good job of it, sometimes too good. Hardware changes almost as rapidly as software. Keeping up with these changes takes help and a good source of information to turn to.

While you could go to the trouble of trying to monitor every hardware vendor's Web site for news and information, the information you get is often biased and not representative of the facts when taken as a whole. There are two excellent Web sites that all gamers should know about that allow us to keep up with the changes in the hardware market. These two sites are Tom's Hardware Page and Sharky Extreme.

Tom's Hardware Guide (www.tomshardware.com)

Tom's Hardware Guide offers gamers a thorough look at all the hardware they need to know about in order to have just the right components under the hood of their computers. Although not specifically a Web site dedicated to reviewing hardware just as it relates to computer gaming, Tom's Hardware Guide does cover everything that a gamer needs to keep up on and more.

A great deal of insider information is presented on Tom's Hardware Guide and sneak peaks at upcoming hardware are always available. The information given on this site is often both highly technical for those true geeks out there and summarized plainly for those who aren't so technically oriented. Many of the benchmarks given for things like video cards, motherboards, CPUs, and such are presented in gaming terms that gamers can understand. Often popular games like Quake 3 or Unreal are used to show the performance levels of various hardware combos rather than generic benchmarking numbers that no one has a reference for.

One of the best things about this site is the fact that direct comparisons are done between nearly all competing hardware devices so that gamers can get a thorough range of information from which to make the best selection when going out to do a little computer hardware shopping. Tom's Hardware Guide also pays attention to hardware that you'll find at Best Buy or CompUSA and not just the ultra high-end stuff only available by buying directly from the manufacturer.

Sharky Extreme (www.sharkyextreme.com)

If you want to see if someone agrees with the info on Tom's Hardware Guide, you should check out Sharky Extreme. The information presented here about hardware related to gaming is just as insightful as it is on Tom's Hardware Guide. Like Tom's Hardware Guide, the information on Sharky Extreme can sometimes get a little technical for your average person. But, since most gamers are bigger geeks than the rest of the world, this rarely poses a problem.

Sharky Extreme is significantly more focused toward reviewing hardware for gaming purposes than Tom's Hardware Guide is. Nearly all the benchmarks and reviews that are done about hardware and expressed in gaming terms that most gamers will be familiar with. Sharky Extreme also reviews hardware not directly related to gaming but often used by gamers. Items like portable MP3 players are looked at in details as well as the typical gamer items like video cards, CPUs, and motherboards.

You'll also find a great many technically oriented game reviews on Sharky Extreme. Something you won't find on Tom's Hardware Guide. All this bundled with the fact that Sharky Extreme also helps gamers keep tabs on the best CPU prices makes this site a weekly must visit place.

LAN Party Web Sites

Ah, now we come to an aspect of gaming close to my heart. LAN Parties. As I've already mentioned many times, LAN Parties are growing rapidly in popularity and there are several sites dedicated to promoting them.

Blues News has already been covered as a general gaming information site that has a very large section of LAN Party postings. But, there are a few others that online gamers should be aware of if they are looking for a good LAN Party to hit on a slow weekend. Note that these sites are general LAN Party promoting sites and not sites specific to any one LAN Party event. The sites listed here will help you locate a LAN Party or link you to a LAN Party Web site.

LAN Party (www.lanparty.com)

LAN Party, the Web site, is probably the best Web site to monitor for upcoming LAN Party events in your area. Most LAN Party organizers use LAN Party, the Web site, to notify the public of their upcoming events. Posting a LAN Party notice to LAN Party, the Web site, is free of charge and easy to do.

On this site you'll find posting for LAN parties all around the world, not just in the US. The party database is easy to browse and can be done by region in order to slim down the number of events listed to just those in your area.

LAN Party, the Web site, also offers Web hosting services for parties sites if you run an event but don't know where to post your complete event information. This is typically a fee based hosting arrangement as you would find with any other Web hosting service.

LAN Party, the Web site, also posts news items daily about events in the gaming world related to LAN Parties. The site also offers tips and advice on how to run a good LAN Party. If you're new to the LAN Party scene and are planning on running a medium or large sized event, this site is definitely worth checking out thoroughly.

Gamer Comment

Jenner (a.k.a. Martin Lessa)

"LANparty.com has a bunch of parties listed. Sometimes it's a little frustrating seeing all these parties in Australia or Germany and not be able to find one in your area. But, it is the best place to use to find out where the nearest LAN Party to you can be found."

The LAN Party Ring (www.bangg.org/lanring)

The LAN Party Ring, shown in Figure 4.12, is an organization of LAN Party Web sites that are all linked together by a common HTML graphic block and link arrangement that you'll find at the bottom the main page of each member site. This link area allows you to travel around the member sites quickly and see what the ring has to offer.

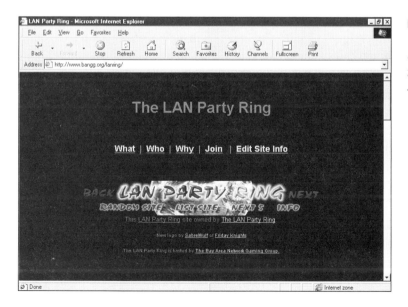

Figure 4.12

The LAN Party Ring Organization Site joins a number of game group sites.

The LAN Party ring is a free service to any Web site that is related to LAN Parties and all you need to do to join is go to the organization site and apply. The appropriate link code and graphic reference will be sent to you via email and you can apply the code and graphic reference to your own site and join the ring. Information about your site and your event will be held in the ring database, which can be browsed by anyone who would like to find a LAN Party to attend. This will increase Web traffic to your site and give a fledgling LAN Party Web site some much needed exposure to the right demographic of Web users.

The LAN Party Coalition (www.lanpartycoalition.com)

The LAN Party Coalition is a new organization started to help promote and organize LAN Parties in the Midwest. Sites like Blues News and LAN Party offer locations to post event information on but until recently LAN Parties have been primarily independent events that are difficult to maintain for several reasons.

The costs involved in running a medium or large event can be fairly high. Hardware has to be purchased (hubs, cabling, computers to act as servers, and so on), promotion for the event has to be done, a location has to be secured, sponsors need to be contacted, Web pages have to be designed, and many other things have to be done before the event can even begin, much less hope to survive. The concept behind the LAN Party Coalition is as an assistance resource that helps LAN Parties get going and even help each other out.

Let's assume that a group in Dayton Ohio wants to run a LAN Party in July and a group in Indianapolis Indiana wants to run an event in June. Both groups have resources like hardware, mailing lists, and other items that they could share between each other so that both events can be a success. Certain members of the group in Dayton might be well skilled in one area and the group in Indianapolis skilled in another. Both groups might be willing to lend a hand at running each others' event. This is the concept behind the LAN Party Coalition; putting event organizers in touch with each other and helping to organize the cooperation between events.

Another aspect of the coalition is to help mediate scheduling conflicts of LAN Parties in the same area that might cause gamers to have to decide between attending two outstanding events. As LAN Parties get more popular, you're going to find several in the same area and scheduling conflicts are bound to happen. Rather than get into an adversarial relationship, two or more events would all benefit from coordinating their events so that they don't conflict with each other.

The LAN Party Coalition is something that our event in Indianapolis (Battle Connection) is fully supportive of and we hope to get the information out as loudly as we can. If you run an event or are planning on trying a larger event, check out the coalition site and contact them to begin the assistance process. They are more than willing to lend a hand.

The Least You Need to Know

➤ There are many kinds of gaming related Web sites from player linking sites to sites offering proprietary games to gaming vendor Web sites to gaming information Web sites to LAN Party related Web sites.

➤ Utilities like ICQ, AOL Instant Messenger, and Yahoo Clubs can be valuable tools in helping gamers communicate.

➤ Services like MPlayer, Heat.Net, and Def-Con can be used to help players connect up but are often unnecessary.

➤ Information Web sites like Blues News and GameSpot can provide some interesting and insightful reading material on all aspects of online gaming.

➤ Many Web sites like iEntertainment and Won offer unique games but sometimes require a subscription fee and a client piece to be downloaded and installed.

➤ Hardware information Web sites like Tom's Hardware Guide and Sharky Extreme are important places to monitor for information related to gaming hardware.

➤ LAN Party sites like LAN Party and the LAN Party Coalition can be valuable resources for those gamers who are trying to run an event themselves.

Part 2
The Big Fight

Games have simulated fighting since prehistoric times. Chess has its origins in ancient fighting tactics. Even the games kittens play train them to be hunters later in life. With their ability to track so much data, computers are naturals to simulate battles.

It's no exaggeration to say that fighting games revolutionized the computer game field, from pioneering 3D graphics to introducing online team or competitive play. So, gear up for battle—whether in the dark corridors of First-Person Shooters, the battlefields of real-time strategy simulations, or the giant robots of mech games, prepare to test your mettle and your metal!

Chapter 5

First-Person Shooters

In This Chapter

➤ The First-Person Shooter genre

➤ The current hot titles

➤ Upcoming titles

➤ FPS gaming strategies

Imagine walking down a dark hallway in a futuristic battle realm. You hear footsteps. You abruptly stop and turn around, seeing nothing but darkness lit occasionally by flaming torches. You continue moving forward. Suddenly, a metallic "caw-chunk" sound rings out behind you and a grenade flies past your head. You duck down a passageway to the right, spin around and blindly launch a missile toward your unseen attacker. A scream. A splatter. Your enemy's head bounces out of the night and lands at your feet. Ducking back into the real world for a moment, you glance over to your buddy sitting at the computer next to you and he is glaring at you. Thus is the way of the *First-Person Shooter*, or *FPS*.

The First-Person Shooter Genre

Without a doubt, the FPS is the most popular type of game in existence today. Why? Because it places you in the action. It gives you the opportunity to explore artificial worlds and conquer them. Your success or failure is based on your skill and reflexes and not a random simulation. You can team up with your friends or fight against them. A FPS takes place from the first-person perspective—you see your surroundings from the same point of view as if you were really there. This is the closest you're going to get to virtual reality for quite some time. The ability to design your own environments and appearance adds to the wide appeal.

As you're probably aware, though, FPS games have garnered their share of controversy lately. Many people—informed and otherwise—have spoken out against the violence that is typical in First-Person Shooters. Personally, I have a bit of a problem with this line of thought. I've been playing these games for years and I've never contemplated carrying it over into real life, and there are literally millions of players around the world for whom that's true as well. Today's games are just that—games. Perhaps at some point in time, games will be indistinguishable from reality, but we're hardly at that point now. Nonetheless, I'll be sure to point out the bloodier of the games that are available—as either a reason to avoid, or, for some, a selling point.

The FPS genre all started with a little game called Castle Wolfenstein, which placed the gamer in a castle overrun by Nazis and their guard dogs. The ability to move freely and fluidly within a seemingly 3D environment was a new experience for users, and they loved it. The programmers at id software quickly followed the popular game with another smash hit—Doom. Doom carried more unpolitically-correct imagery and a more enhanced graphics engine. People were hooked. For a while, it seemed that Doom had hit the limits of what was possible with a FPS. Then, games such as Duke Nukem 3D appeared and took FPSs in a new direction. Adding humor and a touch of raunchy realism, Duke Nukem brought the game to a whole new audience.

As processors became faster and graphics accelerators became commonplace, programmers suddenly had a new palette of tools to work with. Detailed interactive environments sprung to life, and the FPS that we know and love today was born.

Contemporary First-Person Shooters

Now that you know what a First-Person Shooter is, let's take a look at some of the more popular games. A few of these titles have been around for more than a year… In game time, that's an eternity and is indicative of more than just a flashy appearance and brand name. The popularity of FPS games means that a lot of games come out. A majority of these are just plain bad or at least unimaginative and boring. Don't start thinking that just because a game is new, it's better. Longevity is a good thing in gaming! You can download demos of many of these games at www.gamespot.com. Now, on to the titles.

Quake, Quake 2, and Quake 3 Arena

id Software: www.idsoftware.com

Install and Play	8	Story Line Depth	3
Control Simplicity	8	Strategy Simplicity	8
Multiplayer Quality	9	Team Playability	7
Multimedia Quality	7	Modifiability	9
Kid Friendly	3	Online Stability	9
3D Accelerator Support?	Yes		

From the people who introduced the world to FPS titles comes what, for many people, is the pinnacle of the FPS genre as it exists today—the Quake trilogy. The original Quake fully realized the potential shown by Wolfenstein 3D and Doom, and its two sequels have for the most part expanded game frontiers even farther. Figure 5.1 shows a scene from the latest Quake "Quake 3 Arena".

Figure 5.1

Quake 3 sports incredible architecture and effects.

Stunning graphics and incredible multiplayer support make Quake 2 and the new Quake 3 Arena appealing to the eye and to the online gamer. The Quake series builds fantastic environments with amazing architecture. Unfortunately, id software has been stuck in a rut with level design. Although beautiful, the levels in Quake 2 and 3 are dungeon-like and not as varied as some other games. Quake also lends itself to the camper player—offering a lot of hiding places for snipers to hide out. Luckily,

87

there are plenty of user-created maps that address some of the shortcomings in the supplied maps.

If you're looking for a game that offers a great one-player mode, you might want to consider running Quake 2 instead of Quake 3 arena. Quake 3 is primarily a multi-player game. As a single-player game, it doesn't offer the variety and adventure of Quake 2 which features a variety of missions as a marine in the vanguard of an attack on an alien planet. For online multiplayer games, however, Quake 3 is fantastic. None of the Quake games rely on the one before it, so you can pick up anywhere in the series without feeling like you've missed something. The online "Quaking" community is vast and vocal. Modifications and maps are available to suit just about anyone.

Fansites: www.planetquake.com, www.quakenews.com, www.quakeland.com

Unreal and Unreal Tournament

Epic Software: www.unrealtournament.com

Install and Play	7	Story Line Depth	8
Control Simplicity	8	Strategy Simplicity	8
Multiplayer Quality	8	Team Playability	7
Multimedia Quality	7	Modifiability	8
Kid Friendly	5	Online Stability	8
3D Accelerator Support?	Yes		

The main competitor to the Quake series is Unreal Tournament. The Unreal series started with the groundbreaking game Unreal and is continued with the multiplayer arena style game Unreal Tournament. The Unreal game engine does not sport some of the features of Quake 3, such as curved surfaces. It does, however, have some unique features of its own. For example, throughout the Unreal games you'll see startling reflections, particle effects, such as fire, and incredible liquids.

The original Unreal game offers fantastic single-player gameplay—with scenes that play out like a big-budget Hollywood movie. Wide outdoor areas, complete with wildlife, are available for exploration. If you play Unreal by yourself, you're definitely going to be startled by both the effects and fluidity of the game. Unfortunately, multiplayer support was horrible in the original game. Connection problems, constantly having to update your software and awkward movements led to a horrible online gaming experience. Luckily, Epic Software has taken the game engine and created Unreal Tournament.

UT is the direct competition to Quake 3 Arena. There is an ongoing debate as to which game is better—but that's a decision you'll have to make yourself. Offering arguably better level design than Quake 3 and a greater selection of weapons, UT definitely shines. Unreal Tournament has a rather strange user interface—complete with its own windowing system. This can be a bit confusing for someone used to starting other games and jumping into the action. Figure 5.2 shows a few of the Unreal configuration options.

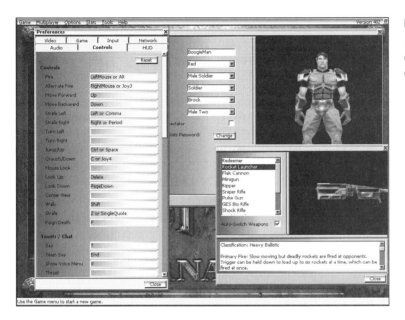

Figure 5.2

Unreal sports a rather complicated interface for a typical FPS.

Overall, I highly recommend Unreal as a single player game, and Unreal Tournament as a multiplayer alternative. Even if you already are a big Quake fan, you can't go wrong with Unreal. The original single player version of Unreal does not have a demo available, but Unreal Tournament does. If you're hesitant to pick up Unreal, download the UT demo... then imagine lush landscapes and cinematic effects added to the stunning demo graphics. That's Unreal.

Fansites: www.planetunreal.com, www.unrealnation.net, www.unrealuniverse.com

Kingpin: Life of Crime

Interplay Software: www.interplay.com

Install and Play	7	Story Line Depth	5
Control Simplicity	8	Strategy Simplicity	8
Multiplayer Quality	3	Team Playability	3
Multimedia Quality	9	Modifiability	3
Kid Friendly	1	Online Stability	3
3D Accelerator Support?	Yes		

89

If fighting aliens and other bizarre creatures isn't your cup of tea, perhaps you should try something a bit more realistic. Kingpin is an ultra-violent game—it's dark, grim, and more than a little splattered in blood. Your enemies are real people, and the weapons are real weapons.

The textures and special effects in the game draw you into a dark city environment. Grimy streets and buildings are everywhere. Fire burns in the alleyways. Not a very nice place to be. The violence in this virtual word is extreme. Decapitations and mutilations are normal. If you attack and injure a player, they run away—leaving a trail of bloody footprints behind them.

Unfortunately, while Kingpin does create a realistic environment, the enemies and weapons are less than lifelike. Despite the appearance of being human, the characters in Kingpin pose unrealistic speed and agility. Weapons don't pack quite the same punch as their real-world counterparts. Don't expect to throw a grenade and do damage; you're going to be disappointed. If you're looking for a realistic simulation, this isn't it.

Kingpin also falls short in the Internet gameplay area. Connections are rarely stable and you're not likely to find many other people to play with. As a single-player game, it's quite an experience, but if you're interested in a virtual online bloodbath, you'll be better off with Quake or UT. For a truly realistic killing experience, try Rainbow Six.

Fansites: www.planetkingpin.com, www.urbangangsta.com, www.poisonville.com

Rainbow Six and Rainbow Six: Rogue Spear

Red Storm Entertainment: www.redstorm.com

Install and Play	8	Story Line Depth	5
Control Simplicity	7	Strategy Simplicity	3
Multiplayer Quality	8	Team Playability	9
Multimedia Quality	7	Modifiability	3
Kid Friendly	5	Online Stability	8
3D Accelerator Support?	Yes		

Rainbow Six is unlike any game you've played before. Based on the popular Tom Clancy novel, you're a member of a special attack unit charged with carrying out precision attack and rescue operations in a variety of locations. The game aims to realistically simulate the experience of searching for, and attacking, other human opponents and rescuing hostages. Rogue Spear is the second installment of the popular series. Figure 5.3 shows the complex paths you can instruct your team to take.

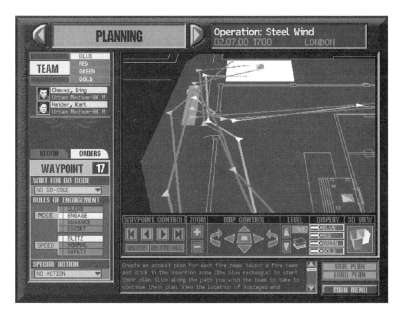

Figure 5.3

Rainbow Six lets you plan every aspect of your attack.

Unlike games like Kingpin that claim to have realism, yet are only realistic in texturing, Rainbow Six aims for realism in gameplay. The graphics are nice, but not outstanding—but they are not what make the game. You must play the game as if it were an actual mission. No running around blindly shooting…no charging into rooms…why? A single shot can kill you. If you're accustomed to Quake-type shoot fests, you're going to die very quickly. The good news is that if you're playing an inexperienced enemy, they're likely to die very quickly, too.

The same rule applies to the computer enemies—the game places more emphasis on stealth and a single well-placed shot from a sniper or a quick burst from a submachine gun than hosing down indestructible bosses with megadeath weapons. However, the artificial intelligence isn't perfect. Enemy terrorists have been seen calmly strolling by the bloody bodies of their compatriots without raising an alarm.

Rainbow Six and its sequel have a strong single-player component. They allow you to plan and coordinate your attacks on the enemy with either online teammates or a computer controlled team. Missions can be over in a matter of seconds, or can go on for what seems like an eternity. For most people, this is a game you either love or hate. If you're used to getting a quick fix from a game, then this probably won't do it for you. On the other hand, if you're looking for an FPS that has a real strategy element, then either of the Rainbow Six games are for you.

Fansites: www.planetrainbowsix.com, www.rogue-spear.com, www.rainbowsix.net/

Descent 3

Interplay Software: www.interplay.com

Install and Play	8	Story Line Depth	6
Control Simplicity	6	Strategy Simplicity	8
Multiplayer Quality	8	Team Playability	8
Multimedia Quality	9	Modifiability	5
Kid Friendly	8	Online Stability	8
3D Accelerator Support?	Yes		

If you're not into killing creepy crawlies or humanoid-ish aliens there's an alternative FPS that might be for you. Descent allows you to pilot your tiny ship and destroy hundreds of beautifully designed enemy craft. The original Descent storyline cast the player as the pilot of a ship probing an asteroid complex where rebellious robots are holding miners as hostages. The Descent game broke the FPS mold by introducing full freedom of movement in three dimensions. You can rotate in any direction and move wherever you'd like.

The Descent series has typically involved controlling your vessel in a series of interconnected tunnels. In Descent 3, although, you also fly to the surface of the outside planet. The graphics make use of the latest video accelerators to create a stunning experience. Lighting effects and fantastic sound make the environment seem real. The physics model is equally well designed. When you shoot an enemy, it spins around in the air, rather than just taking a hit. There is no true up or down—you can find yourself flying around for a few minutes, then realizing that you've spent the entire time upside down. Despite having a large number of controls, Descent 3 remains incredibly easy to play. You can quickly map a few commands to your keyboard, mouse, or keyboard, then jump into the action. In Figure 5.4, the author is about to be blown up.

Multiplayer mode in Descent 3 includes a variety of options that keep the gameplay fresh. Connections are very stable, and the action is smooth. Whether you're looking for a single-player action game, or would like to whiz around in zero-G with your friends, Descent 3 is a great game to add to your library.

Fansites: www.planetdescent.com, www.descent.org/descentia, www.descent-x.com

Figure 5.4

Descent 3 features excellent light effects and realistic zero-G physics.

Aliens Versus Predator

Fox Interactive: www.foxinteractive.com

Install and Play	8	Story Line Depth	6
Control Simplicity	7	Strategy Simplicity	8
Multiplayer Quality	6	Team Playability	4
Multimedia Quality	8	Modifiability	3
Kid Friendly	6	Online Stability	8
3D Accelerator Support?	Yes		

You've all seen the movies, right? With Alien Versus Predator you can finally take over the persona of your favorite movie monsters and wreak havoc on humans, predators, or aliens. Pick your favorite creature and let the mayhem begin! In Figure 5.5 a Marine is about to meet a very nasty predator.

Figure 5.5

In AvP, you can play as an Alien, a Predator, or (why??) a Marine!

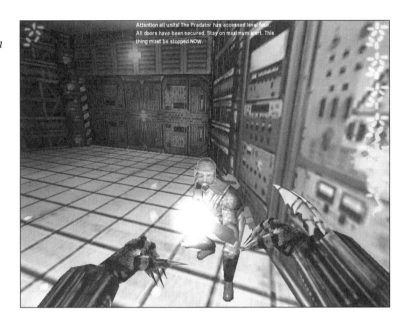

Alien Versus Predator is a game that was obviously designed for fans of the Predator and Alien movies. You control the character of your choice—an Alien, a Predator, or a Colonial Marine. Each character has the special abilities that are unique to that being. Predators can switch between different types of vision and become invisible. Aliens can move with cat-like quickness and crawl along walls and ceilings. Marines...well, marines have flame-throwers, if that's your thing. Unfortunately, even with these special features, the action boils down to typical "who can kill whom faster" gameplay.

Multiplayer online support is included, but isn't the primary focus of the game. If you're looking for a great online Alien Versus Predator game, you'd be better off downloading a total conversion for Quake. AvP is a nice game if you're really into the movies and want the best possible movie experience. As a single-player game it can be fun, but as a multiplayer online title, it falls short.

Fansites: www.planetavp.com, www.avpnews.com, www.avsp.net

Blood and Blood 2

Monolith: www.blood.com/

Install and Play	8	Story Line Depth	6
Control Simplicity	7	Strategy Simplicity	8
Multiplayer Quality	6	Team Playability	4

Multimedia Quality	8	Modifiability	5
Kid Friendly	6	Online Stability	6
3D Accelerator Support?	Yes		

Look at the game's title. What do you think you'll be seeing a ton of in this game? Blood, as you might have guessed, is filled with a lot of red stuff. Unlike games like Kingpin that attempt to portray violence in a realistic way, Blood places the player in a gothic and truly miserable environment that combines elements of sorcery and Old West-style gunslinging.

The graphics are outstanding and offer a nice break from the high-tech/retro look in games such as Quake and UT. The music sets the mood for the game and the occasional comments uttered by the characters will make you giggle with evil glee. Blood is a game that delights in its own make-believe evil—it isn't an attempt to provide any sort of realism. Controls are simple to master, but after playing for awhile, many of the areas begin to look alike. Figure 5.6 shows why Blood is named "Blood."

Figure 5.6

Blood is a game filled with…you guessed it, blood!

As a multiplayer game, Blood, as with many games, falls a bit short. There are connection and lag problems that plague the title. Like so many other games, this seems to be designed for single player action, then have multiplayer support added as an afterthought. If you'd like a fun, bloody, gothic game, this is a good bet.

Fansites: `www.planetblood.com`, `www.bloodshack.com`, `www.lithtimes.com`

Shogo: Mobile Armor Division

Monolith: `www.shogo-mad.com`

Install and Play	8	Story Line Depth	6
Control Simplicity	7	Strategy Simplicity	8
Multiplayer Quality	6	Team Playability	4
Multimedia Quality	8	Modifiability	7
Kid Friendly	7	Online Stability	8
3D Accelerator Support?	Yes		

Remember the good old days of running home after school to watch Robotech? (Ummm...probably not—that's just me.) Who wouldn't want to control a giant anime-style "mech" and tower above the city, making your enemies tremble with fear. Shogo does just that—it let's you control your very own giant robot. (For information on other games that offer a giant-fighting-robot flavor, see Chapter 7, "Mech Games.")

Tech Tip

Anime and Mechs

Anime is the Japanese artform of animation. Willing to take more risks and playing to a wildly varying crowd, Japanese animation might seem a bit unsettling to Americans. Characters die, and there is nudity and sexually explicit scenes in some titles. It's a very different world.

One type of anime centers around the use of mech or mechanized armor. Characters don huge metal robot-like suits to do battle with their foes. Weapons are exaggerated and spectacular. The perfect sort of subject for a video game!

Shogo is designed around the Lith graphics engine, which handles all the effects that you've grown accustomed to with ease. It also scales the environment perfectly whether you are operating on foot as a human, or have climbed aboard one of the giant mech suits that are available. Special effects are taken straight from the similarly themed anime. Giant missile trails and huge explosions—if you want them, you've got 'em! What's more, you can actually transform the robots into other vehicles. Transformers, here we come! Look at all of the lovely explosions in Figure 5.7!

Figure 5.7

Be a big robot and blow things up. Fun!

Multiplayer support is great. While not as ingrained into the minds of gamers as the Quake series, the variation in Shogo makes it an arguably better multiplayer game than the bigger titles. If you have any desire to stomp on your enemies from inside of a towering suit of metal, pick up Shogo and get to work!

Fansites: www.planetshogo.com, www.shogo-mad.com/ring/, www.thehaus.net/Shogo/

StarSeige: Tribes

Dynamix: www.dynamix.com/

Install and Play	8	Story Line Depth	9
Control Simplicity	7	Strategy Simplicity	5
Multiplayer Quality	10	Team Playability	10
Multimedia Quality	8	Modifiability	9
Kid Friendly	6	Online Stability	7
3D Accelerator Support?	Yes		

If you've played a few multiplayer online games and think you know what they're about, think again. Tribes is an entirely unique experience that redefines what an FPS can be. Rather than following the same old shoot-everything-in-the-corridor approach, Tribes unleashes armies upon one another across sprawling landscapes.

Unlike most other fantasy FPS games, Tribes stresses teamplay. You become a member of a tribe and work with your teammates to overthrow the enemy tribes. The victor of the game isn't necessarily the fastest moving group, but the one with the best strategy. Running blindly into an enemy camp isn't likely to get you very far—sneaking up from behind and encircling the foe is. Figure 5.8 demonstrates the immense landscape you're conquering.

Because of the complexity of organizing and carrying out missions with other people, the game can be a bit intimidating at first. You'll want to find a group of friends to play with and form your own tribe. There are hundreds of tribes already in existence and they often behave like exclusive clubs. It's best to get yourself organized before taking on any of these experienced groups.

Figure 5.8

Tribes battles span across a huge landscape.

Tribes is a great game, and one of the only *true* team games that you're going to find. From start to finish, the game is well thought out, and well executed. If you want a game that you can truly get into, and you're not afraid of working with other people, Tribes is a must-have title.

Fansites: www.planettribes.com, www.tribesplayers.com, www.insomniax.net/

Battlezone and Battlezone 2

Activision: www.activision.com

Install and Play	8	Story Line Depth	8
Control Simplicity	8	Strategy Simplicity	7

Multiplayer Quality	5	Team Playability	5
Multimedia Quality	8	Modifiability	7
Kid Friendly	8	Online Stability	4
3D Accelerator Support?	Yes		

Remember playing the original Battlezone arcade game from Atari? The feeling of power behind driving a huge lumbering piece of metal was phenomenal. If you'd like to take control of an updated version of that game, the Battlezone series from Activision is for you.

In the original Battlezone, you drove a tank around and shot other tanks. In the new Battlezone, you do much of the same—but this time you have a whole new arsenal, and a brand new hovertank. Unlike the original, there are many new features. For example, if your tank is about to be destroyed, you can jump out, gun down enemy pilots, and commandeer their vehicles. You can also use raw materials to build new weapons and other structures. There are basic strategy elements that go beyond your normal run-and-gun games and add depth to the experience.

Graphically, Battlezone is impressive. When the first of the new BZ games appeared, it was touted on magazine covers as being the graphical standard by which other games would be judged. The sequel, Battlezone 2, continues to push the envelope and requires quite a powerhouse of a system to show its true splendor. In Figure 5.9, several baddies are about to make yours truly disappear.

Figure 5.9

Battlezone has incredible environments and slick graphics.

In the area of online play, these games are, sadly, lacking. Lag is a definite problem, as are slight inconsistencies in control between single player and multiplayer mode. If you're looking for strategy, you'd be better off with Tribes. On the other hand, if you'd like a good mix of high explosives and heavy metal, try one of the Battlezone games.

Fansites: www.planetbattlezone.com/, www.bz2.com/, members.xoom.com/Epistaxis/bziq.htm

Half-Life

Activision: www.activision.com/

Install and Play	9	Story Line Depth	10
Control Simplicity	8	Strategy Simplicity	7
Multiplayer Quality	5	Team Playability	5
Multimedia Quality	8	Modifiability	7
Kid Friendly	8	Online Stability	7
3D Accelerator Support?	Yes		

Half-Life is a great game. Buy it! Using the Quake 2 engine, Half-Life provides an excellent graphical experience and a compelling storyline. Half-Life plays like a movie. Rather than beginning the game as a pumped-up, tough-as-nails Marine, your character is a geeky scientist—glasses and all. But quickly your world is turned upside down and you must find a way to save the world. This game has your usual shooter elements, but requires you to actually think to figure out where to go next.

Half-Life's main appeal is in single-player mode. The storyline is excellent, as is the intelligence of the computer controlled characters. You'll have to interact with computer characters throughout the game, and it's easy to forget that they're not human. The Half-Life world is totally engrossing and is as close to a true real-time action/adventure game as you're going to find. Most games have a plot that you can basically ignore as long as you kill everything in sight. In Half-Life, you can't do this, and you won't want to! You'll need to interact with others, and pieces of your environment, as shown in Figure 5.10.

Unfortunately, multiplayer mode is not as much fun as single-player mode. Perhaps this is just a side effect of getting a little too pumped by the single-player storyline. Multiplayer mode is your standard shooting fare. There is very little to set it apart from the rest of the pack. For single player games, Half-Life is a must buy. If you're primarily interested in multiplayer action, you'd be better off with Quake 3 Arena or Unreal Tournament.

Fansites: www.planethalflife.com, www.halflifehq.com/, www.halflifefiles.com/

Figure 5.10

Interact with your environment, talk to other people, and blow up soda machines in Half-Life!

Upcoming Titles

So, you've seen a few of the current First-Person Shooters, but what does the future hold for the FPS? There are many titles that are currently in development that the gaming community is eagerly anticipating. Each new year brings a new generation of games that push gaming technology to its limits. If you're a hardcore gamer, you know the great fun of constantly having to play catch-up with the wonderful world of computer hardware. Unfortunately, after you take a look at a few of these new games, you're going to want to be sure that you can play them all, in their full glory.

Daikatana

Ion Storm: www.ionstorm.com

When someone from id Software does something, you can be sure that it's going to be big. Daikatana is a new action/role-playing game designed by John Romero, previously of id Software fame and one of the co-creators of the landmark Doom series. One of the most anticipated games of 2000, Diakatana promises to wow its players with exceptional graphics and an interesting storyline.

Travelling through the past to avenge the death of a famous doctor and set the future right, you will meet up with a giant cast of characters—more than 70 unique creatures, in fact! During your journey, you will meet up with two other characters that will help you in your quest. The multiple-character control system will be a groundbreaking feature in FPS style games.

Diakatana also promises to deliver a full-featured multiplayer system, with multiple deathmatch modes and capture-the-flag options. The game should be available by the time you read this.

Messiah

Shiny Entertainment: www.messiah.com

In development for several years, Messiah is finally going to see the light of day. I remember the first time I read about Messiah—it sounded incredible. Curved surfaces, beautifully modeled characters, and high resolution textures. The initial screenshots looked amazing. Rather than build on an existing game engine like the popular Quake 2 engine (even Daikatana does this!), the Messiah team has created their rendering software.

In Messiah, you play a cherub...yes...a cherub—named "Bob". Sent to Earth by God to discover why the Earth is inhabited with evil, you must make your way through the environment and eliminate the bad guys when you find them. You might be wondering how a little baby with wings could possibly do any damage. That's where the beauty of being a heavenly being comes into play. Instead of relying on your current body to beat the foes, you can possess other characters in the game and use them. You have to see this sequence to truly appreciate it.

Messiah will also support multiplayer capabilities and a completely open game engine to enable gamers to develop their own modifications. Messiah should be definitely interesting. Hopefully it will turn out to be as good as its long-running hype.

Tribes 2

Dynamix: www.dynamix.com

Building on the success of the first Tribes game, Dynamix hopes to have similar success with Tribes 2—the second version of the hit game. Tribes 2 promises to offer all the features that were in the original game, plus a ton of new options. New vehicles and a streamlined control system are but a few of the changes you should see.

The Tribes game engine is also being refined. Levels will be more graphically intense, with new atmospheric effects and an improved physics model. Networking will also be improved with brand new code. Tribes 2 aims to create a completely realistic multiplayer environment with unsurpassed stability.

As long as Tribes 2 doesn't "dumb down" the gameplay that was found in the original title, it stands to be a big hit for gamers in 2000 and beyond.

Oni

Bungie Software: `oni.bungie.com`

Bungie Software has had an interesting existence. Creating some of the first FPS games available for the Macintosh, Bungie later went cross-platform and programmed the award-winning Myth series of strategy games. Now, Bungie is back with Oni, an anime-style FPS that wants to take FPS gaming in a different direction.

How many games have you played where you point your weapon at a character, fire a few times, and it dies? Almost all FPS games follow this model. It really doesn't matter if the creature you're firing on is shaped like a monster, a human, or a big gray rectangle. In Oni, this all changes. Rather than blasting at pixels indiscriminately, you can take on the enemies in hand-to-hand combat. Jump up, kick a gun from their hands, grab the gun, and use it while you can. Close and personal combat is the name of the game.

The graphics in Oni are unique. Rather than focus on high-resolution textures, the levels are designed much like the scenery in anime—solid colors with subtle shading. Early screenshots from the game reveal huge levels and fantastic architecture. There is little doubt that Bungie is onto something big. Look for this in early 2000.

Halo

Bungie Software: `halo.bungie.com`

Besides the upcoming Oni, Bungie has an even bigger game in store for fans. Other than the title "Halo," very little is actually known about the game other than its amazing graphics engine. Early speculation is that this will be a game similar to Tribes, but with significantly enhanced graphics. Be sure to check out the Halo Web site for screenshots and movies. When this game hits, it's going to be big.

With graphics cards like the Voodoo 4 and 5, and the GeForce 256, the year 2000 promises to be an exciting one for gamers. You can be sure that these games, and many more exciting titles will be released in the near future.

FPS Gaming Strategies

No matter what title you're playing, there are a few simple strategies that you can follow to minimize the amount of time you spend hugging the ground. Here is a list of strategies that work for me in deathmatch play. Your mileage might vary.

Use a Mouse or Trackball

Have you been using a keyboard to control your character? Pushing on the numeric keypad or page up/down to move your head around? Chances are you've been killed quite a bit while trying to aim and lock onto your opponents. The reason that *they* can get the quick shot off is because they're using a roller controller for aiming. Using a trackball or a mouse to look around (typically called Mouselook-mode in control configuration menus) enables very precise control of where you're shooting. It can take a while to get used to, but you'll find that a mouse or trackball will improve your ability to score dramatically.

Run-n-Gun

Never stand still. *Never.* You must learn the art of moving while aiming and shooting. Taking this a step farther, to beat the best deathmatch players, you must be able to aim in one direction while running another. This skill can definitely take some getting used to. It's best to practice this by yourself before trying it on others. For example, find a wide-open room and pick a point in the center on the floor. While running at full speed in a circle around the point, try to shoot the point. When you can successfully do this, you'll have a very useful talent that can be applied to your standard gameplay.

Reconfigure Your Controls

Games do not necessarily come out of the box with the best possible control configuration. Try laying your hand on the keyboard in a comfortable position. Note where your fingers are, then map these keys to the most useful commands. You can map secondary commands to the set of keys that are over one row from the primary grouping. This lets you quickly shift to alternative controls without having to look at the keyboard. Try to configure all your FPS games to use a similar layout; that way you don't need to relearn games each time they are played.

Speed and Agility

Never walk. There are very few instances when walking is useful in a FPS. Most games have an always run mode that makes it much easier to stay in high gear. If you notice that other players can easily overtake you, you're probably not running! Besides being speedy, be sure to learn how to fully control your character. If you can duck or squat, do it! The smaller a target you are, the more difficult it is to hit you. Furthermore, if you are ducked down, a player will usually have to aim to hit you, rather than just shooting straight forward.

Learn the Maps and Levels

You'll obviously end up doing this automatically by playing games in single-player mode—but it can be very useful to practice for multiplayer games by getting used to the levels that you're going to play. Knowing where to hide and how to reach weapon/ammo caches can come in quite handy when there are a group of bad guys on your tail with a rocket launcher. You might be a bit hesitant to do this because it seems like cheating—just remember that the people you're going to be playing against have had the same opportunity, and they aren't nearly as scrupulous as you!

Have Fun and Take It Easy!

Don't ever take a game too seriously. If your arch-rival beats you three times in a row, it's not the end of the world. Games are about having fun—much of what happens on a given day is random blind luck. If you find that your stress level is increasing during a game, it's time to step away, turn your computer off, and take a walk outside.

The Least You Need to Know

➤ FPSs, or First-Person Shooters, place you in the game and in the action. You see the game from the point of view of the hero and are often called upon to wipe out hordes of evildoers with a variety of weapons.

➤ Most FPS games offer at least some single-player options. In today's connected world, however, multiplayer online play is the focus for many new games. If you don't have an Internet connection, you're missing out.

➤ FPS games generally operate in teamplay or deathmatch modes. Teamplay operation lets you team up with your friends to fight against others. Deathmatch games are an every-man-for-himself type of happening.

➤ There are many FPS games available that will push your PC to its limits, but there are even more exciting advances just around the corner. As long as there is newer and better hardware available, there will be a FPS that supports it.

HMMMN...

Chapter 6

Real-Time Strategy Games

In This Chapter

➤ What is a Real-Time Strategy Game?

➤ Micro or Macro—Is One Better Than the Other

➤ The Three Basic Online Game Styles of RTS

➤ Advanced Tactical Theory of RTS

➤ Tips and Reviews of Some of the More Popular RTS Games

Tired of driving or flying simulators? Fed up with fragging in the paintball shooters? Maybe you're ready for the big picture. Maybe it is time to command armies and become a great general. If strategy appeals to you in a computer game more than reflexes, then this is the game genre for you, Commander.

This chapter will first define what RTS is, then cover the general theories of gameplay in this rapidly growing genre. Beginning commanders will come away with a better understanding of how to win, while the seasoned general might not only learn a few tips but might also become a better team leader. After I discuss theories, I'll focus on a few of the more popular games.

What the Heck Is Real-Time Strategy?

Real-Time Strategy games, or RTS as they're commonly called, are like a combination of Chess, Risk, and amphetamines! They involve strategy and a small degree of luck; however, because they are played on computers, the players play simultaneously—unlike the turn-based method shared by chess and Risk—hence the speed factor. Three things all RTS games have in common are building an economy, building an army, and building up the tech tree. Doing this faster than your opponent gives you the sense of urgency and excitement.

All RTS games have a playing field or map in which much of the playing field is obscured until one of your units can see it. You have an overhead view of the playing field so you can command and build units and structures. You start out with a few resources and basic units and begin to build up your base. While building higher units and researching technology, you seek out your opponent and attempt to prevent him from building up as fast as you build, ultimately defeating him in the end by overpowering his armies.

In essence, this is what happens in an RTS game:

➤ You establish a base and build fighting units, each of which has unique costs, strengths, and weaknesses

➤ Your fighting units seek out the enemy

➤ Other units gather resources that let you expand your base or build better units

First and foremost, a player needs an economy to meet the other two criteria—army and technology tree. It is very important to gain income without over- or under-building tech and armies. You need to find a good flow of income from your miners, harvesters, or trucks, depending on the game, while steadily producing grunts. Grunts are the basic fighting units, usually infantry. Depending on the actual game, you will find that balance quickly; at least for the first 15 minutes of the game. Figure 6.1 shows a barracks in the game Dark Reign; barracks allow you to construct soldiers called mercenaries.

The Initial, or Rush, Stage

This first 10 or 20 minutes is called the *rush* and for many of the more experienced onliners, the game ends within this time. A certain amount of economy, (mining), is needed for the rush. Any more is a waste of resources. For example: I'm Freedom Guard in Dark Reign and the map is small and it is a 1v1. I will build three Barracks first, after setting my taelon tanker to double up on the water hole, and take the enemy out by destroying his tankers at his water hole. This cuts off his income and gives me a great advantage. Or, I can 6 pool 'ling rush as a zerg on StarCraft and completely destroy my opponent before he even gets one offensive unit made if his base is within 100 pixels of mine. If these terms sound strange to you don't worry. Those were just two examples of some of the RTS games that will be touched upon later in the chapter.

Figure 6.1

Three barracks are building 16 mercenaries very quickly in Dark Reign.

The important thing to remember is that many online RTS games rarely go past the first 10 or 20 minutes, which is known as the rush stage. By practicing, you should be able to balance economy with production fairly easily during that stage. There are many more RTS games than the two I've already mentioned. For this chapter, I'll stay in general terms with a few examples and save the tips for the later part of the chapter when we touch on individual games. These will only be a few tips compared to the countless tactics and results of each game.

I'm talking in general terms of all RTS games so if you wonder what a 6-pool means don't sweat it as it is not as important as the overall message is; especially if StarCraft is not a game you are interested in. Point is that in the RTS venue the first 15 minutes can be critical in online gaming. It is at this time the enemy can rush and catch you completely unprepared. And if you think 1 versus 1 is tough try defending solo a 2 versus 1 assault at the 10-minute mark of a 2 versus 2 game. By the way, an attack before 10 minutes is considered "cheese". However, it is part of the game and therefore legitimate unless all players agree beforehand not to attack before a certain time limit. Sometimes, given the game and map you are playing, a rush is not only a viable plan, but it is a necessary plan.

The Mid Stage

After 15 to 20 minutes the game begins to enter mid-game stage, unless players continue to produce only grunts and send 'em out to the enemy. This is called *vending*, and I will discuss this later in the Macro versus Micro section. There are two main things that occur during mid-game. You begin to expand your bases to increase economy and you begin production of midlevel units. Figure 6.2 shows a Dark Reign game in the vending stage.

109

Figure 6.2

An expansion being built in Dark Reign. Notice the main base is to the left on the minimap.

Expanding bases is required to raise more income, and can carry additional benefits as well. This can be as simple as building another water refinery next to a new water hole on Dark Reign or as complex as sending an MCV (Mobile Construction Vehicle) to a whole new area of the map so you can make additional ore refineries next to a fresh mineral field. The latter example comes from Command and Conquer's sequel, Red Alert. These additional war factories, shown in Figure 6.3, provide the benefit of shortening tank production time. This leads me to the midlevel or mid tech unit production stage.

Figure 6.3

A new expansion base well protected by tanks in Red Alert. The main base is in the upper-right corner of minimap.

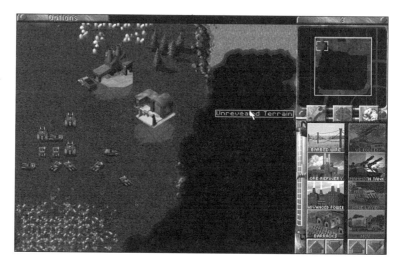

At this point, tech level units are produced and your armies are beginning to take size. Tanks, aircraft, and spellcasters are a few examples of the mid tech, depending on the game's genre. At this stage, you should have at least tripled your mining units and have good recon of the map so you can try to stop your enemy from expanding as well. Team games that go past rush stage rarely proceed past mid stage. In a 1 versus 1 or a Free For All, the game sometimes goes to the long stage, or upper tech tree.

The Long Stage

It is difficult to give a time frame for when the game reaches the long game or final stage. Different RTS games play at different speeds. However, there are distinctions to be noted at this stage. By this time you should have very good recon of the map and three or four bases while ready to expand to a fifth or sixth when needed. Your research up the tech tree should be nearly complete, if not finished, and you should be producing capital units. Capital units are the slower moving, heavily armored units with tremendous firepower. The juggernaut of Age of Empires or the Battle Cruiser of StarCraft are examples. After you have a sizeable force of capital ships the game is about over and your opponent will surrender.

Now that we have covered the basics of RTS let's talk about the two playing styles.

Macro Versus Micro, or Old School Versus New School

There are two basic playing styles for RTS and the discussions in the channels or on the forums have long argued for one or the other. I am referring to macro- and micro-management. Some call it Old School versus New School, and there are many excellent players of both styles. This section describes these styles and tells you which one is better.

Macro-Management: Wave After Wave

A popular playing technique is called macro-management, also known as vending. This playing style is essentially to make very large quantities of the same unit type and throw them at your enemy in waves until he is overpowered. Sounds simple enough, but this can be deceiving. If you decide to play macro you must be able to build your economy very fast to afford the many units. This means you might be vulnerable to a small, early rush force. If you do not get hit early, though, then in late early or early mid game you should be quite strong with a larger army than your opponent has. When you are ready to attack your enemy it is usually wise to send in one unit first for recon, and then send in the first wave if it seems like you can hurt him if not end the game right there.

A few years back when some of the earlier RTS games were popular, macro was common strategy. In Command and Conquer, one of the first RTS games to make a big splash, it was the massive tank rush with three or four war factories behind it, as shown in Figure 6.4, supported by as many refineries. A force of 30 tanks could be built by mid stage and move across the map unscathed. Or in Dark Reign, a quick three barracks build would enable a player to vend grunts quickly. A half dozen of either of these units will destroy a vital tanker truck very fast.

Figure 6.4

In C&C's Red Alert, it does not take long for four factories to make 32 mammoth tanks.

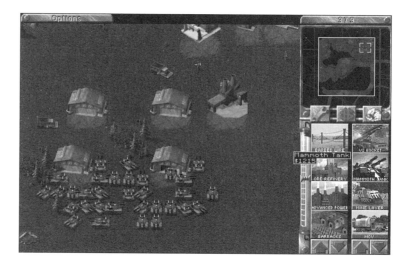

Macro was the favored strategy of those who played multiplayer online back then. This was when networks such as Kali and Ten were new and the games were more restrictive due to the software and hardware. That is why you might hear macro being referred to as Old School. However, even with the newer games with their wider varieties of available strategies, the macro is still popular and usually effective.

The best time to use macro is on relatively open maps with few choke points. A choke point is a bridge, ramp, narrow canyon, or something along that line. Also the map should have a larger than average amount of resources near your base because macro can be quite costly. Remember that getting rich fast is the key to successfully pulling off this strategy. Don't go too long though on initial economy without some sort of grunts in case you get rushed.

Micro-Management: Where Did His Army Go?

On the opposite end is a game style called micro-management or New School. Micro is essentially getting maximum results, usually kills, using only one or a few units. Back in 1996, most of the emerging RTS games did not have a suitable unit for micro. The closest thing I can remember might be the special agent Tanya on C&C's Red Alert. She was capable of blowing up a building as soon as she reached it. She could also pick off enemy grunts as they walked along single file because of her greater range and higher damage. As newer games emerged, more specialized units with high-damage capability were introduced. Although these newer units required micro, or individual control, they weren't as affordable or practical yet as a solid strategy throughout the game. For example, while the Shock Wave in Dark Reign could do a lot of damage, as shown in Figure 6.5, they were too expensive and too slow moving to build an effective strategy around.

Figure 6.5

A bunch of Triple Rail tanks in Dark Reign fall victim to a Shock Wave.

For example Dark Reign, the following year, introduced Shock Waves and Martyrs for Freedom Guard. The Martyr rush would work sometimes but it was more macro then micro. And if you individually targeted each Martyr you might still lose them because they explode on impact, more or less like a running bomb. Shock Waves were very expensive slow-moving vehicles that would do damage by sending a tremor through the ground. Although it required some control and attention it was not viable as a strat due to cost and speed. Also, they self destructed when used, just like the Martyrs. If you could get away with using a bunch of Shock Waves then your opponent was already dead or not close to your skill level.

The best time to use micro is on maps with choke points or maybe islands. This is a viable strategy for maps with fewer available resources or when your opponent is wealthier than you are. Cost-to-kill ratio is much better with micro than macro. It is important to climb the tech tree usually to get these effective units. Just make sure you do not tech so fast as to leave yourself wide open for a simple grunt rush.

Macro or Micro: Which One Is Better?

For the longest time this question has been debated. Some of the top online players have argued for one or the other. Many good players can build an army fast and take you out so quickly you would swear they were hacking (cheating). Other very good players can destroy a small fleet of your capital ships with a few cheap units and you're left wondering where your army or fleet went.

My answer to the question is neither is best. The best players online can do both. They will send a mass initial rush, then maybe tech up for micro units while still sending smaller waves to distract you from the sneaky back-door micro attack. Or maybe your army meets his and numbers seem pretty equal but he wins by targeting your units individually while rotating his damaged units from the front to the back so they do not draw your units' fire.

The important thing for you to do is determine which style you feel comfortable with and play it until you have some mastery over it, and then work on the other style. This is usually the case, with people learning macro first. Other factors on using these styles are of course what kind of player is your partner? is it a team game? Or is it a free for all? This leads me to the next section; which describes the three RTS game styles online.

Some Popular RTS Games

This section will briefly describe some of the more popular RTS games. I will try to give some pros and cons for each one. Also I will cover hardware requirements for the newer games. This should make it easier for you to choose which games you might want to purchase in the future.

Command and Conquer's Tiberiun Sun

I begin this section of the chapter with one of the latest in the popular Command & Conquer series of games by Westwood. Tiberiun Sun, released late 1999 and shown in Figure 6.6, is not an add-on to Red Alert but a whole new game. I tried to arrange the games in this section chronologically by release with Red Alert as the earliest back in 1996 and Tiberiun Sun released only a couple of months ago at this writing. While it was only a little under four years between the games it seemed like a decade to some of the most ardent C&C fans; many of whom claim RTS was invented by Westwood. I am not about to dispute that claim whether I agree with it or not. However, if you are one of those ardent C&C fans, then buy the game and skip on past this part to the next chapter, because I might burst your bubble.

Figure 6.6

Tiberiun Sun features terrain deformation from artillery and ion storms.

Tech Tip

Command & Conquer and Red Alert

Command & Conquer is the game that gives Westwood the claim to having invented the Real-Time Strategy genre. As a member of either the Nod terrorist brotherhood or the United Nations force tasked with stopping them, you construct bases and create soldiers and military vehicles. Red Alert took this model and cast it in the style of an Allied/Soviet conflict. The latter game was notable for its Tanya unit, a highly competent super-agent who could take out soldiers with her long-range rifle and blow up buildings with demolition charges.

Did I save the best for last? No. Westwood completely dropped the ball with Tiberiun Sun. Four years is a huge time frame to make a game. Especially when technology at least triples in that time. So what does Westwood do? They remake Red Alert with prettier graphics, the same stupid ore truck AI, and a game speed so slow that in a four-player LAN I tested this on, it took a real-time of four minutes for a refinery to build. All four computers on that LAN were above minimum specs too. However, Westwood has since released a patch that supposedly speeds up multiplayer game speed.

115

Westwood's idea of new features is queuing, waypoints, and rally points. This was done in Dark Reign two and a half years earlier. There is one fairly new feature though, terrain deformation. If you shell a base or area heavy enough, you will leave craters not only large enough to hinder unit movement but to prevent construction there as well. These craters are usually left by the occasional "act of god" storms. These ion storms or meteor showers are a carry-over from the chronostorm of RA and are quite annoying actually.

Strategy-wise, unit mixes are more important than in RA especially in single-player missions. However in multiplayer on the smaller maps go heavy infantry. On the larger maps, if the enemy doesn't scout you out early I suggest a rush for disk throwers as GDI and for artillery as NOD. Bottom line is, this game is more fun in single than multi. The graphics are nice. The story is engaging. But unless you are a fan of C&C I cannot recommend this one for multiplay. Westwood is releasing Renegade in late 2000, which is supposed to be a FPS within the Tiberiun Sun storyline. Maybe it will hold more surprises or break new ground where this one did not.

System requirements are Pentium 166, 32 MB RAM, 2 MB video, 4X CD-ROM, 28.8 modem, and 200 MB HD.

Age of Empires II

Age of Empires II: Age of Kings, shown in Figure 6.7, is the sequel to Microsoft's popular civilization simulation. With even better graphics than the original, this game covers the Dark Ages to the Middle Ages with 13 different civilizations. It features unit formations, garrisons, and new trade options. One new feature I found useful was being able to call all units to the town hall for defense or just gathering to attack. I recommend this one for single or multiplay. It bumps requirements up to a Pentium 166, 32MB RAM, and 200MB HD.

Figure 6.7

Age of Empires II provides larger maps and even more detailed graphics, plus maybe a history lesson or two!

116

Tech Tip

The Original Age of Empires

Microsoft's Age of Empires was released in 1997 and still enjoys some popularity. It was entertaining and could also teach you some history. You played as one of 12 civilizations from Japanese to Egyptian. The tech tree covers ten thousand years on this one, from the Stone Age to the Iron Age. There is an amazing level of realism in the graphics for a game this size and age. That's also the Achilles' heel for multiplaying, in my opinion. The higher the graphical detail and the animation frame count the slower the game speed.

Warcraft II

Warcraft, shown in Figure 6.8, is an epic battle between the humans and the marauding horde of the orcs. The storyline takes place in a medieval setting of swords, axes, arrows, and catapults. An older game, like the ones previously mentioned, this one has real legs. Blizzard, the company that released it, has sold more than four million copies of the Warcraft series. This includes Warcraft, Warcraft II: Tides of Darkness, Warcraft II: Beyond the Dark Portal, and the latest release Warcraft IIs BNE (Battle Net Edition). The latter is a combination of the other two Warcraft II's plus multiplayer support for the game on Blizzard's hugely popular Internet gaming venue Battle Net. The Battle Net edition also has some new features, including a spacebar hotkey to the last message, user assigned groups, patrols, attack move, fast unit type selection by double-clicking or control-clicking on one, and a few other features that breathe new life in this older game.

You have four resources to gather. Food is from building farms, lumber is from forests with improved efficiency from a lumber mill, gold is from mines, and oil is from sea wells also improved with a refinery. Usually the resources are sufficient and balanced on most maps, however I have run out of gold before. Gold and food are the most basic resources used in producing all units from the peon to the juggernaut.

The game's engine gives a truer FOW (Fog of War) by letting you reveal the map and seeing terrain but not units or buildings if you left the area. On your mini-map you might have scouted an enemy base earlier and his buildings might show up on the mini but you go look again later and twice as many buildings are there now or it was leveled. The point is it is more realistic than in older games where Fog does not return, or more correctly termed, shroud regrows.

Figure 6.8

A Death Knight casts an area effect Death and Decay spell upon several grunts and knights. A good example of micro.

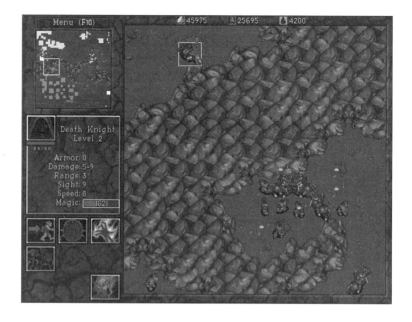

In typical Blizzard fashion the game has both depth and speed. It has a moderately branched tech tree and the spellcaster mages on both sides can research up to five different kinds of spells. Graphics are good but not so detailed as to slow the game play. Two drawbacks to the game however are the lack of really large maps and the fact that the menu panel is way too wide. Although the interface is intuitive to use it seems it could have been more efficiently designed. Other than those two things the game is a good solid choice for either single or multiplayer use. Beginners will be able to learn it with little difficulty but will take time to master it. The hotkeys along with the new features of the BNE version will satisfy the ardent RTS veteran.

Dark Reign

Activision's answer to Blizzard's gauntlet thrown down on the RTS genre, Dark Reign, shown in Figure 6.9, was released in early 1997. As good as Warcraft II was, Dark Reign matched it and maybe surpassed it in one key area: user programmable AI.

Dark Reign: The Future of War is just as its name implies. It is a standard RTS but it has a storyline set in a fictional universe and distant future. The original game pits the mighty Imperium race against the rebellious Freedom Guard. Each race has special units and technology yet both seem closely balanced to play as either micro or macro. I will say though that Freedom Guard tends to own the small map 1v1 due to faster grunt rush as I mentioned earlier in the chapter. If you want the ability to use both races' units and technology you can play as Togran.

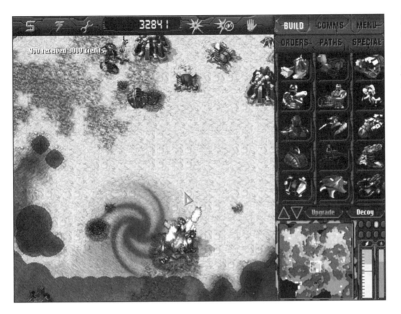

Figure 6.9

The deadly Imperium rift destroys a Freedom Guard power generator in Dark Reign.

A solid game without spectacular graphics or storyline, Dark Reign still proved popular. The reasons primarily had to do with multiplayer mode. The single player mode is fun, but some of the missions are nearly impossible to complete unless you stumble upon the secret (or buy a book that describes the key strategy). The game introduced terrain effect of unit movement and LOS (Line of Sight), which had a much greater impact on multiplayer action. Slopes, gravel, rocks, mud, and roads all have various effects on unit movement and speed. If you just click across the map to move your units, they will take the path of least resistance and while distance maybe farther it is usually faster to the destination timewise.

The other breakthrough is the programmable AI. For the first time in an RTS, a player can set the AI of each of his units individually. You can choose between three priority levels—low, medium, and high—for three categories of behavior—pursuit range, damage tolerance, and independence. A setting I usually use is low, medium, medium. This means the unit will not pursue enemy units unless I order it. It will go to a repair station or field hospital when its damage bar reaches red. It will fire upon threats in sight but will take my targeting as priority. There are also three convenient preprogrammed modes; scout, harass, and search and destroy. These are quite useful and should be used especially in multiplayer games.

If you are looking for more fun you might want to get the add-ons Rise of the Shadowhand and Battles of the Outer Rim. ROTS has two new races with new units, missions, and maps, while BOTR is primarily a multiplayer add-on with an amazing collection of maps specifically designed for multiplayer games. Because of the newer add-ons and due to the patch updates on Activisions net, you should have a Pentium 133, 32MB RAM to really enjoy online Internet multiplay. Also, for Internet eight-player games, a 56K modem is recommended.

119

Oh, and for those of you waiting for Dark Reign 2, it is due out Spring 2000. Imagine combining Dark Reign with Myth2 and you get an idea of this new, true 3D RTS. Although it has amazing realism and a movable field of view, Pandemic assures us that camera movement is not necessary for gameplay. They also insist that the new game engine will not slow down under the ultra realistic physics and graphic rendering. In fact, claimed minimum requirements are a Pentium 200, a 3D graphics accelerator, and 32MB RAM.

Total Annihilation

Okay, now take Dark Reign, add a bit more 3D unit realism, a much larger playing field, and about twice as many units and you have Total Annihilation, shown in Figure 6.10. After the release in September 1997, Cavedog Entertainment gained many awards for its inaugural and highly successful RTS debut.

Figure 6.10

Lose your commander and all other units and buildings explode!

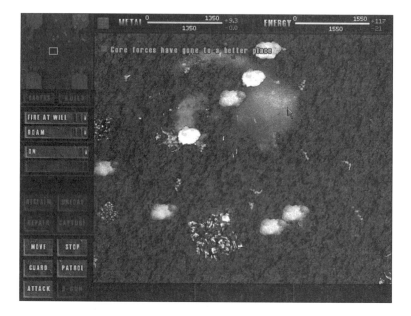

The storyline is traditional: Two sides are warring, the underdogs versus the empire. The venue is traditional: mine the metal and geothermal gases, and then build bases and units. What breaks tradition with TA is the scope of the game. It was the largest game to date when it was released. Maps are up to 64 MB and are hundreds of screens in area. Units are numerous for land, air, and sea battles. It even has aircraft carriers. As impressive as this game looks and plays there is a serious Achilles' heel to it—the commander.

You begin with a single unit that walks and looks like a robot. He is able to make structures and defend himself with a disintegrator gun. He has high hit points and packs a good punch. He is your commander and should he die, you lose the game. This unit must be guarded after the game is well underway. And if your enemy has many air units I suggest you hide your commander under tree cover or under water. This game can easily become a rush to kill the commander, which is unfortunate as expansive as the tech tree is. However, if you can get a game to mid or long stage it can be quite entertaining as long as you stored your commander away safely. Also note that other units can build structures, too, after you make these units so the commander is not needed after you reach mid game. Ctrl+C will take you to him in case you forgot where you placed him. Despite that one weakness I recommend this game for both single and multiplay. ESRB rated it Teen 13+ for animated violence.

Up to 10 players can play on LAN or 4 players on Internet with 28.8 modems. If you have not bought this game yet, I recommend the Total Annihilation Commander Pack. It features the game, two add-ons, and a strategy guide. This gives you a whopping 245 units total, 175 missions, more than 90 multiplayer maps, and 12 3D worlds to play in. You will also need a Pentium 166, 16MB RAM, 4X CD-ROM, and 28.8 modem. Not sure how much HD space is required though.

Starcraft

After making Warcraft II and Diablo, Blizzard had set the bar so high it was beyond outside competition. They were now competing with themselves and in a way that might be true. Blizzard holds two offices: One is in the L.A. area and the other, Blizzard North, is in the San Jose area. So with the reputations of previous hits on the line and parent company Cendant looking for new ownership, Blizzard released Starcraft, shown in Figure 6.11, in April 1998.

Figure 6.11

A Protoss player making Dragoons in Starcraft.

The game has good graphics and funny character voices and sound effects. Repeatedly clicking one unit will make the unit say different things. The game is well drawn and game speed is quite fast for multiplayer mode even on the Net.

You can play as one of three races; Terran, Protoss, or Zerg. Each race has unique units and tech trees. I would recommend Terran for players who like micro. Terran has the most branches in tech tree and requires a good mix of units to be successful with them. Protoss can go either way. I would recommend Zerg for the macro players. It has the least branches in tech and is capable of producing three units (six if zergling or scourge) at a time at each hatchery. While this feature was seriously abused at the beginning, Brood War, the expansion released in December 1998, and its corresponding patch slowed the larvae production at the hatchery by about half.

In fact if you have not bought this game yet, make sure you get Brood War as well. Even though Starcraft can play well by itself, the game does not really seem balanced to me without the Brood War units. You might hear lots of arguments on Battle Net about race balance, although there are not as many as before Brood War was released. In my opinion all else being equal (resources, symmetric map, player skill) that after the top of the tech tree is reached each race has a slight advantage with certain units and spells over other races.

This is a good game with an easy learning curve yet enough depth to make mastery difficult. I would recommend getting this one, in fact, it is my personal favorite in RTS.

Battlezone

Activision resurrected this 1980 classic arcade tank simulator eighteen years later, in 1998. While it still is a First-Person Tank Shooter and it still shares the same name, there is one more thing this game has in common with its predecessor. They both were trendsetting game styles. Atari was introducing an FPS with Battlezone while other games of that era were second-person, such as Missile Command, Asteroids, or Centipede. While the new Battlezone still maintains its first-person roots, as shown in Figure 6.12, it also incorporates Real-Time Strategy.

The storyline is so interesting that with some elaboration it could easily make a marketable, if not blockbuster, Hollywood feature film. An asteroid hit the Bering Strait back in 1952 and left behind an off-world material best described as biometal. Both Russians and Americans salvaged all they could and found it useful for technology. In their desire for more they began to breach the frontier of space setting up mining operations on our moon first. In fact the lunar landing of 1969 was merely part of media propaganda. The landing site was only a few hundred yards from an already established U.S. lunar mining base, and the historical photo of Buzz Aldrin on the moon was actually shot by that base's commander, not Neil Armstrong. On the moon, both the U.S. and Russians discovered alien artifacts that led to subsequent mining operations elsewhere in the solar system. Both are trying to unlock the aliens' archeological puzzle to control the ultimate technology or weapon. There was indeed a Cold War—in the cold of space.

Figure 6.12

Observe the earthrise from the cockpit of your tank while defending your base on the moon in Battlezone.

You're a commander in this space race. In this game, you mine resources and, in a new twist, salvage wrecked battle vehicles. You also build buildings and research technology. You can make multiple units and use them to scout, attack, or defend your base from the competing Russians. Here is where it takes a different direction from other RTSs though. You do all this from within your vehicle. Your tank is like a mobile armed headquarters. From within you can monitor your surroundings with your radar and increase your recon with remote cameras feeding video back to you. You command all your units from your tank so the game has a mix of both strategy and tactics. And finally, if your tank is blown up you are able to eject and run for cover or to a new vehicle.

The game's graphics are exceptional and the game engine powerful and smooth. The storyline is absorbing and the learning curve is not as high as one would think. You'll definitely want a joystick because movement is too hard with keyboard only. The game is indeed fun in single player mode and in multiplayer strategy mode. However as with many FPSs in multiplayer deathmatch it is easy to die many, many times because the enemy knows where you will reappear in the game and sits there waiting for you.

I recommend this game for any age group. If you don't already have it, get the Battlezone Gold pack. It has two authorized add-ons, a demo Battlezone 2, and the BradyGames *Official Strategy Guide*. The guide is quite useful for mission tips in the single player mode.

Minimum game requirements for this one are a Pentium 120, 16MB RAM, 235MB HD, 2X CD-ROM, and 28.8 modem. If you intend to get Battlezone 2, you will need

32MB RAM and a 3D graphics accelerator. Battlezone 2 was released at the writing of this book, December 1999, so I know little about it yet. You can check out www.pandemicstudios.com/bzii or www.activision.com for the latest info.

Myth

Myth, shown in Figure 6.13, is about medieval archers, swordsmen, healers, and villagers at war with ghouls, monsters, and the undead of the Dark. The fantasy storyline is typical but the gameplay is not. What makes this one stand out from others is the player's ability to move the view in a 3D environment. You can literally aim the "camera" or field of view in almost any direction. It's fixed at a downward angle so you cannot tilt up, but you can pan, truck, dolly, arch, and zoom the camera wherever you want. While this is an interesting new feature it also increases the learning curve. It is difficult at first to control the camera independent from the units and you must use the camera expertly in multiplayer games.

Figure 6.13

You can use a positionable camera to choose your view of a fully 3D environment in Myth.

You do not mine resources or make buildings in this game, either. Instead you start out with a given amount of forces and might meet more within the mission. What is unique is that each unit not only has a name (which you can change if you want), but they develop skill with experience. Furthermore, when you complete a mission, your remaining men will begin the next level with you. This option also works for subsequent games in multiplayer mode if the game host has it turned on. One other interesting note here about multiplay: The team captain of your team can control your unit at any time. While this is to prevent you from dying maybe from an unseen danger, it seems this could be problematic. Your captain might want to control the team all alone or he might just send your unit to his death either by accident or not. Definitely suggest joining a clan of trustworthy players if you intend to multiplay often because, this game can quickly breed PKs (Player Killers).

Myth has a fairly good render engine and slow to moderate game speed. The character animations are moderately detailed and the physics of lighting, gravity, and even elements such as rain or snow are faithfully reproduced. If you like gore, this one definitely is bloody. I would not recommend it for preteen players. There is one graphical flaw in my opinion. The game's terrain texture map does not seem to match in tone and color balance to the characters or the structures. It almost seems like two completely different games meshed into one.

Overall the game seems entertaining for single-player mode. Even though there is a good deal of micro in unit placement, movement, even the direction they face, this game reminds me more of Baldur's Gate though than a traditional RTS. I would have to pass on this one for multiplay RTS.

This game came out in 1997 and in mid 1999 a sequel was released called Myth 2 Soulblighter, which has an improved game engine with much better terrain texture. Also alliances can be made and broken during multiplay. And there is no need for the difficult gesture click anymore to get your man to face the right way.

Total Annihilation: Kingdoms

Despite the title, Total Annihalation: Kingdoms isn't a mere add-on to the RTS game I mentioned earlier. The only thing this game has in common with the earlier TA is that it is another hit RTS from Cavedog. This game, shown in Figure 6.14, has an entirely different story and setting.

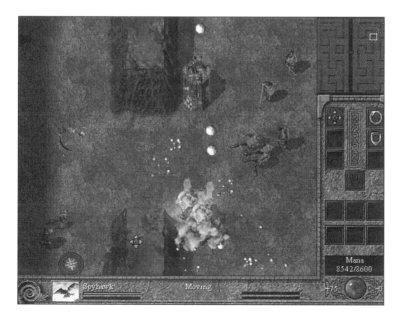

Figure 6.14

Unlike TA, Kingdoms takes place in medieval time.

This game was released in June 1999. While its forebear raised the RTS bar on unit graphics and map size, this one pushes the game engine a little farther. It has a bit better graphics while maintaining game speed. It also features four races, each with a unique tech tree, to choose from instead of just two. These races are battling in a mythical age of serfdoms and sorcery. Experience counts here too. As your units survive melees they rise in skill and change in appearance as veterans. Also there is a new player option of switchable zoom views from close to medium to wide.

Unfortunately, Total Annihilation: Kingdoms suffers from a couple drawbacks in multiplayer venue. First is another similarity the game has to its Cavedog predeccessor, TA. Where TA had a potential Achilles' heel with the commander, TAK has the same situation with the monarch. If he dies, you lose the game. As I mentioned earlier this can be dealt with in TA by guarding or hiding this crucial unit; the same works for this game too.

There's another reason, though, that makes me lean toward not recommending this game for multiplayer use. The game, at the writing of this book, is barely six months old. Yet the online community (a good barometer of a game's "legs") is virtually a ghost town. Two sites that provide some updated info are www.takingdoms.net and www.takingdoms.com. Both are good sites with updates and content. However, neither are posting news daily and the news that is being posted is usually about some third-party icon of the game community leaving in disagreement with Cavedog. Third-party support is a sign of growth within any software industry; a lack of it might put TAK on the critical list.

Hardware requirements are a Pentium 233, 32MB RAM, 80MB HD, 4X CD-ROM, and a 28.8 modem.

Mech Commander Gold

Mech Commander Gold, released September of 1999, is another game that is not an RTS but is also not an FPS or RPG. This is a wannabe RTS that is nothing more than an overhead view of the original RPG Mech Warrior, except now you control up to 12 mech units instead of just one. You do not collect resources nor make buildings in this game. Instead you spend your money on the armament you want before the game starts. Then when inside you can add stuff by finding it in crates or salvaging from wreckage in the field.

Played on mplayer.com this game seems so buggy that player drops seem to be frequent occurrences forcing a remake of the game. Finding players who have time to deal with this is aided by visiting a fan Web site dedicated to the multiplayer aspect of this poser RTS. That site is called Mech Commander Multiplay. It is found at http://mcmultiplay.worldinflames.com and is a nice site. You log in and it sets a cookie, then you will be able to access a database of possible opponents or teammates.

Unless you are a fan of the Battle Tech universe that was born in the 1980s from pen and paper, or of the Mech Warrior computer games that later spawned from Battle Tech's storyline, you will probably want to pass on this one for multiplayer use. However, because the game is decent and the Battle Tech universe is second only to Dungeons & Dragons in worldwide popularity, I don't think they will have trouble selling a couple hundred thousand copies of this game.

Requirements for Mech Commander Gold are a Pentium 133, 32MB RAM, 2MB video RAM, 4X CD-ROM, 210MB HD, and a 28.8 modem. ESRB says Teen 13+ for animated violence and strong language.

Advanced Tactical Theory of RTS

This section offers a brief list of advanced theories. I call them theories because they cannot be measured or tested like build orders or unit statistics. These theories come from my own experiences in RTS for the last three years as well as what I have observed from expert players in RTS. By understanding the following concepts, hopefully, you will have a better grasp of the games and a better foundation on which to make your build orders and strategies.

Know the Map

If you know the map you are playing on, you have a few advantages over an opponent who does not. Besides the obvious edge of knowing where the opponent's start spot might be, you also know where the best resources to expand to are located. However, knowing the map offers more advantages than just those.

Use High Ground to Your Advantage

Most of the newer RTS games use the terrain to factor a unit's movement and damage infliction. This factoring means units on high ground attacking those on lower ground have a greater damage infliction. So, by using upper ground such as cliffs, ramps, or steps your units will prevail easily over an equal number of lower ground units. High ground can also provide protection from detection. If you use a ridge to pass by enemy units on lower ground you can usually pass without his units seeing you from below unless yours fire upon his or he has an air unit nearby to increase his LOS (line of sight). If there are cliffs or walls near his base these might be ideally suited for a ranged unit attack. A few tanks, artillery, catapults—whatever the game might—placed on a cliff near a base can wreak havoc on the unsuspecting enemy.

Use Choke Points to Your Advantage

I touched upon this concept earlier in the chapter. By knowing the map, you also know where the main choke points are if the map has any. Usually maps have main ground chokes near the middle of the map. The points are where the path is narrow

Choke Off Your Enemy's Supply

A *choke point* is a narrow geographic feature that restricts an enemy's ability to maneuver and deploy and allows you to concentrate a large force against a relatively small number of enemies. A narrow gorge that soldiers must traverse single file, or the Panama Canal, are examples.

Keep Your Sight Lines Open

Line of sight, or LOS, refers to the visibility from your current position. An open field has good LOS; it's hard to sneak up on you. Be careful when near trees or hills. You don't know what could be hiding there—but you can use this terrain to your advantage as well.

yet must be used by ground units to access a new area of the map. Bridges and ramps are also examples of choke points. By fortifying at a main choke you can essentially protect more real estate with the expense of fewer resources. This is also useful for containment of your opponent by holding his choke point.

Use LOS to Your Advantage

If you know that the enemy has a base or units on the other side of a wall or narrow ridge, you can use that divider to your advantage. By fortifying with a mix of units including ranged and anti-air, you can dig in, then bring an air unit over to spy over the divider for the ranged units. You can now shell away at his structures and by the time you start you are already in position to defend his counterattack on you by ground or air. Knowing his LOS allows you to rally or build just outside his bases for surprises later on. Remember that he might try this on you too so always check your perimeter regularly, especially in the early game.

Scout Often to Be Prepared

This is not an advanced tip but is a necessity, one that is frequently ignored. You cannot see too much of the map during a game. Many times people feel that the extra resources gained by that one early peon are more valuable than if that peon were used to go scout the map. They are usually wrong, unless of course the map is islands. Always make it a habit to scout and remember to keep scouting throughout the game, especially if you are not familiar with the map. One easy way to scout on maps you know or have explored already is to use waypoints, which leads me to the next series of advanced tips.

Speed Kills

While it is easy to get caught up in strats and build orders, do not forget the R and the T of RTS, the real-time factor. This game genre usually is won by speed, not just strategy. Two types of speed in RTS are unit speed and building speed. Unit speed is how fast you can make units or climb tech tree, while building speed is how fast you can build bases and expansions. There are several things you can do to improve speed, especially for unit speed.

Hotkeys

Hotkeys are predetermined or user-selected keys that activate a certain unit type or building. When hit, they will take you to a certain map location. Right here is an immediate time saver. Rather than scrolling with the mouse across the map you could simply hit *H* and your view centers back over your home base. When you hear a message saying your new tank is ready, hit the spacebar and you are taken to the location of last transmission. Of course, each actual game will have its own variations, but you get the idea.

Not only do hotkeys save you scrolling time but you can usually assign hotkeys to a unit or group of units too. This is a good idea before you mix it up with the enemy. By grouping your forces you can then assign different targeting objectives for each group. By queuing these you increase the damage efficiency of the group.

Rally Points and Waypoints

Rally points are quite a time saver. When a new unit exits the building that made it, it usually just stands at that building wishing it had a magazine to read until you call it into action. But, if a rally point is set, the unit will go to that point and await your command. So, by using hotkeys, queues, and rally points you can literally keep new reinforcements coming to the front while you manage the melee. In fact you don't even have to look at your base or the buildings in most RTS games.

Gotta Have the Moves!

Okay, you know your maps and how to use terrain to your advantage. You are using the queuing and hotkeys to gain some speed. Now do you know the moves? Simply marching a small army across the map to your enemy is not nearly as efficient as it once was in the days of C&C.

Safety in Numbers

Your units are usually most vulnerable when moving across the map. This is because they are spread out in a line instead of clustered together to fight as a group. So, your enemy can actually take them out with fewer units if he is positioned well for an ambush. He can set up some ranged attackers on high cliffs near a choke and pick off your units as they move through. This is normal and easy to forget too, especially if your attention is elsewhere—like fighting at the front.

When moving, try to use waypoints to avoid ambush or detection. Also move your units in smaller stretches, giving them time to regroup some. One thing I find useful, although smarter players will not fall for it as easily, is to group up just outside an enemy's LOS. Then when all the units are positioned and ready to fight as a group, I run a grunt into his view, engage very briefly, and then retreat. If his units are not in hold/guard position, the computer AI will make his units give chase. Then I run the grunt back to his waiting buddies. Remember, the sitting group inflicts more damage than the invading group during the early seconds of the melee. This is because those in back of the invading group have not yet come into range while the front ones take outnumbered damage.

Computer AI

In the more recent RTS games, the player can give some orders as to how a unit should behave. This can be in the form of guarding, patrolling, harassing, search and destroy, and so forth. Some games such as Dark Reign give the player a bit more control by actually setting the unit's aggression. On other games you merely have patrol, guard, move, and attack move. The last, attack move, is on most games now and it is very important.

Attack move simply means when you tell your unit to move they will go to the destination you clicked but they will attack any enemy units that they see along the way. This is particularly useful when engaging group to group. If you don't use it your units will not fight until they reach that destination, thus taking heavy damage before ever firing back.

I use attack move almost all the time but there are a couple instances where I would not, for example, covert operations where I do not want my unit revealing his position. If he fires on enemy units while trying to sneak into the base he will be detected faster. Another time is, as I mentioned earlier, a retreat to draw enemy units. If I stayed with attack move he would not run back but stand and fight until dead; usually that's about three seconds at most. So you will find times during the game when you actually do want a unit or group to move somewhere without stopping at all, but most of the time attack move will be used.

Dance Moves

This does not mean that when you beat an opponent you get up out of your chair and do a silly ritualistic jig as if you just scored a touchdown. Dance moves in RTS are the signature of an excellent micro player. Essentially what these moves are is the perfect timing and anticipation of enemy unit behavior, either human or AI, during the course of a melee. Now you probably think I am talking about mind reading, but really it's just anticipation.

There are certain physics or mechanics to playing these games. One such characteristic is the game speed. Of course there are variables of game speed, from what speed it is set to what conditions or distance the players are from each other. However, except for Internet games, the game speed is almost always constant once underway. If you can get a good sense of timing, more specifically game speed, during the game, you can use it to your advantage with movement during a melee.

During engagement it is usually best to keep your attacking units in motion, especially when it comes to ranged attackers. Often, it takes a while for a ranged attack to arrive, so if your target unit is in motion, it may be somewhere else when the fire comes in.

The point is that dance moves are the anticipated and well-timed movements of your units during an interaction with the enemy. If your timing is dead on, it can not only be rewarding to your game confidence, but it can be devastating to your opponent's. When you lose a melee round and expensive units to an inferior force it truly is angering and mentally hard to recover from in time.

It's All in Your Head

There is very little physical talent to this kind of gaming. The one thing that is physical is eye/hand coordination and reflex time, but not to the degree of a racing simulator or First-Person Shooter. Muscle does not rule this genre; mental ability does.

I have stressed many times to my gaming buddies how important it is to go into the game confident. Mental attitude plays a huge factor here and I'll tell you my theory why it does. This game genre requires planning and multitasking to be good. Unless you consider shooting a shotgun while running or shifting gears while steering multitasking, then you really have not experienced real-time juggling yet.

In short, I go into a live RTS with a plan that I try to implement while interpreting recon info, devising strategies, implementing them, changing them on-the-fly, and carrying them out to defeat my opponent. And, the whole time, I am balancing resource collection to unit production to tech tree climbing. Makes driving a car or playing sniper seem kind of dull in comparison doesn't it?

I am not knocking the other game genres. No, I have a lot of fun with them and who wouldn't? Driving simulators get progressively more realistic, so much so that I will not be disappointed if I die before getting my Lotus Esprit. What I am saying is that with RTS you must maintain a clear train of thought. If you let yourself get sidetracked with either a minor game factor such as a scout unit trying to evade detection or a minor player factor such as trash talk or opponent reputation, then you are not thinking about the plan; present and future.

Remember this: RTS is about the big picture. If you spend too much time thinking about a single unit instead of the whole enchilada, you will likely lose. If you spend time thinking about your opponent's win record or reputation then you will likely lose. Long story short, any distractions will delay your game from where you want to be.

The Least You Need to Know

➤ Real-Time Strategy (RTS) games require both good tactical thinking and quick reflexes.

➤ Most RTS games have some form of multiplayer, and generally work very well over the Internet.

➤ The system demands are often less than other genres. But the more recent games may demand greater CPU horsepower than you might think.

Chapter 7

Mech Games

In This Chapter

➤ A short history of Mech games

➤ Currently available games with Mechs

➤ Strategies for playing Mech games

This chapter will cover some of the Mech games, in which participants do battle with giant robots or war machines. Some people will categorize these games as simulator games. In a way, they *are* simulator games, but based on a hypothetical technology. Most of the games that I would really call simulator games are based on current technology, such as auto racing and flight simulators. But Mech games, I feel, fall in a unique category and thus are in a separate chapter.

The Genre

The idea of Mechs first originated with Japanese animation. Japanese fans take their animation seriously, and Mechs—big fighting robots—are popular among them. It was a natural course of action to take the animation fascination and create computer games.

What makes these games special is that you are in a futuristic machine as the pilot. This is not just any old futuristic machine. This machine has state of the art sensors, advanced hydraulics, megadeath weapons, and legs. What was that? Did I just say "*legs*"? That's right. Here is a list of the features that usually come with Mechs:

➤ Mechs have legs (generally) and are built for war.

➤ They can have weight limits and, as a result, can only carry a limited amount of weaponry and ammunition.

➤ The heavier the Mech, the slower it will move.

➤ Mechs can travel over rough ground, but can have trouble on steep hillsides.

➤ Some Mechs have jump jets that allow them to fly for short distances.

Mech games have a smaller following than, say, Quake or some of the first-person games. Even though Mech games have some of the same fighting action as First-Person Shooters, the Mechs are not as agile as the characters in FPS games. I find Mech games challenging and fun.

Tech Tip

Fighting Robots Stereotype

Since Mech games are based in Japanese animation, such as Robotech and others, enormous fighting robots have almost become a cliché in the anime world. Some of the most entertaining animes parody the fighting robot genre. If you're interested in learning more, use the keyword *anime* with a search engine—you're bound to come up with lots of links.

A List of Contemporary Mech Games

Following is a list of contemporary Mech games. This is not an exclusive list, but includes the current popular games. There are several other games that are listed in the "Others Games" section.

Mech Warrior 2

Install and Play	9	Story Line Depth	8
Control Simplicity	9	Strategy Simplicity	8

Multiplayer Quality	9	Team Playability	7
Multimedia Quality	9	Modifiability	8
Kid Friendly	9	Online Stability	6
Best Controller	Keyboard & Mouse	3DFX/OpenGL Required	No

This is one of the few board games that has made it into the computer gaming arena. It has set the standard among the Mech games. Even though it has been around a while, it is still a favorite for many. Being an older game, an older computer (Pentium 100) would be fine.

The graphics are not outstanding, as you can see in Figure 7.1, but considering the generation when this was made, they're not bad. The best aspect of this game is the game play. Hiding, attacking, tracking, and ambushing all add up to the thrill of this game.

Gamer Comment

Quote From: Reeves (Ethan Reeves)

Comments: "Mech Warrior 2 is an old game, but it's a classic and definitely one of the best games I've ever played."

Figure 7.1

Battling it up in Mech Warrior 2.

Mech Warrior 3

Install and Play	5	Story Line Depth	8
Control Simplicity	2	Strategy Simplicity	6
Multiplayer Quality	5	Team Playability	5
Multimedia Quality	8	Modifiability	2
Kid Friendly	7	Online Stability	5
Best Controller	Keyboard and mouse	3DFX/OpenGL Required	No

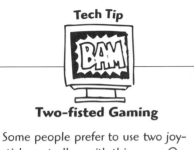

Tech Tip

Two-fisted Gaming

Some people prefer to use two joystick controllers with this game. One is for machine control, the other for throttle and weapon control.

Mech Warrior 3 is much like Mech Warrior 2, with the exception that the graphics are great (assuming you are using a 3D accelerator card). It's obvious that they have spent time creating the mission areas for this game. The drawback is that the original release has a very limited number of missions. There is a new expansion pack called Mech Warrior 3: Pirate's Moon, however, that takes care of this limitation.

Even though there is an expansion, the overall consensus is that Mech Warrior 3 is missing the challenge that made Mech Warrior 2 so popular. The preferred system for this game is a 300Mhz Pentium II with a 3D-accelerator card and more than 500 MB of free disk space. Figure 7.2 shows a cockpit-perspective view of a player targeting an enemy Mech.

Figure 7.2

Cockpit view of a Mech Warrior 3 battle.

StarSiege

Install and Play	9	Story Line Depth	10
Control Simplicity	9	Strategy Simplicity	10
Multiplayer Quality	10	Team Playability	10
Multimedia Quality	9	Modifiability	9
Kid Friendly	9	Online Stability	10
Best Controller	Keyboard & Mouse	3DFX/OpenGL Required	Yes

StarSiege is one of the most refreshing Mech games. You can tell that the designers put a lot of energy into this game, both technically and in the storyline. Technically the graphics are gorgeous. There is a sense of realism with this game as the missions are staged to draw you into the story, which is excellent.

StarSiege will technically run on an older generation game machine (Pentium II-166), but to get your money's worth, I'd highly recommend something a little newer (Pentium III-300 with 3D accelerator) to get the full effect. As you can see in Figure 7.3, StarSiege battles aren't restricted to daylight, either.

Gamer Comment

Game Name: SCORGE (Derek Miller)

"This game rocks. Being able to change my weapons and stuff makes this game."

Figure 7.3

This StarSiege duel is occurring at night.

HeavyGear

Install and Play	8	Story Line Depth	9
Control Simplicity	8	Strategy Simplicity	8
Multiplayer Quality	4	Team Playability	5
Multimedia Quality	7	Modifiability	7
Kid Friendly	8	Online Stability	5
Best Controller	Joystick	3DFX/OpenGL Required	No

Game Name: Cutter (Cody Crocker)

"This game isn't much fun as a Multiplayer game, unless there are a bunch of people to play free-for-all."

This Mech game, shown in Figure 7.4, has a great story behind it. As you play through the missions, the story unfolds very well. This game will play well on older hardware (166MHz system) and does not require anything special beyond that. A 3D card does help the looks though. This game is fine for missions, but Multiplayer is missing something. This game might be better at team battle. One on one becomes a "who can pick the other off first" kind of game.

Figure 7.4

This is the perspective from the HeavyGear cockpit.

HeavyGear 2

Install and Play	9	Story Line Depth	10
Control Simplicity	8	Strategy Simplicity	7
Multiplayer Quality	7	Team Playability	6
Multimedia Quality	8	Modifiability	8
Kid Friendly	8	Online Stability	8
Best Controller	Joystick	3DFX/OpenGL Required	Yes

Even though this is a new product, it still follows the story of the first HeavyGear. In this episode, some of the missions will take place in space, offering full 3D movement. This game is recommended for use with a full gaming machine (233MHz with 3D graphics). You can check out the graphical improvement of this next-generation Heavy Gear in Figure 7.5.

Game Name: RageMage (Unknown)

"I like having the space environment in the game. Moving in space is really tough."

Figure 7.5

Preparing for the attack in HeavyGear 2.

Others

There are several other Mech games that didn't make the list. These games were not left out because they weren't any good. Most of these games are older or just are not as popular.

One of the games is called CyberStrike2. Its predecessor originated on the Genie dialup network and could become expensive to play because of the monthly fees. 989 Studios has since picked it up and completely revamped it to match today's graphic standards. You can even get a demo copy that is online playable (http://www.cs2.net/).

BattleTech: Solaris, shown in Figure 7.6, has all the favorite components of a Mech game. It has heat management, weapons management, jump jets, and online play. GameStorm offers unlimited online play for BattleTech as well as other games for a small fee. BattleTech takes place in the thirty-first century.

139

*This is a cockpit view
from BattleTech: Solaris.*

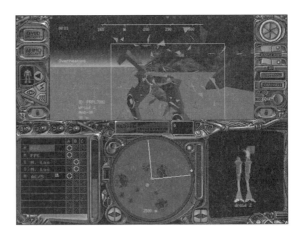

Another game that is a little different is Shattered Steel. In this game, you use a Mech to defend the planet against mechanized alien invaders. This game also allows for online gaming with Kali.

Scarab is also an older game that has online capability. This game doesn't require much of a computer to play online. It has a weak storyline, but you can play teams (up to 6 people). You can also change your Mech midgame during one of the three lives your character has to live.

The only game that doesn't quite fit here is Slave Zero. Not because it's not a Mech game, but because it's new. This game may just break the mold a little. You are piloting a biped Mech, but unlike the bulky tank-like Mechs you and I have grown to love, this one is tall and sleek. It is also agile so it can make humanoid-like moves making the game act and respond more like a First-Person Shooter. GameSpot lists this game in the action genre.

Overall Mech Game Strategies

Playing Mech games is much like playing First-Person Shooter games. You have to run around and destroy the other units. I know, it sounds simple, but there can be a lot of controls and conditions to watch. The action can be just as intense, but there are more factors involved in the game. These are definitely games that become more fun as you become more familiar with the controls and the nuances of the game itself.

Each of the Mech games has its own specialty. One has the ability to change the structural components of the Mechs, while other games only let you change weapons and still others only have preset Mechs available.

I'm going to cover some of the basic combat strategies when playing. Hopefully, these tips can help you master one of these games in this chapter. Then maybe you can go online and develop your own strategy or tactic to help you against the onslaught.

Learn to Torso Twist

One of the first things you should learn to do well is maneuver your Mech around a field while turning the torso in either direction. This gives you a wider firing range without having to change the course of your Mech. You are still limited to the field of view by the cockpit screen. Being able to twist the torso also helps you to see more than what is in front of you.

After you become comfortable with this type of maneuver, you will want to try something a little different. Because, in a battle situation, you are going to be targeted as well as targeting others, you need to avoid being hit and hit the others at the same time. Maneuvering your Mech is very important. Here are some of the basic maneuvers.

➤ S-maneuver: This maneuver is used when avoiding being shot from behind or when approaching a target. You can also use this maneuver to put objects between you and your opponent. It is mainly moving in a zig-zag pattern as you move away or toward an enemy target. Torso twists are very important here. You may have to continually adjust the torso position to see the target when moving toward an enemy and still keep up the zig-zag pattern. You can see from Figure 7.7 what I'm talking about. The retreating S-maneuver even shows the use of and obstacle.

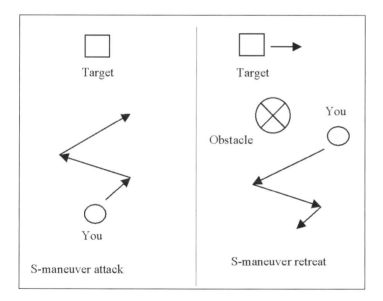

Figure 7.7

Here's a tactical diagram of the crucial S-maneuver.

➤ Perpendicular maneuver: The perpendicular maneuver is used in long-range attacks to give the opponent a moving target. This maneuver keeps your side to the enemy. The object of this maneuver is to keep one side toward your enemy and keep moving. It is always harder to hit a moving target. Being perpendicular gives you the most movement as far as your enemy is concerned.

➤ Circle maneuver: This maneuver, shown in Figure 7.8, is best used when attacking in close proximity. This maneuver requires less skill than the S-maneuver, but more than the Perpendicular maneuver. You will need to respond to the enemy as they make changes in direction and speed.

Figure 7.8

Here's how you do the circle maneuver.

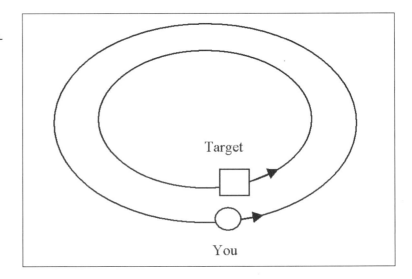

➤ Reverse Fire maneuver: This maneuver isn't one in which you fire behind you, but where you back up while moving and fire on the enemy Mech. Since in most cases, when being chased, it is hard to turn around to return the fire. It is, however, very easy to reverse direction and have the enemy chase you. You can still use a zig-zag pattern or move in any direction, as long as you move to get out of the way of fire.

Protecting Damaged Areas

Becoming proficient in controlling your Mech, learning how to avoid being hit, and protecting those areas that do get hit are your best defense skills for playing Mech games. Using obstacles and using the perpendicular maneuver, mentioned above, are the best ways to protect the damaged areas when you do get hit. When using the perpendicular maneuver, try to keep the damaged area away from the incoming fire.

Target Leading

One of the tricks that will help with targeting is target leading. This is especially helpful when you are tracking a moving target. You can easily target someone who is standing still, moving directly toward you, or moving directly away from you. Hitting a moving target is not as easy as hitting a stationary target.

Hitting a moving a target requires skill, guesswork, and chance. You have to aim just in front of the target and fire. You have to guess how far away the target is and lead the target just enough so that when you fire, your target will have moved into the fire by the time it has reached the target's position (see Figure 7.9).

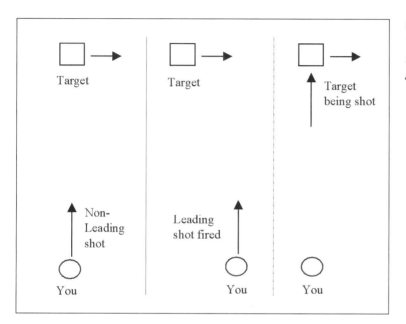

Figure 7.9

You must master the technique of leading your target.

As you can see from the previous example (first section), if you don't lead the target, you will miss. By aiming ahead of the target (seen in the middle section), when the arsenal reaches the target, the target will be hit (last section)—or has a better chance of being hit, depending on your skill.

Heat Tracking

Some of the Mech games, like the Mech Warrior games, have special considerations. The Mech Warrior games have a heat component to watch. If you fire your weapons too fast and too often, then your heat index rises. If the heat gets too high, you can't fire your weapons. You don't want that to happen during a firefight. You can find some water to get in to help keep cool.

Not all the Mech games have the heat considerations. HeavyGear, for instance, doesn't have any heat factors. In HeavyGear, your Mechs are more maneuverable than in MechWarrior and they have wheels that can let them speed away.

The Least You Need to Know

➤ Only a handful of computer games qualify as Mech games, but they're among the most enjoyable, combining strategy, tactics, and science fiction storylines. Diehard Mech players gravitate to Mech Warrior as their preferred Mech game of choice.

➤ Strategy plays an important role in Mech games because winning doesn't just mean surviving—it means taking less damage.

➤ The more skilled you become at controlling a Mech the more it shows up during the heated, heavy battles.

Part 3
Becoming Someone Else

As kids lots of games involve make believe. Even into adulthood, some adults retain this adventuresome spirit through role-playing games. Some of the first computer games duplicated the nature of these games, in which an adventurer wandered around a dungeon with a sword slaying monsters. A similar online tradition continues as gamers join ancient worlds[md]ancient in the computer sense—that is…some more than five years running!

Computers have spawned other virtual worlds, too. Role playing has gone beyond the days when your screen flashed a text message like "You are in a maze of twisty passages, all alike." Today's adventures are akin to starring in a movie that you make up as you go. You create a character with unique attributes and interact with animated figures, many of whom remember how you treat them and respond accordingly later.

So open the mailbox, buckle on your sword or your radiation suit, and come explore the many people you can be!

I AM GILKOR OF THE WOODS!!

Chapter 8

Personal Role-Playing Games

In This Chapter

➤ What a role-playing game *is*

➤ A brief history of role-playing games

➤ Classic role-playing

➤ Hybrid games

➤ The future of online RPGs

In a sense, all computer games that are not classics (like chess or backgammon), are *role-playing games*. If you're playing a flight simulator, for example, you're playing the role of a pilot. Or if you're playing FIFA 2000, you're playing the role of the soccer coach.

But in a true role-playing game, you create a character (or characters) from scratch, assign attributes, equip the party, and *become* the character during the game. Attributes define the base abilities of the character, which typically include physical abilities, such as strength or dexterity, and mental abilities, like willpower. As characters progress through the game, they gain experience, which is usually tallied as *experience points*. Experience points can be used to learn new skills, enhance existing skills or, in some cases, even alter fundamental attributes like strength or dexterity.

A role-playing game (RPG for short) usually involves adventures, puzzle solving, interaction with the environment or other characters, and combat. In this chapter, we'll talk about small-scale role-playing games. In these games, there are usually no more than 4 to 6 characters, and there's a storyline that exists as the reason for the party to be together. But often, more mundane occurrences take place, such as developing new skills at the local training center, or hunting for food so the party won't starve.

This differs from a genre known as *adventure games*, in which you are more an interactive observer. In RPGs, one of the characters is *you*. You choose the character attributes, equip them, alter their appearance. Your character can then advance, get better at certain things (due to your guidance) and matures over time.

A Brief History of Role-Playing Games

In the early 1970s, a small game called Dungeons and Dragons arrived on the scene and rapidly became hugely popular. Developed by Gary Gygax, D&D (as it was called) was originally conceived as a set of rules defining medieval combat, but the players found themselves having as much fun acting out their characters as fighting. D&D became the prototypical pen-and-paper RPG. While other RPGs existed prior to D&D, Gygax's game spread like a fever, even making an appearance in the movie *E.T.*

When computer games began to arrive on the scene in the 1980s, it was natural for role-playing games to make it to the small screen. Computer RPGs take care of a lot of the busywork, like dice rolling and inventory management. Some of the classic computer games of all time were RPGs, including Wizardry III, Ultima IV, and the AD&D Gold Box series from SSI.

All of these games were single-player games, though. However, I spent many a night with the SSI Gold Box games, playing through with friends in "hot seat" mode. When we'd enter combat, different people would take over to run their own character. But to say it was multiplayer would be stretching things.

There were multiplayer games on the Internet already, however. These were called *MUDs*, which stands for *multiuser dungeon*. In the early days, most were text based, so your typing skills had to be pretty sharp to keep up. As Internet connection speeds improved, MUDs started adding some simple graphics capabilities. These multiuser dungeons are the spiritual ancestors of the current generation of multiplayer RPGs.

The Current Classic: Baldur's Gate

Baldur's Gate shipped at the end of 1998, and is still enormously popular well into 2000. The game is based on the Advanced Dungeons and Dragons (2nd Edition) paper role-playing rules. However, the rules have been modified a bit, partly to take advantage of the power of the modern PC, and partly to clear up problems that always exist when translating a paper game to the interactive medium.

Baldur's Gate is an enormous game, taking up five CD-ROMs (six if you buy the Tales of the Sword Coast expansion). You can find out more about Baldur's Gate at

`www.interplay.com/bgate/info.html`

Also, one of the best fan sites out there is the Baldur's Gate Chronicles, which also has information on the sequel (Baldur's Gate II) and Neverwinter Nights:

www.bgchronicles.com/

Baldur's Gate tells the story of a single character (represented by you), orphaned at a place of learning. He (or she—the character can be either sex) sets out to discover his identity and heritage. Along the way, a mystery is encountered. There are a large number of subquests and subplots that keep things moving at a good pace.

Baldur's Gate enjoyed immense support from the user community. For example, the game allows you to have custom sounds and portraits for your characters, and there are Web sites that have amassed large numbers of voice and portrait files.

The Baldur's Gate Perspective

Baldur's Gate is played as if you were looking down on a set of painted miniatures from an angle. This is called an *isometric perspective*, and is fixed—you cannot rotate or change the view. The maps are beautifully hand-drawn. Even though the game is not true 3D, there is a good sense of a three-dimensional world as your characters pass behind or underneath objects.

As in the paper version of AD&D, you gain experience as the game progresses, and your character gains levels, as shown in Figure 8.1, which indirectly translate to better skills and abilities. The game has an experience point cap, however, so your characters can only advance to a certain point; the actual maximum level varies depending on character type.

Figure 8.1

A typical scene in Baldur's Gate.

A Matter of Character

Probably the most critical set of decisions you'll make in Baldur's Gate is creating your character. The type of character, and that character's attributes, will shape how you play the game, and how all the nonplayer characters (that is, the computer-controlled people you encounter) treat you. Figure 8.2 shows one of the game's character creation screens.

Figure 8.2

The Baldur's Gate character creation screen.

Note

Charisma Counts!

Whatever type of character you create, give them a fairly high charisma. That will reduce the cost you have to pay when you buy items.

Baldur's Gate on the Internet

Baldur's Gate was built from the ground up to be a multiplayer game; unlike many games, there's no real distinction between single player and multiplayer. Your party can have up to five characters in addition to the main character, or six total.

Dr. Ray Muzyka, the lead designer of the game, once said that his intent was to recreate the feeling of the paper game. He wasn't talking about rules, but instead referring to the group dynamics that occur around a tabletop game. In that respect, Baldur's Gate succeeds admirably, especially over a local area network.

Connecting and Playing over the Internet

Baldur's Gate does not feature an in-game browser to locate ongoing games over the Internet. However, GameSpy, that essential Internet gaming tool, has built-in support for Baldur's Gate. All you really need to know is the IP address of the game host, although, so if you're playing with a group of friends, the host just needs to supply his or her IP address to the group.

Playing Baldur's Gate over the Internet, however, can be a frustrating experience. For example, whenever conversation occurs with a nonplayer (in other words, computer-controlled) character, the game comes to a halt for *all* the players. Similarly, when entering, buying, or selling in shops, the game also stops while transactions are underway.

However, the game gives tools to the game host that, properly used, can minimize some of the frustration the conversation and shopping sessions cause. For example, you can set the game up so that only certain characters can initiate conversations or shop for goods. This permission system, shown in Figure 8.3, is very flexible, and helps streamline gameplay over the Internet.

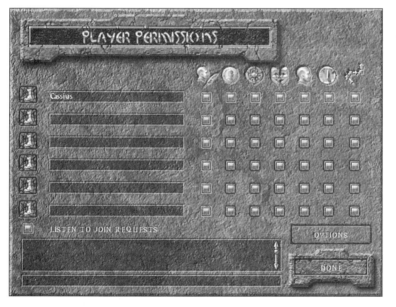

Figure 8.3

Baldur's Gate lets permissions be set for certain actions.

Dealing with Unknown Players

One of the coolest features of Baldur's Gate is the ability to have persistent characters. You can export a character you created out of the single player game and use him or her in a multiplayer game. This ability allows for a very personal element in the game.

Exported characters could create some potential imbalances, however. Imagine a party early in the game, consisting of fifth- and sixth-level characters—it would definitely lack any challenge. The enemies would be relatively weak so as not to pose an insurmountable threat to beginners. Like the conversation problem, Baldur's Gate deals with the issue of character importation by letting the host set permissions. This can run the gamut from allowing everything (experience items and statistics), to allowing only the base statistics (strength, dexterity, and so on) to be imported.

The bottom line is that Baldur's Gate, and its companion add-on, Tales of the Sword Coast, succeed admirably in recreating the social experience of pen-and-paper RPGs. It also gives the host a set of tools to manage multiplayer games, creating a less frustrating and more enjoyable experience.

System Shock 2: Defining the 3D RPG

The original System Shock practically defined a style of action gaming that had serious RPG elements embedded in it. Unlike many action games, running around with guns blazing was often counterproductive. However, System Shock was, at its core, an action game.

System Shock 2 is very much a role-playing game, albeit with action elements in it. Play this like a First-Person Shooter, and you'll find yourself stymied and frustrated. Also, your character grows in skills and attributes over time. Finally, there are three character classes to choose from; whichever you choose affects the overall style of play.

System Shock 2 retails as a boxed, single player game. The designers were originally going to build multiplayer into the core retail game, but deadline pressures prevented it. If you want to experience multiplayer System Shock 2, you'll need to download a patch from www.lglass.com. You install System Shock 2 off the CD-ROM, like most standard, Windows-based game titles.

Unlike Baldur's Gate, System Shock 2 (we'll call it SS2 from now on), is a single-player game with a multiplayer element grafted on. However, the multiplayer element is well-thought-out and works well, within some limitations. As with any true RPG, you work cooperatively with your teammates to make your way through an interesting and compelling story.

The Characters of System Shock 2

Most of System Shock 2 takes place on one of two spaceships. You play the role of a military person assigned to the *UNN Rickenbacker*. When you arrive, however, the *Rickenbacker* seems to have become infested with strange critters and two competing AI (artificial intelligence) constructs. Your task is to solve the mystery of the *Rickenbacker*.

During the character design process, you can choose between three character types. You do this by choosing a service branch in a futuristic, space-based military. Choose the marine, and you create an action-oriented character; enter the Navy, and you develop engineering expertise, including the ability to hack into computers, research items you find, and repair objects (including weapons). Finally, you can also choose to enlist in the OSA, a black ops group that gives your character significant psionic (psychic) abilities. Think of psionic abilities as the pseudo-scientific equivalent of the magic that's used in fantasy-based games.

When forming a multiplayer party, creating a balanced party adds to the fun. Having a couple of marines, one hacker/researcher, and a psi-capable OSA agent makes for a good mix. Hackers can often disable security terminals and break into locked areas. Characters with psionic abilities can launch ranged attacks or add protective capabilities. The marines, of course, can eventually gather heavy weapons.

One of the limitations of the multiplayer System Shock 2 is that all the characters look the same (except for their color), as you can see in Figure 8.4.

Figure 8.4

Here are a set of twins…er, no a group of System Shock 2 player characters. The third player is viewing the scene.

Tech Tip

Not a Shooter!

At its glossy surface, System Shock resembles first-person shooter games like Unreal or Quake II. In fact, it isn't. If you play it like a shooter, you will become frustrated and won't progress far. Instead, you need to take some time to carefully research objects you find, explore each area thoroughly—and slowly. Hack into security terminals to disable security along the way. Whatever your approach, take your time. This is an RPG, not a pure action game.

Figure 8.5

System Shock 2 is a true role-playing game. You manage an inventory, research objects, and have a host of skills and attributes you can improve.

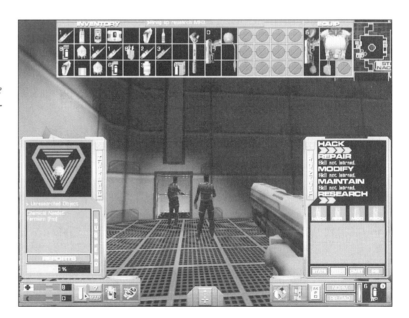

Connecting with System Shock 2

First, if you've got the original, retail version of the game, you'll have to download a patch in order to play it as a multiplayer game. You can get the patch from www.lglass.com. After installing the multiplayer patch, a multiplayer button appears on the opening menu. Like Baldur's Gate, players need to know the IP address of the host system.

When you launch the multiplayer game, each player has the capability to go through the opening sequence and create a character.

Character creation in System Shock 2 is not a sterile roll-the-dice situation. Instead, you pick your service, then go on several tours of duty. Depending on the choices made, characters will pick up differing mixes of skills. In multiplayer mode, each player can go through this process simultaneously. Then the game synchronizes with all the players at the start of actual gameplay. At times, System Shock 2 can suffer from serious lag problems, but if all the players have fast, digital connections this problem is reduced.

Saving games is very flexible. Any user can save, although it should be noted that an individual copy of the game will remember an individual character's stats and abilities, even if you copy in another save game.

Overall, System Shock 2 is fun, entertaining, absorbing, and immersive. If you're looking for a multiplayer RPG with a first-person perspective, System Shock 2 is an excellent title.

Sub-Genres

As computer games became more sophisticated, there came a gradual blurring of game genres. While classic RPGs still exist, like Baldur's Gate, hybrid games have emerged. A hybrid game is one that takes a different genre and adds role-playing elements to it. If System Shock 2 is a role-playing game with action game elements, then a hybrid action game might, while focusing on action, add elements such as character development.

Wheel of Time

For example, Wheel of Time is an action game set in the fictional worlds created in Robert Jordan's fantasy novels. But there are strong RPG elements, as your sole character's attributes improve over time.

Wheel of Time plays much like a first-person shooter otherwise. However, the online aspect of Wheel of Time is quite interesting. Instead of the usual "let's kill everything in sight" mode, the objective is to capture and hold four seals to the prison of the Dark One, an ancient and evil enemy.

At first blush, this might seem like another variant of capture the flag, but it's much more involving. Instead, you can use a game feature called the Citadel Editor to dynamically create defenses on-the-fly, alter your own citadel (fort), and make life difficult for your enemies. It requires you to think on your feet more than many action games. You can find out more about Wheel of Time at www.wheeloftime.com.

Age of Wonders

In a similar vein, Age of Wonders is a strategy game that takes you through a campaign of conquest through a fantasy world. It's a strong, turn-based strategy game in which you gather forces, conquer cities or recruit them to your cause, and defeat opposing armies.

During the start of the campaign, you have the opportunity to customize the leader by assigning schools of magic and attribute points to certain skills. As the game progresses, your character gains experience points, as shown in Figure 8.6, which can be used to add additional skills. If that character is killed in combat, the game ends. A lot of the fun of Age of Wonders is watching your character grow during the campaign. More information can be found at www.ageofwonders.com.

Figure 8.6

Character development of heroes adds a role-playing element to Age of Wonders.

The online component of Age of Wonders is like a compressed version of the campaign. You only play on a single map, although some can be quite large. As the ebb and flow of conquering human or AI enemies occurs, your online hero also gains new skills and attributes. The simultaneous turn option allows for streamlined gameplay in a turn-based game. In essence, all the players are moving at the same time. That means that you occasionally have to be quicker to a goal (say, capturing a city) than your opponents. However, each combat encounter is resolved as it occurs.

Diablo: The Quintessential Hybrid

Blizzard Studios has developed a reputation for high-quality, real-time strategy games, thanks largely to one of the most remarkable games to come down the pike in quite a while. Diablo burst onto the scene in 1996, offering frenetic real-time action from an isometric perspective, but also offering strong role-playing elements.

At its core, Diablo is very much a Kill the Foozle game. Your job is to hunt down Diablo, an evil creature who has been terrorizing the locals with his minions. You play one of three base characters: a warrior, a rogue, or a sorcerer. All can fight and use magic, but they're balanced differently. As you progress through Diablo, your base statistics can be improved, which has a direct impact on what objects you can use. Many advanced items require fairly high-level attributes.

Diablo supports four players working through the storyline. Unfortunately, Diablo also developed a deserved reputation for *player killers*, or PKs for short. A player killer would tag along with a party and wait until the party has accumulated a lot of items, then kill the others and loot them.

You can play multiplayer Diablo either through Battle.net (Blizzard's own game server at `www.battle.net`), an IPX local area network, or via modem direct connect. When playing through Battle.net, Diablo seems to have fewer lag problems than many other games.

Future Online Role-Playing Games

What follows is a brief summary of upcoming personal RPGs with an online component. All of these games should ship in 2000.

Baldur's Gate II

It's natural that there would be a sequel to the hit computer RPG of 1999. Baldur's Gate II will use an enhanced version of the game engine used in the original. However, it will support a higher resolution (800×600) and make use of 3D graphics for special effects, although the game itself will still be a 2D, isometric perspective. Like the original, Baldur's Gate II will support multiplayer parties through the story. You can find out more at the Baldur's Gate Chronicles, `www.bgchronicles.com`.

Vampire: The Masquerade

Vampire is a dark, gothic-style game set in a fictional world created by White Wolf, the pen-and-paper role-playing game developer. Vampire will be fully 3D, and the game will be played from the player's perspective. The player takes on the role of a vampire, but we're not talking Bela Lugosi here. The Masquerade world is a rich, politically complex alternative to our own world. Vampires have their own clans, and live in secret among the mortal folk (called *kine*). The story takes you from medieval Europe to modern cities (vampires live a very long time).

One of the revolutionary aspects of Vampire is its Storyteller mode. In Storyteller mode, an online gamemaster can create and host his or her own adventures. To create a truly new adventure, however, isn't for the technologically faint-hearted. It will require some expertise in programming and level design. Up to four players will be able to play through the boxed Vampire story online. More information on Vampire: The Masquerade can be found at `http://www.nihilistic.com/propaganda.html`.

Neverwinter Nights

Neverwinter Nights looks like it could revolutionize computer role-playing games. The game itself uses a beautiful 3D game engine, but you play from an external view (you see your character on the screen, not through his or her eyes).

Neverwinter Nights is being developed by Bioware, the same studio that created the Baldur's Gate series. Like in Baldur's Gate, Bioware is seeking to replicate the social dynamics of the pen-and-paper RPG experience. However, Neverwinter Nights differs from Baldur's Gate—and not just because it's 3D.

Neverwinter Nights will give budding gamemasters the tools to create their own adventures. The stated goal is to make that creation as easy as possible, though it's unclear how technically savvy the adventure creator needs to be. A game can even have multiple gamemasters. Games can be hosted over a LAN or on the Internet, and Bioware will be putting together a service called Neverwinter.net to act as a match-making service for adventurers and gamemasters.

Unlike Vampire, a particular online adventure could actually have several parties of real players, all competing to complete the same quests, but within a storyline. In fact, servers playing different games can be linked up through portals, allowing characters from one game world to move into another.

All in all, Neverwinter Nights may prove to be the multiplayer role-playing game of 2000. You can find out more about Neverwinter Nights at `www.neverwinternights.com`.

The Least You Need to Know

➤ Role-playing games allow you to create, develop, and act out a character through a series of adventures.

➤ The addition of online capability to off-the-shelf, retail games has vastly expanded the role-playing game experience.

➤ Future role-playing games will even let you design and run your own adventures.

Chapter 9

Persistent Universe Role-Playing Games

In This Chapter

➤ Stories without end

➤ The community factor

➤ Pure role-playing games

➤ Other genres

In the science fiction novel *The Diamond Age*, author Neal Stephenson postulated a world in which fictional adventure would take place on an ongoing basis. Each virtual story would have actors—some actual paid actors, while others are paying customers dropping in for a little fantasy.

In fact, such worlds are starting to sprout up today. Games like Everquest, Asheron's Call, and Ultima Online are creating virtual worlds that continue to function and thrive whether or not you're logged on. More such persistent worlds are on the way.

Most of these persistent world games are *massively multiplayer*. That means that there are hundreds, even thousands of people logged on to the game at any given time, moving, acting, and adventuring in the virtual world. Note, however, that not all massively multiplayer games are necessarily persistent.

In this chapter, we'll survey the various existing and upcoming persistent world games, discuss what makes them fun, and explore the downside.

The Community Factor

Unlike single-player games, there often is no single story that drives a persistent world. There are several factors that make a persistent world viable:

➤ The world is huge, and has many interesting places to explore.

➤ There are a variety of activities to pursue, ranging from exploring dungeons, hunting down monsters, noble quests and even huge multination wars.

➤ The game is open-ended. You can play the game in ways that the designers never anticipated. For example, one player I know became a sort of merchant prince. He played as an adventurer to get to a reasonably high level, then hired others to go on adventures. He would buy and sell commodities, magical items, weapons, and armor in competition with the games' built-in shops. Most of all, he sold information—where to go to find items, interesting locations and so on.

➤ Perhaps most important of all is the community factor. Friendships are made online that often extend into the real world. Groups of people who have never met join together to form adventure parties, and these groups often stay together.

It's this last item—community or social interaction—that gives the persistent world game their real cachet. I often hear about permanent, real-world friendships that are formed by chance encounters of virtual characters. There's nothing like being assaulted by multiple monsters in an online world and having your virtual butt saved by another player.

The flip side of this coin is virtual friendships. These are cases where player characters gather together to go on adventures, but never actually meet in the real world. Sometimes, they never communicate with the real people behind the characters, even by email, preferring to interact as the game characters.

If you'd like to learn more about persistent world games in general, there are several Web sites you can check out, like www.stratics.com and www.rpgvault.ign.com.

The Dark Side

All of this sounds wonderful, but there are some drawbacks, too. Nothing is perfect, and virtual worlds are no more perfect than their real counterpart.

➤ To be successful in persistent world games requires a massive investment of time. While it's true that casual players can have a good time, it's hard to get into that sense of community if you only play occasionally. The huge time investment also precludes other activities—including, sometimes, real-world relationships.

➤ The jerk factor also comes to play. In some games, these dweebs become player-killers, getting a weird kind of joy out of killing and looting every player character they come across. Now, it is possible to simply role-play an evil character, and that isn't necessarily a bad thing. In Ultima Online, for example, a pair of thieves worked together. One would try to pickpocket people. If caught, the town guards would come over and kill the would-be thief. His partner stood by, and if the thief was killed, would pick up the loot off the body. But that's a little different than simply to become some sort of virtual Hannibal Lecter, existing only to hamper other people's enjoyment.

➤ Game limitations can be very frustrating. For example, both Ultima Online and Everquest servers can become mobbed, especially on Friday nights. The net result (pun intended) are weird traffic jams in the game world, especially where loot might be available. It's quite hilarious to stumble into an Everquest location where a particular, high-value item will respawn on a particular monster on a busy night. Hordes of player characters are hanging about, competing to be the one who gets the jump on the monster.

➤ The motivation to continue in the world may be lacking. In standard role-playing games, there's always a story—even if it's a simple "kill the foozle, save the world" story, to keep things moving. Sometimes it's hard to feel you're a hero out to save the world—or even your village—on a Friday night in Everquest.

Commonalities

All of these games have a few things in common. First, they are constantly under development. This is mostly a good thing, because it means that new features, areas, and bug fixes are constantly occurring. The only downside is the occasional wait before a game session to download an update.

The second feature in common is easy connectivity. Since the games were built from the ground up as Internet titles, the ability to connect easily to the game server is built in. There's no need for an additional service, like GameSpy, nor do you need to know arcane IP addresses.

Under the hood, the games handle the issue of Internet lag in varying ways. Everquest seems to have aggressive prediction algorithms, which can sometimes be frustrating in combat situation. Imagine drawing a bead on someone with a bow. You see the monster and fire. But in fact, you were really firing at a phantom graphic, because the monster on the server side zigged instead of zagged. Predicting movement is an unfortunate reality until we all have very fast connections with no lag time.

Finally, the game companies constantly create new adventures and activities for the players. These range from new dungeons to explore to group events of various types. Ultima Online even has different events hosted on different servers.

Ultima Online

While several persistent world games existed before Ultima Online, it was UO (as it's affectionately known) that launched the real craze. The Ultima series of single-player computer RPGs are among the most popular ever created, so it was natural that a lot of gamers were interested in a persistent world version of Ultima.

Set in the mythical world of Britannia, Ultima Online presents a top-down view of the world, as shown in Figure 9.1, much like the single player games. The world of Britannia is fleshed out in great detail, since the designers were able to draw on over 15 year's worth of single-player Ultimas.

For more on Ultima Online, check out www.uo.com.

Figure 9.1

A light traffic day in Britannia.

Unfortunately, the early days of Ultima Online were less than glorious. Although the designers hoped the title would be popular, they succeeded beyond their expectations. The game rapidly attracted a huge number of players, and stretched the capacity of the game past the breaking point. In those dark early days, slow servers and poor performance plagued the game. This might have been bearable, but the capacity of the game itself wasn't up to the task. For example, the designers envisioned a classic supply-and-demand economy—a noble idea, but when the game was flooded with hordes of players, many key resources were exhausted. This depletion created a lot of frustration among players.

There was also a fairly serious problem with PKs (player-killers). While the town guards would hunt down PKs in any city, that wasn't the case in the countryside. A favorite tactic was to lurk near the entrance to a dungeon, then jump the hapless adventurer when they emerged from the dungeon loaded down with loot. But some player killers simply got their jollies running up the kill total.

As time wore on, many of these issues were fixed. On the technical side, new servers were added and existing ones beefed up. Issues with the economy and game capacity were slowly resolved, and the game has become much more playable over time. There's still quite a community of Ultima Online players, and the ones who have stuck it out are having a good time.

Like most such games, you have to spend a lot of time in the game so you can develop an advanced character. The adventures and quests only get really interesting if you've gone up a few levels and have improved your adventuring kit. Also, if you log off for more than a few days, any permanent facility you've created (your house, for example) deteriorates pretty rapidly. One interesting side effect of this is the auctioning of high-level Ultima Online characters for real money on auction sites like Ebay.

Everquest

Everquest was developed for Sony by Verant Studios. The game is set in a pretty typical fantasy world. There are elves, gnomes, dwarves, monsters, and evil sentient creatures set in a Tolkienesque environment. What sets Everquest apart is the lush, 3D graphics and detailed environments. At times, the scenery is simply beautiful to look at—check out Figure 9.2 for a sample.

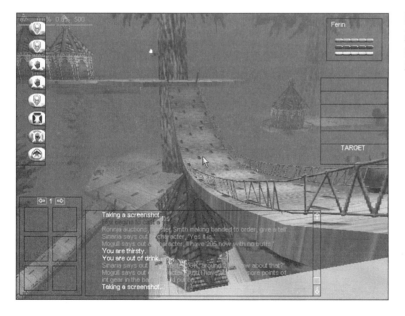

Figure 9.2

Looking out over the tree-tops in an elfin city in Everquest.

You can play the game from either a first-person perspective or a third-person perspective, depending on your preference.

The Everquest world is a rich one, with different factions, races, and cultures. Your character may be treated differently by the local nonplayer character (NPC) population, depending on how they perceive you. Since the game adheres to many of the conventions of modern fantasy literature, it's difficult to overcome prejudices. To Everquest's credit, you can be accepted over time, provided you do good deeds (at least, good deeds according to the locals). On the other hand, there have been race wars in Everquest, in which armies of player characters such as dwarfs fight others of opposing races like elves or trolls. Although all of this is in a fantasy setting, stereotypes of any type seem a little disturbing.

Still, there's no denying Everquest's popularity, and the players themselves tend avoid stereotyping other player characters. In fact, one way to avoid the problem of NPCs treating you like dirt if you're from another region is to be part of a mixed party.

Character creation in Everquest allows you to choose from a number of races and alignments. You have some limited customizability of an individual character, but it's not extensive. Also, you can have up to nine characters per server, though you can only play one of them at any given time.

Everquest's popularity, however, can work against players sometime. It's pretty hilarious watching hordes of player characters combing through areas in immediately adjacent cities in search of monsters to kill. Hopefully, the world will scale up over time, but right now, avoiding weekends is generally a good idea. Figure 9.3 shows a relatively small group of adventurers stocking up at a general store.

Figure 9.3

Shopping on a Friday night. Actually, this shop isn't as crowded as some tend to be.

As you advance your character in Everquest, you can find guilds to join. Guilds are important in that they often hand out new quests, which can lead to the discovery of magical artifacts or powerful, magically enhanced weapons.

Player killing is handled in a unique way. You have to pursue a particular quest to develop the ability to kill player characters. When you succeed, you can attack other player characters—but only those who also have completed that quest. If you don't want to be a PK, just drop the quest item and continue. Note that if you want to participate in some of the epic wars, you'll need the PK ability.

In Spring, 2000 a new expansion to Everquest, called The Ruins of Kunark, will add an entire new continent to the Everquest world. The new section will feature more detailed graphics and a new playable race, the Lizardmen.

For more on Everquest, see the Everquest home page at `http://www.station.sony.com/everquest/`.

Asheron's Call

The folks at Microsoft's gaming group took notice of the success of Ultima Online and Everquest. On the one hand, those games didn't sell millions of copies. On the other hand, thousands of people pony up roughly $10 per month, which is an ongoing revenue stream.

Asheron's Call is Microsoft's answer to Everquest. Like Everquest, Asheron's call is a massively multiplayer, 3D-accelerated role playing game with a fantasy setting. However, similarities to Everquest end there.

Player characters in Asheron's Call are all human, so you never get the chance to play a stocky dwarf or rangy elf. The game makes up for this by allowing a huge amount of character customization. As your character progresses and acquires armor and new clothing, your character's look changes as well. There's also the ability to add detail to the face. Figure 9.4 shows an Acheron character about to zap a baddie with a bow and arrow.

This level of character detail makes up for another lack in the game: the graphics. The graphics in Asheron's Call are certainly adequate, but they don't approach the level of detail in Everquest.

One unique feature of Asheron's Call is how the game focuses on the social aspect of gameplay. The simplest way is through fellowship, which is sort of an extended adventure party. More interesting is allegiance. You see, Asheron's Call supports a sort of feudal hierarchy, in which lesser players can swear fealty to more advanced players. The players who have vassals beneath them actually get a trickle of experience points as their vassals advance.

Swearing fealty isn't permanent, either, so a lord that mistreats his minions will find himself *sans* dominion in a hurry. At its best, the allegiance system encourages advanced players to help out lesser ones. The newbies gain wisdom from the experienced players, who in turn gain some additional experience points.

165

Figure 9.3

Drawing a bead in a dungeon in Asheron's Call.

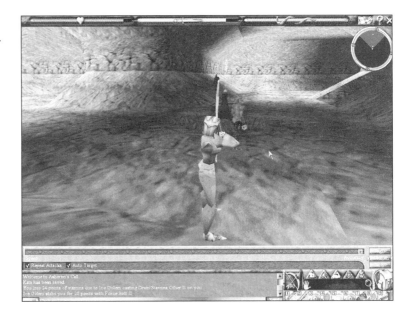

Check out more details about Asheron's call at
www.microsoft.com/games/zone/asheronscall/.

10Six

Unlike the three games we've discussed so far, 10Six is not a role-playing game. Instead, 10Six is more like a massively multiplayer version of the real-time strategy game Battlezone. In Battlezone, you played the game from a 3D perspective, but it wasn't all action. In addition to combat, you also built bases, mined resources, manu-factured new vehicles and researched new advances. 10Six takes this into the realm of persistent world, massively multiplayer gaming.

The basic story of 10Six sets the game in the not-so-distant future. A huge planetoid has entered our solar system, and is loaded with the typical science fiction plot device, in this case a valuable new resource called transium. The powers that be have divvied up the planetoid into 999,999 square plots of land. You, gentle player, have been selected to homestead one of these plots.

Although it's a huge real-time strategy game, you can play it from an exterior perspective, or get right into the action, like Battlezone. When you first start, you're actually protected from external attack—as long as you stick to your tiny plot of

Tech Tip

My Balonium Has a First Name...

Science fiction fans have coined a term for that made-up piece of scientific gobbledygook that becomes crucial to the plot. They call it "Balonium", pronounced "baloney-um."

land. Of course, if you're a gamer, this gets old in a hurry. After you've built up an infrastructure, it's off to explore adjacent plots.

There are several corporate factions in the game, and you essentially are a part of one of them. This membership is handy, because as the game progresses, you have to form alliances with other players who also are allied with the parent company. This way, you can form mutual defense pacts. Thus, if an opponent attacks you, you can call on one of your erstwhile allies to help out.

One insidious part of 10Six are *jitters*. These are insidious in a gameplaying, addictive kind of way. Jitters are another resource on the planetoid (which is named *Visitor*, by the way). Jitters are the building blocks of technology on Visitor. The insidious part is that some jitters are more common than others. The only way to acquire some jitters is to buy them, trade for them, or win them through conquest. It's a feature much like that in collectible trading card games like *Magic: the Gathering*, in which some cards are very rare. Done right, jitters can add an interesting sub-economy to the game.

As in all persistent world games, the game runs 24 hours a day, seven days a week. That means that it's running when you're not logged on. It also means that your base can be vulnerable to attack when you're not present. You can build automated defenses, but the critical thing is to build those alliances with other players.

Since 10Six is a product of Sega's HEAT.NET, you can head over to `www.heat.net/10sixchannel/index.html` if you're interested in playing 10Six.

Upcoming Worlds

The idea of a persistent online world has gripped the gaming industry like a fever. It's not simply the fact that a successful game generates ongoing revenue. In many ways, a virtual, persistent world is a holy grail of gaming. There are a number of upcoming virtual world games coming out in the next year. Many have a unique spin all their own.

Multiplayer Battletech 3025

The original Battletech board game featured turn-based, tactical combat between giant battlemechs. Think of them as tanks with legs, piloted by human pilots pitting their combat skills against enemies similarly equipped. (And for more information on this type of game, check out Chapter 7, "Mech Games.")

But Battletech is more complex than that. The original creators of Battletech envisioned large nation states that encompassed hundreds of star systems. Modeled on the historical era that followed the fall of the Roman Empire, these kingdoms exist after the demise of the legendary Star League. These feudal-style nation states are the remnants of the Star League, and the pilots of the huge war machines are akin to knights of old.

In multiplayer Battletech, you initially take the role of a pilot of a single battlemech. At this level, the game is very much a 3D simulation of a giant vehicle engaged in furious combat on a tactical level. As the battlemech pilot, you and your combat skills are the difference between success and failure. Of course, you're part of a unit, so teamwork is key.

If you desire, you can simply remain a pilot. But if you're more ambitious, you can move up the ranks, taking over command of small units, and even, over time and with some luck, become the ruler of one of the five vying nation states. At all times, you play within the confines of a military hierarchy, so it's well-suited for people who truly want to work in teams.

Battletech 3025 is slated for release in spring or summer of 2000. Information on Battletech 3025 can be gleaned at `www.battletech3025.com`.

Freelancer

Freelancer is the brainchild of veteran game designer Chris Roberts. Roberts was responsible for the seminal Wing Commander series of space combat games, which incorporated some adventure or role-playing elements. But Roberts also created Privateer, a fascinating game set in the Wing Commander universe. Instead of playing a hotshot pilot, you could take the role of a trader, a mercenary, or even a pirate.

Freelancer is very much the spiritual descendant of Privateer, set in a massively multi-player, persistent world. You start out with a minimal ship, and make your fortune through buying, selling, or hiring yourself out as a mercenary. One of the unique features of Freelancer is the space combat system. Past space combat simulators have required pretty good joystick skills, but Freelancer assumes—probably rightly—that the ships of the future will be heavily automated. Combat will be more a matter of choosing your targets and letting the ship's computers handle the gunnery. While this may not be as appealing to joystick jockeys, it will make the game much more accessible.

Not much else is known about Freelancer currently, and the game isn't scheduled for release until sometime in 2001. Microsoft already has their official Freelancer site up at `http://www.microsoft.com/games/freelancer/default.htm`. You can also get a different perspective from Digital Anvil, the creators of Freelancer, at `www.digitalanvil.com`.

Jane's World War

Imagine a persistent online world. Now imagine that persistent online world constantly at war. That's the premise behind Jane's World War, an upcoming persistent world being developed by Electronic Arts.

Jane's World War is not a single game, but will link multiple games together over time. Each world will be capable of supporting more than 100 users, and the war will continue when players are offline, until the war is won. The goal is to have human commanders give orders and determine strategy while individual players fly fighters, drive tanks, or operate other fighting vehicles. All games starting with Jane's USAF will have code that supports Jane's World War.

Motor City

If you yearn for a simpler time, when everyone worked on their hot rods in their garage, hung out at the local soda shop, and raced street rods on city streets at night, then Motor City is for you. Motor City is based on Electronic Arts successful Need for Speed line of arcade racing games. Unlike the earlier titles, Need for Speed: Motor City will have a strong persistent online element.

The game takes place around a somewhat fictional version of Detroit, set during a bygone era not unlike that in the movie *American Graffiti*. You start out with a limited stake of cash, buy a junkheap, and proceed to race your way to fame and fortune. The online game will keep track of your progress, your winnings, and your status. All in all, Motor City looks like a great game for racing buffs who yearn for a bygone era of fast cars and street action.

More to Come

This is just a taste of the future persistent world games. There are certainly more on the horizon, and they'll span most of the possible game genres. The era of virtual worlds and virtual communities, in which we play roles that previously existed only in our dreams, may be upon us sooner than we think.

The Least You Need to Know

➤ Persistent world games are virtual game worlds that continue to function even when you're not playing.

➤ You play as only one of many thousands of players.

➤ The world continues to evolve and change when you're not logged on, which typically means that you need to play frequently to "keep up with the Joneses".

➤ Persistent world games typically charge a monthly (or other periodic) subscription fee.

Part 4

Simulations Galore and the Oldies

When you get right down to it, computers are nothing more than number crunchers. But this ability gives them the marvelous capacity to mathematically duplicate reality. Gamers have enjoyed this facility in many ways since the dawn of computing[md]from flying a virtual airplane to calculating fantasy baseball statistics.

Come see the many ways your desktop machine can contain its own duplication of reality. You can manage a pro hockey team, pilot a World War 2 bomber over enemy lines, and win ten grand on a single poker hand.

Then there are a variety of games that, while (gasp!) two or three years old, have earned a loyal following. Visit our games hall of fame, where classics like Doom and Command & Conquer still thrill.

Chapter 10

Online Sports Gaming

In This Chapter

➤ The Big Leagues—Team Sports Games

➤ Solo Sports

➤ The Racing Life

At one time or another in our lives, most of us have dreamed of being a great sports star. Maybe you wanted to be part of a great team, such as being the star shortstop for the New York Yankees, the key playmaker for Leeds United or goalie for the San Jose Sharks. Or perhaps solo sports turned you on. You yearned to be Arnold Palmer at St. Andrews. Or maybe you wanted to be like Jeff Gordon at Daytona or Bobby Unser at Indianapolis.

On the other hand, maybe your tastes run to more extreme activities like snowboarding, motocross, or monster truck racing. PC sports games allow you to live whatever sports fantasy your heart desires. There's a vast array of sports games available for the PC. While playing against the computer can be a serious challenge, playing against a human opponent is the greater challenge. It's very satisfying to win a hard-fought season in a game like High Heat Baseball 2000, knowing that all the others in the league were baseball fans like you.

It's getting easier and easier to find those online leagues, too. Matchmaking services like Microsoft's Internet Gaming Zone, Sega's heat.net, and Mplayer.com all have organized league play. In some cases, there are even tournaments with prize money—or you may find yourself playing against a real pro.

This chapter is structured a little differently than others. Because of the wide array of sports titles available, it isn't possible to cover representative games from every genre. We'll hit a few high points and exceptional titles, but for the most part, we'll be surveying the online sports gaming scene. That means that if your favorite sport isn't mentioned, don't despair—there's probably a PC game that covers it!

The Big Leagues

For the most part, humans are social animals. We like being around other people, and while solo sports can be tremendously satisfying, many people really like the camaraderie of being a part of a winning team. Big league sports, such as soccer (football outside of the US), American football, baseball, basketball, and others routinely have huge audiences. There's little short of the Olympics to generate the spectacle of a Super Bowl or World Cup game.

Tech Tip

Put It on the Pad

If you plan on playing a team-based game, a good PC game pad is usually a good bet. Most game pads are fairly inexpensive, ranging from $10 to $40. They're very similar to the pads you see on console game units such as the Sony Playstation. In fact, a lot of games in this chapter originally appeared on consoles.

Even in this arena, though, there are a staggeringly large number of PC games that cover various team sports. On the American side, there's a pile of football games, several good baseball titles, hockey games, and basketball. Toss in international titles, and you'll find soccer, rugby, and even that mainstay of the Commonwealth, cricket. There are no doubt others I've missed, but suffice it to say that if there's a team sport you crave, then there's probably a PC game based on it.

However, not all of them are easily playable on the Internet—and many are still not multiplayer beyond a single computer. For example, Microsoft NFL Fever 2000 allows two players to play, but only on the same PC equipped with dual game controllers. One of the best soccer games around, FIFA 2000, does allow play over a local area network, but not over the Internet.

Note that most of the team games available are two-player games. That is, you play one entire team, while another player handles the opposing team. No one has yet designed a multiplayer sports game so that each onscreen player is represented by a real person. Games like soccer, basketball, or hockey would lend themselves well to that, although baseball and cricket might be less interesting for a large number of players as someone would likely be stuck in the outfield.

Still, there are a number of very good team sports that are Net playable. Let's touch on several key examples.

High Heat Baseball 2000 (and 2001)

High Heat Baseball 2000, by 3DO, has become the modern classic baseball game. In the early days of PC gaming, Earl Weaver Baseball was the standard, and every baseball game since then has failed to measure up—except High Heat Baseball 2000.

What's more, HH 2000 is playable over a local area network and the Internet. As of this writing, 3DO was prepping High Heat Baseball 2001 for release.

High Heat Baseball 2000 has all the features you'd want in a PC baseball game. When you're playing in action mode (that is, actually playing the batter or pitcher), it's a fully 3D-accelerated game with solid, if unspectacular graphics (Figure 10.1). However, if you're one of the reflex impaired, you can play it in manager-only mode (though you may not find many online players willing to play this way).

Figure 10.1

High Heat Baseball 2000 in action.

The game is also highly configurable, as you can see in Figure 10.2. You can set options such as how the designated-hitter rule works, how many innings to a game, how long the season runs, and so on. You can also do a round-robin playoff including up to eight human players. There's a player editor, which allows you to modify player capabilities, and even a minor league management function that lets you bring up promising stars from the minors.

The three major online gaming services—the Internet Gaming Zone, Mplayer, and HEAT.NET all support matchmaking for High Heat Baseball 2000. Make sure your ping time is less than 200ms for adequate performance.

Figure 10.2

There's a lot of customization built into High Heat Baseball 2000.

Tech Tip

Ping Time

Ping time is a measure of the responsiveness (or *latency*) of your Internet connection. It's measured in milliseconds, and represents the amount of time it takes for a data packet to travel between servers. The lower the ping time, the better. You can run the ping command that comes with Windows (by clicking the Start Menu, choosing Run, and then typing **ping** followed by the server name or IP address). However, many multiplayer games have built-in ping utilities, which are easier to use. Also, many of the matchmaking services report the latency to you in one form or another.

While logging on to one of the matchmaking services and playing a quick pickup game can be fun, it's a lot more entertaining to get a number of your friends involved for season play. Figure 10.3 shows the screen you'll use to create a playoff game. However, make sure you and your buddies understand that it's a fairly serious commitment. The games themselves don't take that long, but getting through a full, eight-player playoff takes effort and patience.

In the end, High Heat Baseball 2000 is one of the most multiplayer-friendly sports games around. Now what are you waiting for? Get cracking and set up your own league!

NHL 2000

Electronic Arts Sports is one of the leading game publishers in the industry, and their EA Sports franchise is one of the most widely known. The company has set a formula of releasing a new version of a game around the time the season for that sport starts each year. EA's NHL hockey game has gone through several iterations, but NHL 2000 is one of the best yet. It's widely played on matchmaking services such as Microsoft's Internet Gaming Zone and heat.net. You can see some of the ice action in Figure 10.4.

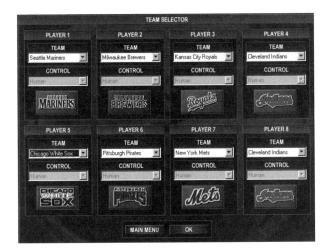

Figure 10.3

High Heat Baseball's play-off setup screen.

Figure 10.4

NHL 2000 in action. The graphics are simply stunning and gameplay is fast and furious.

You can even import a bitmap graphic of your own face and put it on the best player in the game. NHL 2000 has just about everything you'd want in a hockey game, including an advanced fighting mode! If this isn't pandering to your audience, I don't what is.

Madden 2000

Like NHL 2000, Madden 2000, shown in Figure 10.5, is one of EA Sports's regularly updated titles. The 2000 version of this popular football game now supports Internet

Tech Tip

Avoid the Lag Time Penalty Box

Because of the fast and furious action in NHL 2000, the game is sensitive to lag time on the Internet. Make sure you and your opponent see ping times of well under 200 milliseconds for best performance. Anything less can interfere with play.

play (as well as play over a local area network). Like many similar titles, Madden 2000 supports either an arcade action mode of play or a coaching mode, in which you pick the plays, but the AI actually runs the play. You can see some of Madden 2000's many options in Figure 10.6.

Unlike NHL 2000, which is supported by the larger matchmaking services, EA Sports has taken control of the Madden 2000 online gaming experience by creating a custom Web site, `http://www.eafoot-ball.com/`. When you launch an online game from Madden 2000, you're connected to the EA Football matchmaking service. It works quite well. You can play against other humans in action mode or coaching mode. The site often hosts tournaments as well.

These three titles are fairly typical of team sports on the Internet. Today, not all the major league team games support online play, but by next year, most will. Then you'll be able to pick your favorite team sport and challenge your best friend on the other side of the country to a match.

Figure 10.5

Madden 2000 sports attractive graphics and improved AI over earlier versions, as well as an online play mode.

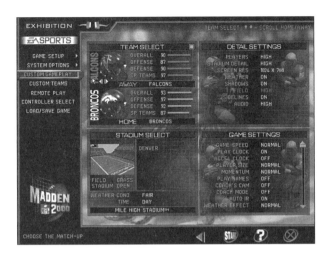

Figure 10.6

Madden 2000 is highly configurable and allows you to play in action or coaching mode.

Solo Sports

There are large numbers of games that revolve around team sports, but if you stop and think about it, there aren't that many big league team sports. What you end up with are several games from different publishers, covering the same sport. How many football games do you need?

Solo sports are different. There are dozens of these, covering a staggering array of different individual sports. They range from the prosaic, such as Brunswick Bowling and the Bassmasters fishing simulation, to the adrenaline rush of games like NASCAR 3. There are also the quieter games, such as Links LS2000 (golf), and Virtual Pool. You'll also see extreme sports, such as snowboarding and inline skating PC games.

One important sub-genre of solo sports is racing games, which we'll cover in the section following this one. We'll just hit on two fairly popular solo games, but bear in mind that there are many, many games out there.

Links LS 2000

Easily a perennial bestseller, the Links series by Microsoft (who acquired the original publisher, Access Software, several years back) is one of the oldest franchises in computer golf still around. There are other good golf games, but they're always measured up against Links. This year's model is Links LS 2000.

Links LS 2000 ships on three CDs, but the third CD just contains movies (AVI files) of the courses. These are loaded by the tour program that comes with the game. Links has a huge number of options, and you can play just about any variant of this ancient game that's recognized. There are a number of player models available—for both men and women—but the only Pro models are Arnold Palmer and Fuzzy Zoeller—no female pros, alas.

Links is an extremely popular series, and has offered online play for a number of years. In fact, you can still find Links 98 available on some of the matchmaking sites. So you'll find no shortage of Links players online, eager to match their skills against yours. Be aware that if you commit to an 18-hole foursome, it could take some time. Like the real world, it's considered bad form to drop out once you start.

Figure 10.7

Links LS offers a plethora of online play options.

Note

Be a Virtual Spectator

One other nice thing about online play is that you can drop in and just watch a match. This option allows you to see how other good online players play—which clubs they use in certain circumstances, which mode they like to play, and so on. There's quite a number of online play options, which gives you a great deal of flexibility. Best of all, you never have to worry about getting conked by a stray ball.

Over the years, a passionate online community of Links players has formed. Access (and now, Microsoft) has catered to those players, and there's now an officially sanctioned tournament, the LS Tour. But be aware that these are *serious* players, so make sure you've brushed up on your skins game before taking part.

If a pickup game is more your style, one of the best sites for Links LS 2000 is the Internet Gaming Zone (www.zone.com). If you have a Zone account, just head over to the Links LS 2000 section, shown in Figure 10.8, where you can join a game or even check up on this virtual realm's sports news.

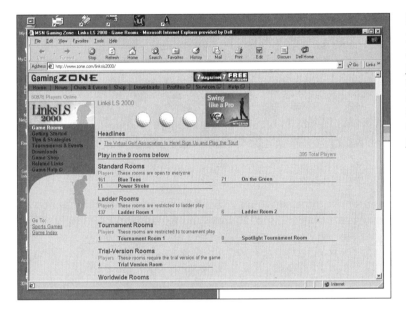

Figure 10.8

The Internet Gaming Zone has extensive support for Links LS 2000, including pickup games, ladders, tournaments, and even the ability to try out the demo version multiplayer.

It's a little cumbersome to actually get into a game—simply finding a free game can be a chore. Once you've become a part of the community, though, you can set up times and games to meet with your online golfing buddies. Figure 10.9 shows the screen you'll see displaying the virtual games going on, including the ones you can join.

In the end, Links LS 2000 is an absorbing game in its own right, but the flexibility, online options, and ease of play make it a compelling game even if you're not a golf fan.

Figure 10.9

As you can see, there are a lot of Links fans.

Brunswick Bowling

About the last thing you might think that would make a good computer game is bowling. But Brunswick Bowling is a surprisingly good little game, with lots of good options and variations. The graphics are very good, and the whole affair has a sort of spit and shine associated with much more elaborate games. (Fishing might be pretty far down on your list too, but as you'll see, there are good fishing games out there too.)

Brunswick Bowling is supported by most of the online matchmaking services. The game is very easy to pick up, and there are occasionally tournaments online as well. Figure 10.10 shows a virtual bowler lining up a shot.

Figure 10.10

Brunswick Bowling: a surprisingly fun title that captures the spirit and feel of the game.

Racing Games

When you mention racing games, most people will think of an arcade racer, like the Need for Speed series, or a serious racing simulation, like the NASCAR Racing titles. But racing games actually encompass much greater variety than those initial thoughts might imply.

Take TrickStyle, for example. Here's a nice little offbeat game in which you ride on a sort of antigravity skateboard through various landscapes and cityscapes. Along the way, you get points for performing stunts as well as for winning races.

Then there's Pod Racer, from LucasArts. If you saw *Star Wars, Episode I: The Phantom Menace*, you'll certainly remember the scene in which young Anakin Skywalker raced through the desert at breakneck speeds on a sort of high tech chariot pulled by jet engines. You, too, can relive this by becoming a champion pod racer in your own right.

Another charming, but slightly goofy game is Plane Crazy, which is supported by several online matchmaking services. Plane Crazy is an arcade racing game, but you fly oddball aircraft that resemble 1930s style racing planes through weird and exotic courses.

A very different sort of game is Microsoft's Midtown Madness. When you first start out, it seems to be an average racing game with ho-hum graphics. However, when you discover the "Cops and Robbers" mode (only available multiplayer), it becomes a sort of Mr. Hyde to the racing game's Dr. Jekyll. In Cops and Robbers, you race through the city and pick up a bag of gold. Other crooks and cops try to ram you to shake loose the gold. It's not unlike capture the flag, but more frenzied and hilarious.

Finally, there's BoarderZone. At first blush, BoarderZone resembles TrickStyle—but it's a tad bit more serious. BoarderZone is a snowboard competition game. There are both racing modes and stunt modes. The graphics are drop dead gorgeous and the physics are reasonably realistic.

Note

Grab Your Wheel of Fortune

It's worthwhile investing in a good computer steering wheel and pedals if you plan on doing a lot of online racing. Racing games—even the offbeat ones—are often much easier with a wheel/pedal combination than with a joystick, gamepad, or keyboard. The steering wheel metaphor is a strong part of our driving culture, and the familiarity is very comforting when playing a racing game.

Let's take a look at two highly popular autoracing titles as examples.

NASCAR Racing 3

NASCAR Racing is one of the most popular spectator sports in the country. There's something visceral about watching drivers muscle 3,000-pound stock cars around an oval track for 400 miles. The NASCAR Racing simulation series, as developed by Papyrus Studios, has been around for nearly a decade now.

In NASCAR Racing 3, shown from the driver's perspective in Figure 10.11, the series finally makes the transition to Windows gaming. Previous versions were DOS-based, and while multiplayer was possible, the setup process was arcane and difficult. However, the gameplay has been uniformly excellent, with the developers at Papyrus working hard to create an accurate simulation that's also fun.

Figure 10.11

Moving through the pack in NASCAR 3.

NASCAR 3 builds on the successes of the earlier game with somewhat improved graphics and more courses. While Daytona still isn't included (because of licensing reasons), the variety is now greater, including added road courses.

NASCAR supports multiplayer on both local area networks and online. The major way to play online is through the World Opponent Network (won.net), an online service hosted by Sierra Studios, NASCAR's publisher. It's very simple to find a quick race, once you've gotten an account through WON, as Figure 10.12 indicates.

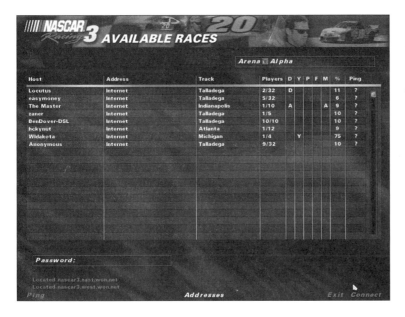

Figure 10.12

Finding people to race with NASCAR 3 is very simple, due to the in-game browser for won.net.

One thing you should be aware of before jumping into an online race: This is a serious simulation. If you jump into a race and try to drive casually, you'll be eaten alive. Practice against the computer opponent. Get comfortable with manual gearshift. Learn how to read the groove on the track, and be able to follow it. Become experienced drafting behind other cars. Learn the ins and outs of car setup. Once you've done that, you'll be ready—and even then, you'll only be a middle-of-the-pack racer for awhile.

WON supports a very active community of NASCAR racers who are constantly uploading new car *skins* (paint jobs) and setups. You can learn a lot by perusing the forums, too.

Note

You Might Not Be Able to See Distant Opponents

As you play NASCAR 3, you'll see cars popping in and out of view. This is perfectly normal. The game automatically adjusts various parameters to try to maintain a smooth frame rate, so it sacrifices displaying all cars in order to make the game run faster. It also tries to predict the location of cars when playing online, so be sure your connection speed is as fast as possible.

Need for Speed: High Stakes

If NASCAR3 represents the epitome of the racing *simulation*, then Electronic Arts's Need for Speed franchise is the quintessential arcade racer. The action is always hot and heavy in any Need for Speed game, and you'll find that drivers are not at all polite or cautious. You'll be bumped, nudged, and outright rammed off the road by other players, so being aggressive is rewarded.

The Need for Speed series has supported multiplayer since Need for Speed II came out in 1997. High Stakes, shown in Figure 10.13, is the latest incarnation of this incredibly popular series.

Figure 10.13

Need for Speed: High Stakes combines fast action with gorgeous graphics.

In any Need for Speed game, you typically drive exotic, but familiar cars. Electronic Arts has licensed the appearance and names of a number of high-priced sports cars for various games. These include the McLaren F1, various Ferraris, Lamborghinis, Porsches and more. Starting with Need for Speed III, the game added a hot-pursuit mode, in which you could play the role of a policeman trying to chase down these mad speeders—or you could try to get away from the cops.

High Stakes was the first of the series to have online play built right into the game. You first have to get a free account at www.earacing.com. After that, you can log on automatically from within the game itself.

When you're in the EA Racing Lobby, you'll be presented with a choice of game types, as you can see in Figure 10.14. Pick a game type, enter or host a game, and you're off. If you just want to race only with opponents of your choosing, you can password protect the game.

Figure 10.14

The EA Racing lobby. If you create a game, you can password protect it so only people you know can get in.

In the end, you'll find that Need for Speed: High Stakes is great for an adrenaline rush. I've hosted multiplayer games in which all the players were sweating profusely within a couple of races. This is one addictive racing game, so if you've ever wanted to drive one of these exotic cars with reckless abandon, this is your game.

Virtual Heros

If computer games allow us to play out our fantasies, then sports games are probably the most accessible form of the art. Most people would have to make a stretch of imagination to identify with a dwarven cleric or the pilot of a 30-foot tall attack robot. But most of us have played sports, and perhaps have even been successful. The coolest thing about sports games is that you can learn them and play them without the hours of training or dedication required by a Jeff Gordon or Mia Hamm. By the same token, however, you can seek out like-minded people and share some great gaming experiences.

So break out that gamepad or steering wheel, log on to the Net, and start your engines!

The Least You Need to Know

➤ Online sports games span a wide variety of team and solo sports.

➤ Most of the major matchmaking services support various sports games, but a few will have dedicated Web sites.

➤ You can play out your sports fantasies on the Net in the sport of your choice.

Online Simulation Games

Simulations are created to mirror reality, even if that reality may be a fictional one, as in a starship simulator. The difference between a simulator and an action game can be subtle, but simulators generally try to immerse the user in a reasonably realistic way, modeling something that's real or could be real.

The Toughest Challenge

Simulation titles are among the most difficult games to create. Because the game designer is trying to emulate reality as closely as possible, there are a host of challenges that don't exist in games that are invented out of whole cloth. Take flight simulations, for example. If a game models real aircraft, there are any number of actual and wannabe pilots who will pick apart the flight models, instruments, and even squadron markings on a realistic flight simulator.

Simulations are also among the most hardware-intensive games available. While First-Person Shooters might strain the graphics hardware of a PC system, sims tend to hit CPU and memory in equal proportion to graphics. Think about a combat flight simulator with dozens of aircraft in the air. Each aircraft has to have AI, flight dynamics, and avionics calculated. In a modern jet sim, if missiles are launched, each one needs to have the physics calculated. Ground and water vehicles might be moving and fighting, too. All in all, sims can chew up the horsepower of a modern CPU and beg for more.

Most sim designers take this into account and have all manner of settings to allow you to tweak the game for your system. The good news is that flight sims are no more demanding on Internet connections than any other fast-paced game title.

There are three types of simulations: civil aviation sims, combat flight simulators, and space flight sims. In the latter two, there are both standalone games (that are multiplayer) and massively multiplayer sims. We'll look at both types.

Note

Grab a Joystick

Simulation games, more than almost any other type of title, need the appropriate game controller. For combat flight simulators, you really need a good joystick as a minimum. Don't get a generic joystick, but one designed as a flight stick. Examples include the CH Products F-16 Combatstick (modeled after the control column on the real fighter jet), the Saitek X36, and the Suncom Talon series. If you want even more control and realism, add separate rudder pedals and throttle controls.

Civil aviation flight buffs should definitely opt for a good flight yoke, but beware of cheap yokes, which break easily. The best low-cost yoke, the FlightSim Yoke, is made by CH Products and comes in both game port and USB versions. There are also very pricey ones designed for pilot training, but available to flight sim users.

Without further ado, let's dive into the world of simulation games and see what's in the air.

Civil Aviation Flight Simulators

For the longest time, the market for civil aviation flight simulators was dominated by a single title, simply called Flight Simulator. Several years ago, Microsoft bought out BAO, the creator of Flight Simulator, and now develops new versions completely in-house.

Recently, there have been a slew of new civil aviation sims released, including Fly!, Sierra Pro Pilot, and the Flight Unlimited series. But Microsoft's latest title, Flight Simulator 2000, shown in Figure 11.1, is still the top gun, and a huge number of add-ons come out yearly to support this perennial best-seller. Let's take a closer look at Flight Simulator 2000 and its support in the online community.

Figure 11.1

Here's a Beechcraft King Air over Chicago's O'Hare International Airport in Microsoft Flight Simulator 2000.

Flight Simulator 2000 comes in two flavors, the standard and the Pro edition. The Pro edition layers on extra cities, more aircraft, and even discount coupons for real-world flying lessons. However, either version works fine in online flying. The best support for Flight Simulator 2000 comes from the Microsoft Gaming Zone (www.zone.com), but Mplayer (www.mplayer.com) supports it as well. You can also hook up for casual group flights, provided all the flyers know the IP address. Figure 11.2 shows an independent multiplayer site, SquadWar.com (www.squadwar.com).

FS2K, as it's colloquially called, is a huge title that ships on three CDs in the Pro version and 2 CDs in the basic version. You get 12 fully fleshed-out cities, a dozen aircraft in the Pro version, and one of the most complete tutorials in any game title. You can simply fly around, buzzing the local cities, or fly in a disciplined and realistic manner, although the game does lack a real-time air traffic control feature in single-player modes.

Figure 11.2

Flight Simulator 2000 offers flexible multiplayer configuration options.

There are numerous add-ons from Microsoft and third parties, ranging from additional scenery and aircraft packs to elaborate adventures with structured goals and gameplay.

You might wonder exactly what people do in a civil aviation sim. After all, you're not flying around shooting down bandits. However, civil aviation is an exacting and detail-oriented practice. Some sim pilots are current, former, or future real-world pilots who enjoy the opportunity to practice procedures without the hefty expense of flight time. Others enjoy the challenge of flying the perfect pattern or making a landing in a windstorm. Still others just like to buzz around the scenery (you can't cut between the World Trade Center towers in real life).

Interestingly, there are also more online options than in many combat sims. There's a community of virtual air traffic controllers, for example, which adds a tremendous amount of realism to your virtual flying experience. (For more information on the virtual air traffic control system, start at the International Virtual Aviation Organization, www.ivao.org).

Did you know there are also virtual airlines? A virtual airline is a group of like-minded flight sim pilots who are fascinated by the idea of being a commercial aviation pilot. They are assigned to routes and regular flights, just like real pilots, and fly the route in the simulator. There are a number of virtual airlines, depending on how much you want to fly and whether your tastes run to large aircraft (like the 747) or smaller, regional airlines. You can find out more at http://www.planetaviation.com/virtualairlines/.

However, most enthusiasts simply get together and fly in tandem or in groups. They share tips, practice formation flying, or simply see who can fly the most efficient paths from one area to another. It's a wonderfully sedate and refreshingly nonviolent hobby.

In the end, if you're fascinated by civil aviation but don't have the desire or where-withal to fly real aircraft (which can cost $50 an hour and up), then Flight Simulator 2000 is an excellent choice given the devoted community of enthusiasts and multi-player possibilities. Being bored is not an option.

Standalone Combat Flight Simulators

Combat flight sims have an appeal that stretches beyond simply flying around and shooting things up. Most good sims either have a strong historical flavor or capture the workload a modern jet pilot has to live with. A good historical sim, such as Rowan's MIG Alley, can be an educational experience as well as a visceral adrenaline rush.

However, if you're used to playing First-Person Shooters, getting used to a flight sim can be more challenging than you might expect. On the one hand, you typically don't rack up dozens of kills in a session, so the pace seems a little slower. On the other hand, you get to manage real-world physics in the best of the sims. Imagine lining up the perfect shot—but just then, your plane stalls, and you enter a flat spin. One moment, your itchy trigger finger is about to be gratified, the next moment, you're frantically trying to remember the spin recovery technique you skipped reading in the manual.

Tech Tip

Watch Your *Six*

One key concept to understand in a combat flight simulator is the idea of *situational awareness* or SA as it's sometimes called. Simply put, situational awareness is your understanding of the existing 3D environment around you, including location or direction of friendly and enemy aircraft. (That's why it's vital to keep an eye on your *tail*, or *six o'clock*, as well as that bandit you're chasing.) But it's more than that; it includes an understanding of energy management. After all, no aircraft has infinite power, and gravity truly does suck, so understanding your aircraft's power envelope is critical to being a successful sim pilot. The best of the aces during World War II not only knew when to attack, but when to avoid attacking—even when the situation might have looked perfect.

193

There are a large number of good combat flight sims. Some are so hyperrealistic they have a tremendous learning curve, but there's a terrific sense of satisfaction when you master them. Combat sims are divided up (somewhat arbitrarily) into *study sims* and *survey sims*. A study sim is one that focuses in great detail on a single aircraft. Falcon 4.0 or Jane's FA-18 are examples of Study Sims. Survey Sims let you fly a variety of aircraft, but often give up some detail in the process. Survey sims don't require the steep learning curve of many study sims and tend to be more fun out of the box. A lot depends on your own personal preferences on the matter. Falcon 4.0 not only accurately models the F-16 Fighting Falcon, but an entire hypothetical ground war—you're truly just one facet in a larger action. A title like MIG Alley lies somewhere between the two—several aircraft are modeled, in relatively good detail, but it's also very accessible to new users.

Let's take a look at three representative combat simulators.

European Air War

European Air War, by Microprose (now Hasbro Interactive), had an unusually long gestation period, and at one time, nearly the entire development team was replaced. Usually, this bodes ill for any game, but EAW, as it's fondly called, turned out to be one of those titles that hit a wonderful sweet spot. It's reasonably realistic, yet very accessible. It has some marvelous historical flavor, and when you fly through a huge formation of B-17s, with AAA explosions filling the air, you get a real sense of how it must have been, as you can see in Figure 11.3.

Figure 11.3

Chasing down BF-109s in a P-51D while escorting a B-17 raid over Germany in 1945.

In European Air War, you have the choice of flying careers for either the Allies or the Germans. There's a lot more variety on the Allied side, including British aircraft such as the Spitfire, Tempest, and Typhoon. You can fly P-51s (both B and D variants), the P-47 Thunderbolt, and two different P-38 models of american aircraft. The Germans offer several different Messerschmidt BF-109s, a couple of FW-190 models, and several twin engine fighters such as a BF-110 and Ju-88.

When EAW first shipped, the game proved to be somewhat problematic when playing over the Internet, but Microprose later issued a 1.2 patch that fixed most of the multiplayer problems and added more to the game (such as higher resolution modes). In addition, EAW has garnered terrific support from the user community. User-created add-ons that are must-haves include *Enemy Coast Ahead* (*ECA*), which is an editor that lets you fly aircraft not normally flyable in the standard game. The *Meatwater Sound Pack* significantly beefs up the sound effects in the game, adding more realistic engine and gunfire effects, among other things. There are also hosts of new art and paint schemes and a user-created campaign. Most of these can be found at www.combatsim.com.

Multiplayer flying in EAW is a treat, although you can only fly single missions. However, you can fly cooperative, team mode or simple deathmatch-style play. EAW supports a variety of multiplayer connection options, as you can see in Figure 11.4.

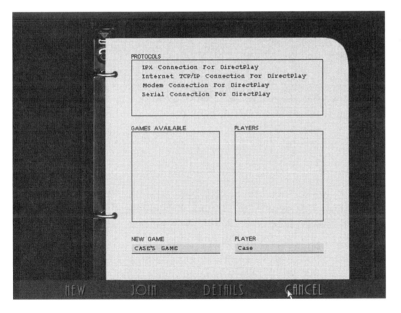

Figure 11.4

EAW supports these multiplayer connection options.

Most of the online matchmaking services offer support for EAW, and there's a sizeable EAW community on the Microsoft Gaming Zone.

European Air War came out in late Fall of 1998, yet it still has a loyal following. It's among the best of the World War II combat sims available, and you can still find it in your local shops.

MIG Alley

MIG Alley was the term coined by allied pilots during the Korean Conflict to describe the hotly contested skies over the Korean Peninsula. When the US entered the Korean War in 1950, the North Koreans could only field a very limited force of aging propeller aircraft. On November 8th, 1950, Chinese MIG-15s tangled with US P-80s in the world's first jet-versus-jet conflict. One MIG-15 was shot down, but the P-80s were outclassed by the faster, more agile MIGs.

In addition to being a superb combat simulator, MIG Alley is interesting because it captures the end of one era—prop aircraft as viable fighters—and the beginning of the jet age. You can check out the action in Figure 11.5.

Figure 11.5

These F-86s are conducting a fighter sweep over the Korean peninsula in Rowan's MIG Alley.

Flying in MIG Alley is different from other sims. The F-86A Saber moves much faster than a prop fighter, but doesn't have any of the advanced avionics of a modern jet fighter. The net result is that you're trying to line up the nose of your Saber, with its four 50-caliber machine guns, with your Mark I eyeball at 500 knots. It requires some good, seat-of-the-pants flying; no fire-and-forget missiles here.

Note

Evolution of the Pilot's Workload

The workload of the fighter pilot has increased over the years. During World War II, all you had were your eyes (the "Eyeball, Mark I") and radios. Chuck Yeager became a top fighter pilot in part because he had 20/10 vision, and could spot aircraft further away than most people.

During the Korean War, the concept of the FAC (forward air controller) was added. These were spotters who would radio locations of targets or enemy formations to allied planes. Also, the sheer speed of the early fighter jets made for a greater workload.

During the Vietnam era and later, avionics—aviation electronics—became more complex, and pilots had to watch radar, operate computers, and manage "smart" weapons like heat-seeking and radar-guided missiles. Later technological advances led to the "fire and forget" missile, but they're much more expensive.

Curiously, the most complex aircraft of the modern era, including the upcoming F-22 Raptor, try to simplify the pilot's workload by automating much of the process. The F-22, for example, won't let the pilot stall the plane.

In addition to good local-area network connections, MIG Alley offers Internet play either via direct TCP/IP connection or through the heat.net matchmaking service. The sim offers three different multiplayer options: standard free-for-all (deathmatch), team play, and Quick Missions. Team Play is the most fun for six or more players. If you only have a couple of players, Quick Missions is actually great fun, because it allows AI-piloted aircraft into the mix, and lets you fly cooperatively with a human wingman against AI opponents.

In summary, MIG Alley is a superb single-player combat simulation modeling an era of history that's been ill served in the past by other sims. It has a terrific dynamic campaign, excellent graphics, and fun online play.

Figure 11.6

Heat.net lets you easily set up Internet MIG Alley sessions—and it's free.

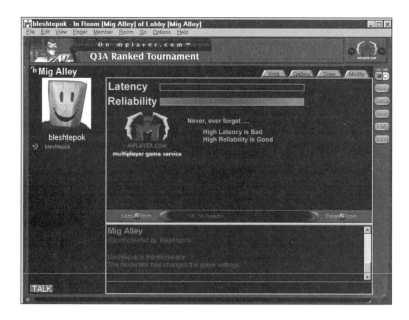

Jane's USAF

Jane's USAF is a classic survey sim. You can fly eight different aircraft, ranging from the massive firepower of the A-10 Thunderbolt II (or the "Warthog") to the whisper-quiet F-117A, from the brute force of the F-105D Thunderchief in Vietnam to the sleek F-22A in a hypothetical future conflict.

Tech Tip

Who's This Jane Person?

Electronics Arts licensed the use of the Jane's name from Jane's Publishing for its line of realistic combat simulations. Started by J. F. T. Jane in the late 1890s, Jane's Publishing began with books covering the naval forces of the era in great detail. As the technology of warfare evolved, Jane's added annual volumes on aircraft, armored vehicles, small arms, and more.

Today, the Jane's books are widely read by anyone working in the defense industry. In the past, classified information has appeared in Jane's publications, not through leaks, but through the smart analysis of the Jane's staff.

Like any product that covers this much ground, USAF does tone down some realism features. The control setup, for example, is very similar from one aircraft to the next. This means that the F-22A might be somewhat limited relative to the real capabilities of the fighter when it ships. At the other extreme, the Vietnam-era fighters sport more sophisticated HUDs (heads-up displays) than they really had. Still, USAF is quick to learn and is great fun as both a single-player game and online. You can see the workhorse F-15 Eagle in the thick of things in Figure 11.7.

Figure 11.7

The action heats up around your F-15 Eagle in Jane's USAF during an attack on an enemy airfield.

While USAF supports multiplayer options via LAN, online play is handled directly through Jane's Combat.net, a matchmaking service hosted by Electronic Arts. You can reach the combat.net site at `http://www.ea.com/cf_janes/jcn/index.html`.

Let's take a closer look at the Jane's Combat.net site. It's a great example of how a gaming matchmaking service should work. First, there's the main screen, shown in Figure 11.8, which shows you all the available game types.

To play, select the game of choice, then type in a username and password. After you log in, you're presented with the main lobby for the game. You simply click on the game you want to play. The top player is hosting the game, and the others are listed below. When you're ready, USAF is automatically launched. As you play, your statistics are captured and displayed on a killboard, shown in Figure 11.9, which is persistent.

Figure 11.8

Here's the main Jane's Combat.net page.

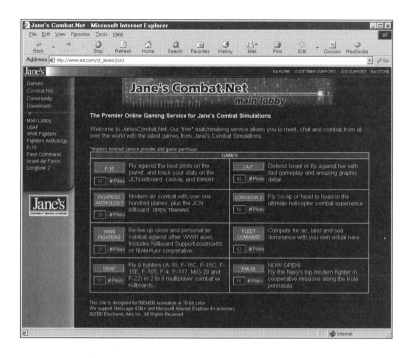

Figure 11.9

The Jane's Combat.net killboard for USAF lets you compare your rankings.

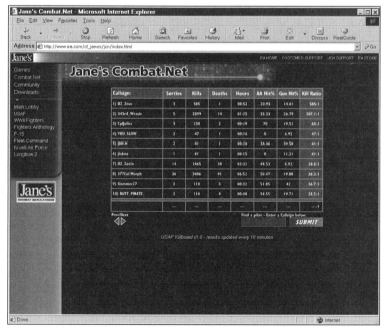

The only downside to USAF online play is that it's limited to single missions. If there were cooperative (or team) multiplayer through the campaigns, it would be nearly perfect.

Freespace 2

Let's move beyond the restrictions of earthly gravity and current technology into the world of the far future. There are a number of space combat simulations. Most try to offer varying degrees of realism (though there is no sound in space), so they aren't simply action games. Some have fairly sophisticated military campaigns.

So let's move to the far future. If you've ever watched the TV series *Babylon 5*, you've probably been amazed at the scale of the space fleet combat. You have sleek destroyers, powerful battle cruisers, and mammoth dreadnoughts engaging in long-range space combat, using weapons of unimaginable power. Buzzing around are the tiny space fighters and tactical bombers, dogfighting and trying desperately to even the odds in the larger engagement around them.

If the thought of being an ace space fighter pilot in this kind of scenario excites you, then Freespace 2 is your salvation.

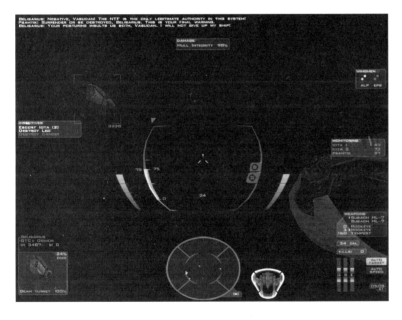

Figure 11.10

Flying between two opposing capital ships who are about to engage isn't the smartest thing to do.

Freespace 2 requires 3D acceleration; there is no software mode. The graphics scale up to as high as 1024×768 in 32-bit color, and the special effects are quite good. One thing that sets Freespace 2 apart from other similar games is the sense of scale. Capital ships are huge, and flying near one can be an awe-inspiring event. While the single-player game is excellent, Freespace 2 really shines in multiplayer.

Unlike many games, you can fly the campaign in multiplayer mode. The game is saved after a completed mission. You can connect up online, or through pxo.net, the built-in matchmaking service for Freespace 2. Other game sites support it as well, including heat.net and the Zone. There are a host of game options, including campaign, co-op, deathmatch and others.

Figure 11.11

Freespace 2 has more multiplayer options than most.

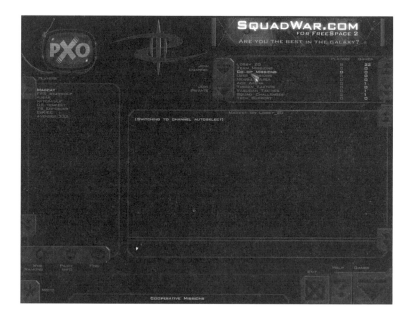

Situational awareness works a little differently in Freespace 2 (and other space-fighter sims) than terrestrial-flight sims. On the one hand, there's no gravity to worry about, so you never have spins and stalls. But energy management is more critical, because you have a fixed energy supply that feeds engines, weapons, and shields.

One unique online feature of Freespace 2 is Squad War. Squad War is essentially a battle for territory between two units of human players. Pxo.net assists with the matchmaking service, and keeps track of the territory captured or lost by each unit. It adds a bit of persistence and consistency to an already fine game. Also, if you have enough players, you don't all have to be fighter pilots. There are tactical bombers in Freespace 2, which are capable of delivering ship-killer missiles and bombs. Of course, they're also more vulnerable, so fighters are needed for escort.

In the end, Freespace 2 is a superb, well-rounded game with a great single-player story, a plethora of multiplayer options, and the Squad War semi-persistent game tossed in. If you've always wanted to strap yourself into the seat of a space fighter, check it out.

Massively Multiplayer Sims

Most of the single player games we've seen so far only support up to eight players. But real battles often have hundreds or thousands of combatants. What I call massively multiplayer simulations cater to the audience of pilots who want to be part of something much larger. (Here, we're defining massively multiplayer as more than 32 players).

One of the earliest commercial massively multiplayer games was a simulation: Air Warrior. Air Warrior is still popular in its third generation, although its online version looks crude by modern gaming standards. Air Warrior offered offline play as well so pilots could practice with new aircraft, but the true enjoyment is always competing with human pilots.

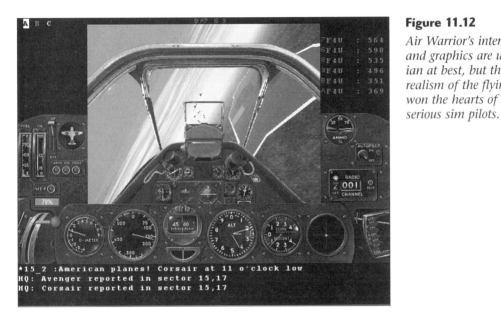

Figure 11.12

Air Warrior's interface and graphics are utilitarian at best, but the overall realism of the flying has won the hearts of many serious sim pilots.

In the last year, multiplayer-only sims have begun to sprout. We'll take a look at a couple of the most recent, including a game that has an interesting twist on the simulation genre.

Fighter Ace

Fighter Ace is Microsoft's entry into the massively multiplayer sim genre. As such, it's an excellent introduction to this style of gaming while offering some substance for hard-core users. Fighter Ace, shown in Figure 11.13, is offered exclusively on the Microsoft Gaming Zone (www.zone.com).

At its heart, Fighter Ace is a simple, objective-oriented combat simulator. As the name implies, you only fly fighters; unlike similar games, there's no option to man a bomber crew, for example. There is an arcade mode, which is actually set by the server at the Zone, and a more realistic mode. The realistic mode does model stalls and simple spins, as well as some weather effects and energy bleeding (that is, when you turn, you lose speed).

Figure 11.13

Fighter Ace's simplified interface and decent graphics make it a fun, if lightweight, sim.

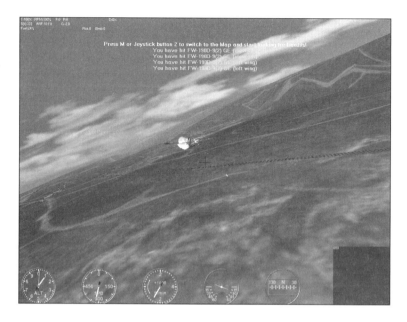

There's standard competition between different fictitious nationalities and a territorial mode. Of the two, the territorial mode is most interesting. Your nation gains territory by taking out enemy objectives such as airfields. It's actually pretty entertaining, and after flying for a while, you forget about issues of realism and focus on the objective at hand. Not surprisingly, you connect through Microsoft's Gaming Zone, as shown in Figure 11.14.

Figure 11.14

Fighter Ace's online connection occurs through the Zone.

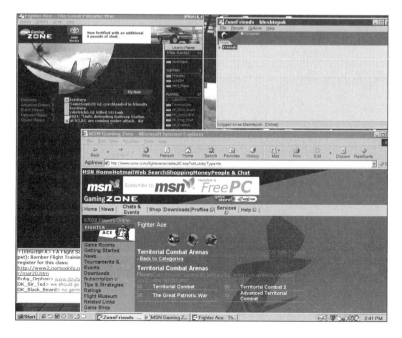

Fighter Ace is a free download, but costs either $1.95 per day or $9.95 per month to play. If you fly more than about once a week, the $9.95 per month fee is a great deal. There's a relatively small but strong Fighter Ace community at the Zone, and it seems to be growing steadily. In the end, it's the community that brings you back to any massively multiplayer game more than just the gameplay.

Allegiance

Allegiance is a different animal altogether.

On the surface, Allegiance appears to be a massively multiplayer space-combat sim. In fact, most of the players in the game will be flying space fighters, trying to take out other fighters, resource collectors, enemy bases, or enemy capital ships.

But it's more than that. You can fly bigger ships, with turret guns that are staffed by human players. But that's not even the most interesting part. What's more interesting are the roles of the commander and the investor.

For the commander, Allegiance is less a sim than a real-time strategy game—except that many of the units are real people.

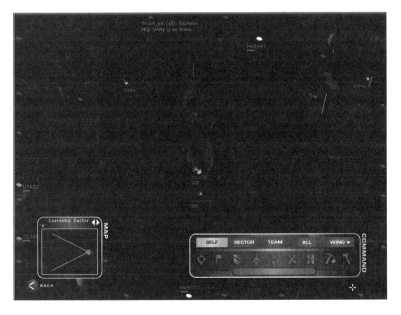

Figure 11.15

The commander gives orders through the command screen. Issuing orders is much like moving units in a real-time strategy game.

However, the commander has to be both good at the strategy of the game and good at working with the players who are his resources. It's a rude shock when you select a unit and tell it to go somewhere, and it does something completely different. You certainly can't blame bad AI. As one online forum post lamented, you can have an excellent set of hotshot pilots, but they'll lose the game to a bunch of average pilots if their commander is much better.

The role of the investor is also interesting. While the commander can play this role, it's best to have a dedicated investor. Usually, the commander is up to her arms in alligators trying to keep the game moving in a winning direction. The investor manages the technology development tree, as shown in Figure 11.16. Like the commander role, this seems a little like the tech tree in a real-time strategy game—except that the investor has the power to give the sim pilots upgrades or not. Of course, sim pilots who might feel slighted could simply refuse to properly perform their mission.

Figure 11.16

The investor manages the income from the miners (who are exclusively AI pilots), manages the research tree, and allocates upgrade resources to pilots.

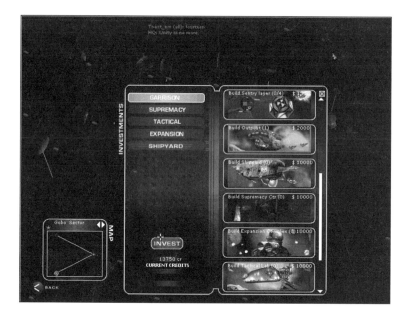

Note

Save Your Downed Buddies!

One tactic to try, if you have enough players, is to have one player in a slower, more highly armored ship act exclusively as the SAR (search-and-rescue) unit, much like a Seahawk helicopter would do on a modern aircraft carrier.

Of course, there are one investor and one commander in a given game. The rest of the players are flying spacecraft. There can be hundreds of players in a single game. The arena isn't just one big area, either. There are *jump gates*, which allow you to instantly transition to additional areas, and must be defended from incursion by enemy forces—or provide your side with an invasion point. There are multiple factions, too, each of which has individual strengths and weaknesses.

Pilots not only fly combat missions, but rescue missions as well. When a ship is destroyed, the game can be set up so the pilots don't simply respawn or return to the base. Instead, they eject in a survival capsule that must be retrieved by another friendly pilot.

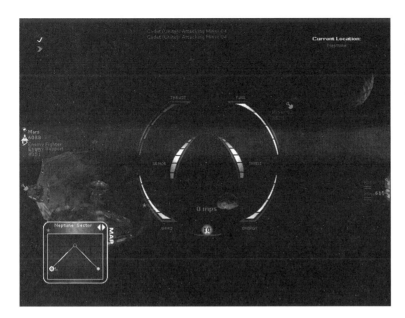

Figure 11.17

From the cockpit of a fighter, Allegiance resembles many similar space fighter games, but it has much more depth.

Allegiance differs a little from other massively multiplayer games. Out of the box, the game supports up to 32 players on a server, which allows connections on a LAN or from the Internet. However, if you want to experience Allegiance on a truly massive scale, you need to get a paid subscription to the Allegiance Zone on the Microsoft Gaming Zone.

What it comes down to is that Allegiance is something different—a genre breaker, not simply a mixed genre game. To win, you have to pull together a team of players good at specialized tasks, work together well, and take care of each other. In the end, that's what victory is all about.

Simulated Realities

Simulations are all about simulating reality—although with something like Freespace 2 or Allegiance, it might be a fictional reality. While simulation games are more complex than other genres, they are also multifaceted, giving you the opportunity to really feel the workload of a fighter pilot, or understand how a combat campaign is really conducted. You're allowed to play out your fantasies of what it would be like to be at the controls of an F-15C Strike Eagle conducting a bombing run, or trying to bring in a 737 for a landing at Hong Kong International on a rainy day.

The Least You Need to Know

➤ Simulation games have the goal of creating environments that reflect a realistic world, such as a flight simulator.

➤ Simulations often demand a lot from your PC hardware, and are often the most complex type of game title.

➤ Multiplayer options abound, and flying in a virtual squadron is rewarding and great fun.

Online Card Gaming Sites

Historically, games have been about getting people together in a shared social experience. Whether it was a foursome for bridge, rummy with the kids, or pinochle with the guys, card and board games have been standard fare for social gaming for hundreds of years. Now, the Internet lets us expand our traditional social games into virtual communities. No longer will we have to wait until the group frees up time. You can find a new group every single night of the year, if that's your fancy.

The New Demographics

These days, when online gaming is mentioned, people unfamiliar with online gaming usually think of one of two things: First-Person Shooters or massively multiplayer role-playing games. First-Person Shooters have gotten a lot of publicity, rightly or wrongly, because of their violent content. Games such as Everquest and Ultima Online have received tremendous publicity in the mainstream media because of their large and loyal following, not to mention their addictive nature.

But in fact, these players, the real-time strategy game players, and simulation buffs make up a minority of online gamers. In fact, the majority of online gamers aren't kids or even young adults. Instead, they're older adults, often senior citizens, who gather at popular gaming sites to play classic games, especially card games. After you get behind the demographics, you'll find enthusiastic, civil, and thoughtful communities of game players.

Card games have always been highly social games, so the various sites try to mimic the social aspects by having strong chat capability built into the games.

Play for Free!

In this chapter, we'll take a slightly different tack. Instead of investigating specific games, we'll check out the various popular Web sites that offer card and other classic games. After all, Hearts is Hearts—or is it?

Note

Get the Latest Version

Because most of these sites use Java or Shockwave for some of the free games, make sure you have the most recent update of your favorite Web browser. After all the update is probably free, too!

The good news about all these types of games is that they are, for the most part, free. The Web sites make their money off advertising and the other premium games. But the high population of card game players means lots of traffic, which translates into lots of hits on the site. Most online card games can be played in the browser or in a Java or Shockwave applet. This means that users don't have to download large files, nor do they have to buy a CD-ROM to play the games.

It's probably the free nature of the games that first attract users, but it's the additional features that keep players coming back. Let's check out the various major sites.

Site Reviews

Some of the major gaming matchmaking sites also offer card and classic games, while some of the mainstream portals only offer these types of titles. Let's examine some of the more popular ones.

Microsoft Gaming Zone

The Microsoft Gaming Zone is one of the more popular gaming destination sites. Like many good Microsoft products it was acquired by the company, not created from scratch.

The Microsoft Gaming Zone offers 12 distinct card games, consisting of a mix of retail, free online, and premium online games. The four free titles are bridge, cribbage, spades, and hearts, as shown in Figure 12.1.

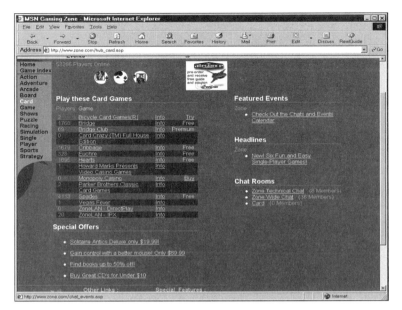

Figure 12.1

The Microsoft Gaming Zone card room. Note that the vast majority of players are in the free games.

The one premium game is Bridge Club, which is a highly competitive but friendly group who play a variant of Bridge known as *Duplicate Bridge*. It's an interesting variant, because it removes most of the luck from the game through matching up hands. Because it's more skill-based, the sessions can be highly competitive.

All the free games do require a small download, but even if you're on a modem, it's fairly painless. However, don't be fooled just because the games are free; some of the players here are very sharp. The good news is that rooms are sorted by capability level, so if you're a casual player, you can probably find a room that fits your skill level. There are casual rooms, more competitive rooms, ladders (which are ongoing tournaments), and ranked rooms. You can check out the Hearts competition in Figure 12.2.

Each of the free rooms also has regularly scheduled events and tournaments. When transitioning to a game room, you have to click through an ad page, but the ads are otherwise not too intrusive. The Zone even offers popular variants of each game (such as the Jack of Diamonds variants in Hearts).

Note

Pull Rank

If you're a good player, consider playing in the Zone's ranked rooms. Every score and win is recorded and stored at the server end. So every time you come back in, you're ranked against other players, and know exactly where you stand.

Figure 12.2

The Hearts room on the Zone is pretty typical of the free games. There are lots of players, and the action ranges from serious competition to light-hearted, casual play.

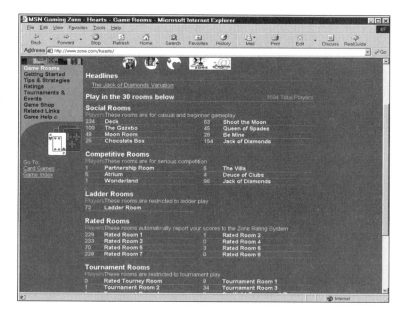

Pogo.com

Pogo.com began life as TEN (the Total Entertainment Network). Originally, TEN was a subscription-only service offering matchmaking service for retail multiplayer and custom games. Unfortunately, the subscription model never took hold, so TEN reinvented itself as Pogo.com, a free service offering lighter, more casual games.

All the pages on Pogo.com look similar; there's no attempt to distinguish the look of various pages until you actually enter an individual game room. Pogo does pop up somewhat obtrusive ads when moving into the game rooms, but once in the room, the only ad is a banner at the top of the page. One nice feature is the ability to look in on a game and check out the scores. If you start a game, you can also customize the type of game quite easily, selecting common variants before beginning, as you can see in Figure 12.3.

Like the Zone, Pogo offers special events and tournaments, some of which have cash prizes. Except for the somewhat intrusive advertising, Pogo is well thought out and a good site for card games (and other classic games).

Pogo.com also has partnerships with several large Web portals, including Excite@home and the Go Network, so if you hit the Excite Web site at http://www.excite.com/games/online_games/, or the Go portal at http://www.go.com/Center/Games/, you can play Pogo online games there as well.

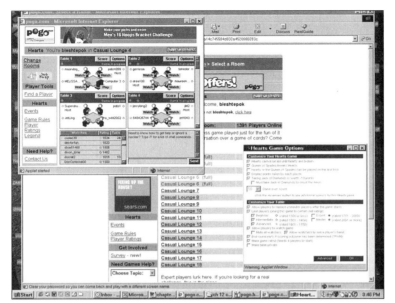

Figure 12.3

A Pogo.com game room. Note the button for options, which allow you to customize the type of game, and the level of play.

Mplayer

Like TEN, Mplayer started life as a subscription-only matchmaking service. However, as the viability of the subscription model faded, Mplayer transitioned to a free matchmaking service, supported by advertising. Mplayer supports serious gamers in retail versions of games such as Unreal Tournament, but also has a fairly active card game community.

Mplayer's card game support is fairly extensive. Like the Zone, Mplayer supports retail card games (such as Vegas Games) and free, Web-only online card games. Like most similar sites, most of the action lies in the free card games. Mplayer does have events such as tournaments, but the list of titles isn't quite as extensive as the Zone.

Yahoo

The granddaddy of all Web portals is also a gaming site.

If you head over to `http://games.yahoo.com`, you'll find an extensive list of card games available. Yahoo makes extensive use of Java applets for the various card games. Yahoo offers an extensive list of free games, but the amenities are somewhat limited, as shown in Figure 12.5. Yahoo does have different sections for player ability, making it easy to find like-minded people. There's a ladder system for keeping track of players who want to participate in the ladder, but that's about it.

213

Figure 12.4

MPlayer's card game rooms are a little generic-looking.

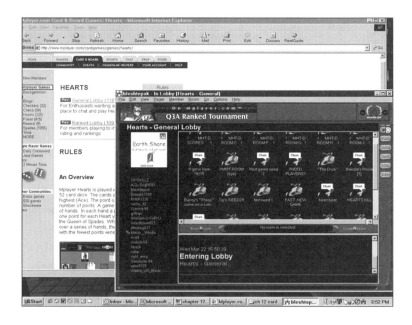

Figure 12.5

Yahoo's card games offer casual play and a variety of options, but there's not a lot of sophistication to the gaming site.

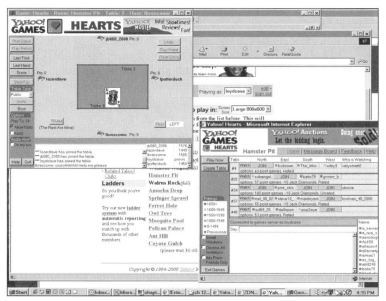

However, Yahoo is something much bigger than just a gaming site, so you can jump from the gaming site to another part of Yahoo and back. But if you're a fairly serious player, check out the Zone or Mplayer. The one exception is Pinochle: Yahoo's gaming site is the only one of two card sites to offer Pinochle, so if you're a fan of this highly addictive card game, it might be worth closer inspection.

IEntertain

This site began life as the Web site for IMagic, a full-service developer and publisher of CD-ROM games. However, the most successful game for IMagic turned out to be the online-only Warbirds, a WW2 fighter simulation. After losing money on CD-ROM games, IMagic morphed into IEN (Interactive Entertainment Network) and is now an online-only entity.

However, IEN's nonpremium offerings seem to be almost an afterthought. Even the list of games seems ill conceived. There's Poker, Euchre, Solitaire, and a bunch of other games that can best be described as obscure. Missing from the list are popular games such as Hearts, Bridge, and Spades. This is not the place for card game players in general.

World Opponent Network

WON is a matchmaking service originally started by the Sierra Online division of Havas Interactive. It acts as an in-game matchmaking service for many of Sierra's popular retail games, such as Half-Life and NASCAR Racing 3, but has an extensive list of free card games under the Hoyle license, as shown in Figure 12.6.

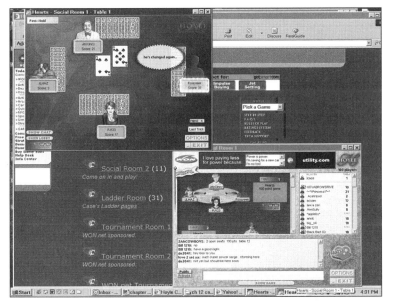

Figure 12.6

WON is a solid matchmaking service with a somewhat busy, but fun, user interface.

One game I remember fondly from college days is double-deck Pinochle. There was more than one occasion where a Friday night game met Saturday's sunrise. If Pinochle is one of your interests, the WON has a busy Pinochle community (among others). There are good players, tournaments, and other scheduled events for all the card games.

One interesting feature of WON is the capability to have a free Web page. While you could theoretically use it for anything, most of the pages are dedicated to the various games offered by WON, whether free or retail.

Other Traditional Games

In addition to card games, all of the sites listed here offer matchmaking services for other types of games, too. One stable is Backgammon, the ancient game of strategy and luck in which you move checker-like pieces around a field in set patterns. Another popular game is the Japanese game Go, a deceptively simple game that is nearly a topic for a book unto itself.

Chess is another hugely popular game and sites like the Zone offer chess matchmaking services and frequent tournaments. They rank matches as well by the standard numeric Chess rankings.

Precursor to the Future?

Online card games, along with their classic board game counterparts (such as, Backgammon, Chess, and others) are hugely popular. These types of games are not graphics or audio intensive, but they show what can be done. Already, several larger game companies are looking at putting up Web versions of their old classics.

Someday, we'll all have multi-megabit bandwidth, and there will be even more choices. But if you're into card games, you don't have to wait, nor do you have to pay a single cent for hours of fun and camaraderie. Pinochle, anyone?

The Least You Need to Know

➤ Card and other traditional games are far more popular than the more heavily publicized games such as Quake III and Starcraft.

➤ Most matchmaking services offer free gameplay for these classic games.

➤ Even Internet portals, such as Yahoo, have gotten into the act of hosting card and traditional board games.

Chapter 13

Oldies But Goodies

In This Chapter

➤ Check out the origin of the popular First-Person Shooter genre

➤ See how real-time strategy games first made their splash on the scene

➤ Learn some tips on getting older games to function properly under Windows

---

Some of the Old Timers who have been around the gaming world for a while will remember the good old days when games were games. They ran in DOS and the really cool ones used 16 colors. Now that was something to play. Now, of course, we would laugh at those games and have trouble imagining why anyone would want to play something as ancient and as backward as the games of old.

Well, let me tell you something, those were the games that many avid gamers today cut their teeth on when the gaming industry was young. Some of the very early games were text based, such as Zork where you were given a text instruction and responded with text actions. I remember playing Zork on an Apple IIe.

After Zork came an outburst of games; some continued the text-based tradition of Zork, while graphic games kept making leaps. For example, a company called Apogee released a series of two-dimensional side-scrolling adventures called Captain Comic. These games were fun and offered challenges in the tradition of video games like Mario Brothers. Epic Games released a number of these games, as did Apogee, MicroProse and several others. Some of these games are still available as you can see from Table 13.1.

Table 13.1—Classic Game Downloads

Game Title	Web Link
Zork	gamingplace.siol.net/adnl/dlzork1.htm
Captain Comic	ftp.fastgraph.com/fg/misc/comic5.zip
Jill of the Jungle	ftp.cdrom.com/pub/games/dos/action/jill/jill.zip
Duke Nukem	ftp.cdrom.com/pub/3drealms/3drealms/share/1duke.zip
Duke Nukem 2	ftp.cdrom.com/pub/3drealms/3drealms/share/4duke.zip
Raptor	ftp.cdrom.com/pub/3drealms/3drealms/share/1rap12.zip
Castle Wolfenstein	ftp://ftp.cdrom.com/pub/3drealms/3drealms/share/1wolf14.zip

Then came the revolutionary game called Castle Wolfenstein. This game was a graphic masterpiece giving the appearance of three-dimensional space, as you can see in Figure 13.1. The graphic clarity wasn't as smooth or as detailed as the games today, but it was fantastic for its time. You got to travel down hallways, enter rooms, shoot bad guys, and find secrets. I'll bet that none of this sounds familiar to you.

Figure 13.1

In the classic Castle Wolfenstein, you're a prisoner escaping a Nazi fortress.

Older FPSs

Now I've mentioned some of the real old *First Person Shooters* (FPS). That was only the start of the FPS genre. Those games could be played only by one person at a time. They weren't multiplayer. Technically, to be put in this book, the game needs to be multiplayer. This is, however, an online game book. So let's talk about some of the games that have the capability to be multiplayer.

One of the things to look for, if it is a concern of yours, is the kid friendly component to the game. Most of the FPS games are pretty violent. We have tried to provide some rating for each of the games to give you an idea what they will be like. A quick reminder: The rating scale is 1 to 10 where 10 is a high, positive rating and 1 is a low, negative rating.

Doom and Doom 2

Install and Play	9	Story Line Depth	7
Control Simplicity	8	Strategy Simplicity	8
Multiplayer Quality	8	Team Playability	8
Multimedia Quality	5	Modifiability	8
Kid Friendly	5	Online Stability	5
Best Controller	Keyboard & Mouse	3DFX/OpenGL Required	No

The history maker has to be Doom. After the game came out, all I heard from gamers was how cool the game was and that I had to play it. I have to admit that it was pretty cool at the time. And this game would allow you to play against other players. That *was* cool! Shortly after Doom hit popularity, there were other releases with the same type of interface. At the core of Doom was a game engine. This engine made it possible for programmers to use one core program and create different environments. This spawned the Hexen and Heretic FPS games. The best part of these games was they introduced the third dimension. The characters in the games could (gasp) climb stairs. This added a height aspect to the games that we had not seen with the earlier Castle Wolfenstein.

These games were intended to be played from DOS because the Windows environment was limited and took up valuable memory resources. The play options were not limited to local machine. You had three choices—IPX, Modem, and serial—as shown in Figure 13.2.

Figure 13.2

Available choices to play against others in Doom.

Allowing people to play together over the modem introduced the Dwango Company that provided a location for people to dial in and play one of these FPSs against other people. Of course there was a small fee for providing this service. Connecting to other players directly was easy too. Provisions were made to keep a phone address book; you could host a game or connect to a game, as you can see in Figure 13.3. This was all wonderfully easy, but only allowed two people to play together at one time.

Figure 13.3

From the Doom Modem Menu you can set up your connection.

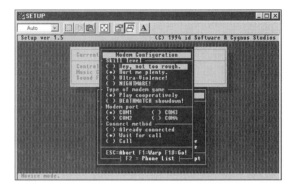

The networked games were just as easy to set from the game interface, as you can see in Figure 13.4. You just had to make sure that the DOS network drivers were installed for the IPX protocol. You can set the port number before launching into the game. (You can look at the end of this chapter to see how the network drivers were installed.)

Figure 13.4

You can play up to three other players on a LAN.

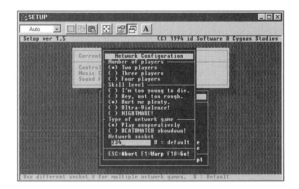

The premise of Doom and Doom 2 is that the player is a marine, as shown in Figure 13.5, trapped in a base that has been taken over by demonic monsters. Your mission is to clear the base of this alien scum without dying. You can find secrets with weapons, armor, and medical kits to help you complete your task.

Be careful. These creatures are around every corner. You never know when you will be attacked next.

Figure 13.5
You can fight it out in Doom.

Redneck Rampage

Install and Play	9	Story Line Depth	9
Control Simplicity	9	Strategy Simplicity	8
Multiplayer Quality	9	Team Playability	9
Multimedia Quality	8	Modifiability	6
Kid Friendly	6	Online Stability	8
Best Controller	Keyboard & Mouse	3DFX/OpenGL Required	No

Yee Haw! Redneck Rampage by Interplay (www.interplay.com) is a fun FPS that adds a hillbilly-ish sense of humor, as Figure 13.6 indicates. The game has the usual features of killing the bad guys and saving the planet. In this game, aliens have landed and cloned some of the people of a local town called Hickston. Your job is to rid the area of these poor pathetic individuals and get your pig back. You find beer and whiskey to drink, moonpies and pork rinds to sustain you. But don't drink too much alcohol or you'll be too drunk to shoot straight.

Although this is not a new game, you might still be able to find it on the shelf of your favorite computer game store. There have been a couple updated releases of the game also. All these games can be played online, so you and your friend can whoop it up, drink beer, and eat moonpies.

Figure 13.6

Shootin' chickens in Redneck Rampage.

Duke Nukem 3D

Install and Play	9	Story Line Depth	8
Control Simplicity	8	Strategy Simplicity	9
Multiplayer Quality	9	Team Playability	9
Multimedia Quality	7	Modifiability	9
Kid Friendly	3	Online Stability	8
Best Controller	Keyboard & Mouse	3DFX/OpenGL Required	No

You are on top of a building and you see your ride get blown from the sky. That's how the opening animation starts in 3DRealms's Duke Nukem 3D (www.3drealms.com). Your challenge now is to reclaim good old Earth from the aliens who are busily taking it over, as seen in Figure 13.7. You wander in and out of buildings, through tunnels, in rooms and into the atomic sewers to find and destroy the aliens. Don't kill any of the exotic dancers, though, or you will have to deal with instantly appearing aliens out for revenge.

This was one of the first games I played over a network with several other people. We would play some team, but we had more fun playing deathmatch. Can you imagine 8 to 10 people all fighting, jumping, flying for the best weapons and positions?

Figure 13.7
Duke is about to blast an alien on the far building.

Duke Nukem 3D does contain some adult content, but also has a parental lock that is password protected. The only switch is to turn the adult mode on or off. Some of the other games just have warnings, but don't have a way to control the violence.

Shadow Warrior

Install and Play	8	Story Line Depth	7
Control Simplicity	9	Strategy Simplicity	8
Multiplayer Quality	8	Team Playability	7
Multimedia Quality	8	Modifiability	6
Kid Friendly	5	Online Stability	8
Best Controller	Keyboard & Mouse	3DFX/OpenGL Required	No

As a ninja in Shadow Warrior (see Figure 13.8), you have the weapons of a ninja: throwing stars, sticky bombs, plus the conventional guns that we enjoy in the First-Person Shooter games. You can regain your health by punching the dummy or collecting first-aid packs.

Lo Wang (your character) makes comments and statements that are hilarious as you are playing along. There are radio-control cars to play with in the game as well as subways to ride.

Figure 13.8

About to slash an attacker in Shadow Warrior.

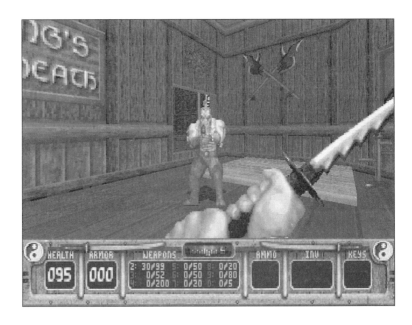

Quake

Install and Play	8	Story Line Depth	6
Control Simplicity	9	Strategy Simplicity	8
Multiplayer Quality	9	Team Playability	9
Multimedia Quality	7	Modifiability	9
Kid Friendly	6	Online Stability	8
Best Controller	Keyboard & Mouse	3DFX/OpenGL Required	No

The war isn't going so well. Most of your marine troops are being overwhelmed on the alien planet. Your job is to save the day by infiltrating the encampment and teleporting to the alien home world where it's kill or be killed.

Quake, shown in Figure 13.9, has an advanced game engine. It shows with the graphic details and the smooth animation. The better your graphics card the better this game looks.

Figure 13.9
Kill or be killed in Quake.

ROTT

Install and Play	8	Story Line Depth	8
Control Simplicity	8	Strategy Simplicity	9
Multiplayer Quality	7	Team Playability	9
Multimedia Quality	5	Modifiability	4
Kid Friendly	7	Online Stability	7
Best Controller	Keyboard & Mouse	3DFX/OpenGL Required	No

Rise of the Triad or ROTT for short. You have four characters from which you can choose. This is a combination of a First-Person Shooter and packman game. The object is to kill the guards and scientists and gain points by collecting silver spinning disks.

The premise of the game is that you and the other three are overrun by enemy forces. The boat you came in on has been discovered and the only way out is by going into the Monastery.

This game was one of the first with the capability to launch a *server*, or host machine, as shown in Figure 13.10, and have others connect to the server to play. Generally, games allowed someone to host a game. Usually the host of the game also plays on the game machine. Setting up a server allows a separate machine to run the server and everyone else can connect to the server and have better performance (theoretically speaking that is).

Figure 13.10

Networking options for ROTT.

The other unique and new feature of this game was the capability to change the screen size. You could actually change the viewing area of the active game. This allowed you to choose playing or action area on the screen. In all the earlier games, the viewing area was determined and set by the programmer.

Older RTSs

What is an RTS? If you haven't discovered the answer from an earlier chapter, then I'll simply say that *RTS* stands for *Real-Time Strategy* game. If you want to know more, I'll refer you to Chapter 6, "Real-Time Strategy Games," where it is covered in depth. Besides, I'm just going over some of the older games anyway.

Real-Time Strategy games have to be my personal favorites of all the game types. Some of the first games I used to play were strategy games. RTS games give me the challenge that I look for in a computer game.

Command and Conquer

Install and Play	9	Story Line Depth	6
Control Simplicity	8	Strategy Simplicity	7
Multiplayer Quality	9	Team Playability	8
Multimedia Quality	7	Modifiability	3
Kid Friendly	8	Online Stability	9
Best Controller	Keyboard & Mouse	3DFX/OpenGL Required	No

I remember back when…Well, I'm sure you don't want to hear about the war stories now. Command and Conquer was always a big hit at the LAN parties I attended. The best part about the RTS is that you can ally with others on the map and work together to battle. We have had six and eight people playing with teams of two or three. You can imagine that the battles can get intense as you and your teammates have to defend multiple fronts.

Most RTS games require that you manage resources, as shown in Figure 13.11, to build units to use to fight and defend. The resource in Command and Conquer is Tiberium, which is harvested, then processed. Buildings are constructed and units are trained or built. It's very important to create a balance of the various units. Having all one unit type might work in defeating the enemy, but having a diverse assembly can be much more effective.

Figure 13.11

Evil Nod units are about to finish off the GDI base.

WarCraft II

Install and Play	9	Story Line Depth	3
Control Simplicity	8	Strategy Simplicity	8
Multiplayer Quality	9	Team Playability	8
Multimedia Quality	7	Modifiability	3
Kid Friendly	9	Online Stability	9
Best Controller	Keyboard & Mouse	3DFX/OpenGL Required	No

WarCraft II follows the standard RTS layout. WarCraft II differs from Command and Conquer in that there are more resources to collect, as you can see in Figure 13.12. There is also more micro managing of the units. With Command and Conquer, the harvesters would collect Tiberium without intervention. In WarCraft II, the peasants need to be set to a task, such as cutting wood. If the wood runs out at the location the peasant was cutting, he will not look for more wood to cut. You will have to set him on the next task.

Figure 13.12

Human camp being finished by a team of humans and orcs.

With WarCraft II you will also need to balance combat units with the harvesting units. Otherwise, the enemy can walk into your camp and wipe you out. Don't let this happen to you.

Dealing with Older Games under Windows 9x

Older games should work just fine under Windows, with emphasis on *should*. We all know that, sometimes, older programs, especially games, act peculiar under Windows. When you run across the older programs that don't work any more, they might be fine under DOS. If you were to run the program under DOS, it would work just fine.

How to Boot to DOS

What is the best way to run DOS when Windows 9x is installed? The *best* way is to switch to DOS at bootup. If you try to use the "Restart in DOS mode" option that Windows gives to you at shutdown, Windows might not be fully shut down and might still interfere with the game.

To ensure that you are running only DOS, press and hold the F8 key on your keyboard after the BIOS for your computer has initialized, but before you see the Windows slash screen (the one with the little blue bar at the bottom that seems to be moving). You should see a menu with a numbered option for starting in DOS mode. If you get the splash screen and you don't get the menu, you waited too long. You will have to restart the computer and give it another try. Don't fret if it takes you a couple tries. Even I have trouble from time to time starting in DOS mode.

Another option is to create a DOS boot floppy disk. This gives you the freedom to make changes and modify which drivers get loaded without having to make changes to your currently working system. You can format the floppy disk from a DOS window by clicking **Start**, choosing **Run**, and entering the command format a: /s. This will copy the needed system files onto the floppy disk when it is finished formatting.

The other way to format is floppy disk is to use Windows Explorer and choose to format with the system. Here's how to accomplish this procedure.

Note

Use a blank floppy disk

Be sure that the floppy disk is empty or has no valuable data on it before formatting. I would hate to see you format and lose the last copy of your great-grandmother's secret recipe for liver pate.

1. Click **Start** from the taskbar.
2. Go to Programs, then click **Windows Explorer**.
3. Find the A: drive and right-click the icon.
4. From the menu, click **Format**. You'll see the dialog box shown in Figure 13.13.

Figure 13.13

Setting up to format a floppy disk.

5. Be sure that the box is checked for Copy system files.
6. After you have selected the floppy disk type (usually 1.44MB), click the **Start** button and let the floppy disk format.
7. Click the **Close** button when you are finished.

Loading CD-ROM Drivers

When booting to DOS, you might want to use your CD drive to access the games or the game data. Because you have been using Windows, you have not needed anything special to activate the CD drive. Windows does this automatically. When you boot to DOS, you will lose the ability to access the CD drive unless drivers are loaded.

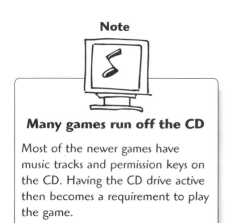

Many games run off the CD

Most of the newer games have music tracks and permission keys on the CD. Having the CD drive active then becomes a requirement to play the game.

The drivers get loaded when you boot to DOS. What are these drivers and where can I find them? Normally the drivers are shipped with the CD drive. Today, computers come with the CD drives preinstalled and the operating system doesn't need the DOS drivers to activate the drive so you might not have the drivers loaded.

Then what can I do? If you know who the manufacturer of the drive is, you can go to their Web site and download the driver. You can go to `winfiles.cnet.com/drivers/drives.html` and look up the driver for your CD drive. Now I bet you are asking, "How do I know who the manufacturer of the CD drive is?" If you go to the Control Panel of your computer and open the **System** icon and select the **Device Manager** tab (see Figure 13.14), you will see a category labeled CDROM. Click the plus and your CD drive item will appear. Then each item should show the manufacturer and the model.

Figure 13.14

Checking on the CD drive installed in your machine.

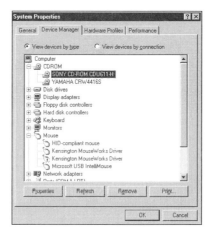

Now that you have the driver, what do you do with it? It will need to be loaded. There are two files that control which drivers get loaded in DOS. These two files are called `autoexec.bat` and `config.sys`. They are both text files and can be modified with Notepad. Some of the manufacturers provide little programs that automatically modify these files with the appropriate settings. Then, after the changes have been made to the files, you can copy the two previously mentioned files and the driver files to your boot disk and you are ready to boot you computer from the floppy disk and still access your CD drive.

Tech Tip

How to find Notepad

Notepad can be found by clicking the Start button, then choosing Programs, then Accessories and then selecting it from the list. Double-clicking on a text document also launches Notepad.

Here is an example of what the config.sys file should look like. There should be one line in the file that takes this format:

```
device=btdosm.sys
```

or

```
device=aspicd.sys /D:oemcd001
```

Everything past the equal sign will be unique for your CD drive and might not be the same as what I have shown here. Your drivers might have a different name and/or different settings. Mileage might vary. The driver that is shown after the equal sign is what you will want to have copied on your boot disk or the CD still will not work from DOS.

The autoexec.bat file will have a line like the following:

```
MSCDEX.EXE /D:oemcd001 /L:F
```

Again, as earlier, mileage might vary. The common denominator in the previous line is MSCDEX.EXE (see Figure 13.15). The second part refers to the device identifier (in case there is more than one CD device in your computer). The last option is the pre-selected drive letter assignment.

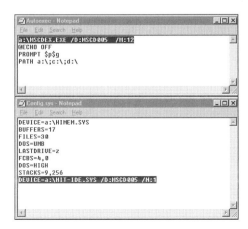

Figure 13.15

Autoexec.bat and Config.sys file examples for a Hitachi CD drive.

Loading Plug and Play Drivers

I shouldn't really have much to say about the plug and play drivers, after all, they are plug and play. (We used to call them plug and pray.) The plug and play feature that your hardware might have is designed to allow Windows to directly determine which drivers are needed to make the device operate. DOS does not have the capability to query the devices and load the driver for the device. Most manufacturers will provide DOS drivers along with the plug and play drivers. Refer to the manufacturer's instructions for installing their drivers.

Some of the manufacturers will provide installation applications that will modify the appropriate files and install the needed files in the correct locations. That can be the hardest thing about doing manual installs. If the files aren't in the correct place then it just won't work correctly.

The easiest option is from Windows: **Start—Shut Down** and select the **Restart in DOS Mode**.

Loading Old IPX DOS Network Drivers

Most of the older games use IPX over the network. Loading them isn't that hard at all. You can load them manually or add them to the Autoexec.bat file so that they load when you start in DOS. (Again, this would best be done on the boot floppy disk.)

First you will want to start LSL.COM. If you need the files, you can get them from http://www.battlecon.com/battlecon/dosnetworking.html. Some of the cards will need the newer 2.16 version of the LSL.COM file to work.

The second file that you will want is the Ethernet card driver. This file can be obtained from the floppy disks that were shipped with the card or from the manufacturer's Web site. I like to use the 3Com Ethernet cards, so the file I would use is the 3c5x9.com file. This is the driver for the card. Included with the download from the manufacturer is a file called NET.CFG that contains the information about the card and the frame type to use. This file can be edited with a text editor to make changes as needed. You will need to keep this NET.CFG file, shown in Figure 13.16, with the others.

The last file you will need to start is IPXODI.COM. This file is the final networking layer needed for the games to communicate over the network. If you automated this process with a batch file, the commands should look like the following:

```
LSL.COM
3C5X9.COM
IPXODI.COM
```

This assumes that all the files are in the same location as the batch file including the NET.CFG file.

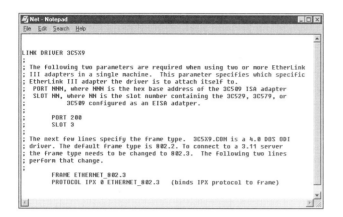

Figure 13.16

Example of the NET.CFG file contents.

As an alternative, boot to DOS mode from Windows and run Start Net to start the networking services.

You can search the Internet and find some useful information about connecting computers in a DOS network. Be careful though; some of the information might be old or not applicable to your situation.

As you begin to experience some of the older games and compare them to the new hot games as they come out, you will see differences in the look and feel of the games, the simplicity of the game strategy, and control of the games. As the technology of the games improves so does the level of difficulty. If you find an older game that you fall in love with, stick with it. There are others who will like the game too and will want to play with you.

The Least You Need to Know

➤ Almost from the beginning, computers have been the platform for some fascinating games.

➤ The hottest three-dimensional shooters have their origins on a couple games that still retain a loyal fan base.

➤ Although a relatively new genre, Real-Time Strategy games are based on a couple now-classic titles.

➤ You can play older, DOS-based games on your Windows computer, but you may have to do a little simple tweaking first.

Part 5
The Gaming Community

As an online gaming enthusiast, you're hardly alone! The Internet is remarkable for its ability to bring people together, and gamers were among the first groups to take advantage of this potential.

Now's your chance to join the community of online gamers. You can check out nifty online discussions, learn about secret game codes, download crucial utilities to give you that extra edge, and compete against gamers from anywhere on Earth. What are you waiting for? Fire up your modem and join the community!

OOOOOH...

Chapter 14

Other Important Online Sites

In This Chapter

➤ Choosing New Hardware and Finding the Right Drivers

➤ Gaming Tips Beyond Your Wildest Imagination

➤ Cheaters Never Win...Except in Computer Games

➤ Gaming News

➤ The Planets Network

When you are gaming online, it's important to remember that having the game is only the first step in mastering it. If you want to get the full gaming experience, you should connect with other players via tips sites, new sites, and others. You should also make sure all your drivers are up to date. This chapter will introduce a wide variety of online resources to complete your gaming experience.

Choosing New Hardware

Computers are like cars in some ways. You might not be able to find a good bargain that still has all the features you want. And you might find certain parts become obsolete faster than others do. You might have a perfectly good machine, but feel its sound or video just doesn't perform to your standards. Fortunately, upgrading these components is much easier than going under the hood of your 1965 Dodge Dart!

There are many types of video cards and sound cards that will make your gaming even more realistic. If you are in the market to upgrade a card or curious as to which is the best, you should visit one of several sites that review computer hardware. One such site is deja.com. As you can see from Figure 14.1 below, Deja has an abundance of information.

Figure 14.1

The deja.com page lets you search and post news articles.

Here's how to check hardware ratings at deja.com:

1. Open your browser and click in the Address (or Location) bar at the top.
2. Type www.deja.com.
3. On the left side of the screen, you will see a table of contents; point to Computing and Tech (don't click yet), and a submenu will pop out to the right.
4. Click on **Add-In-Cards and Components**.
5. Click on the ratings tab to see how the current video cards are ranked.

You might choose from two categories, 2D and 3D combo graphics cards or 3D accelerator cards.

Whichever one you choose will show you a table of many cards ranked on several different criteria; ease of use, performance, compatibility/stability, and cost/benefit.

This process should give you a good place to start if you are looking for a new piece of hardware.

Another good site for reviews of hardware is the Ziff-Davis site, ZDNet. Go to http://www.zdnet.com and click **Buying Guides**. Doing so takes you to the Computer Shopper site that walks you through choosing the best piece of hardware for you.

After a visit to this site, you should know everything you would ever want to know about a graphics card. It will tell you what the card does, how it does it, and what is the best one on the market right now.

Finding the Right Drivers

The two sites I just discussed give you a jump on what to buy and why. But if you already have the hardware that you want (or, like the rest of us, all you can afford right now), you might want to update the drivers. A *driver* is the piece of software that enables your video card, joystick, or any other piece of hardware to interface with the operating system and work correctly.

Sometimes a good piece of software can get you almost as much as a new piece of hardware. Well, it's cheaper anyway. If you bought your computer more than a year ago, chances are, there is a driver for your video card or your sound card that will enable it to run more efficiently than the driver that shipped with it. However, you should be warned that the latest isn't always the greatest. Avoid drivers that are still in the beta testing stage. The best place to find a driver for your graphics card, sound card, or input device is at the manufacturer's site. I know what you're thinking; "I have no clue what type of graphics card I have." Don't worry, it's not that difficult to figure out if you know where to look.

The first place to look for your video or sound manufacturer is in the box. If your computer came with any paper manuals, they might tell you which graphics or sound card you have. This is a long shot, considering how many computer manufacturers today seem to think online manuals are the way to go.

Fortunately, you can see which device your Windows computer is using by looking in the Device Manager. The device manager can be found in the Properties screen of My Computer or in the Control Panel represented by the System icon. To access Device Manager:

1. Right-click the **My Computer** icon.
2. Click **Properties** in the resulting menu.
3. Click the **Device Manager** tab, as shown in Figure 14.2.
4. These are the hardware devices that are installed on your computer. (Scary, isn't it?)
5. Click the plus sign beside the Sound, video and game controllers selection.
6. Select the controller you would like to know more about and click the **Properties** button. An example of the Properties dialog box is shown in Figure 14.3.

Figure 14.2

You can see a list of all your hardware devices in the Device Manager.

Figure 14.3

You can see all the properties of a piece of hardware in its Properties dialog box.

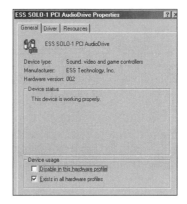

Here you can find the manufacturer of your device.

After you have found the manufacturer of your device, you can do a simple search on the name of the manufacturer with a search engine such as Lycos, Infoseek, or Ask Jeeves to find that manufacturer's Web site. Most manufacturers have Web sites with names that are pretty easy to figure out, such as http://www.creative.com for Creative Labs.

Table 14.1 lists some of the more popular multimedia hardware sites.

Table 14.1—Major Hardware Sites

Company	Website
Matrox	http://www.matrox.com
STB Multimedia	http://www.stb.com
3dfx Interactive	http://www.3dfx.com

Company	Website
3d Labs	http://www.3dlabs.com
S3 Inc.	http://www.diamondmm.com
nVIDIA	http://www.nvidia.com
ESS Technology, Inc.	http://www.esstech.com
Creative Labs	http://www.americas.creative.com
ATI Technologies, Inc.	http://www.ati.com
Alliance Semiconductor	http://www.alsc.com/
Anubis	http://www.anubis.co.uk/
AOpen, Inc.	http://www.aopen.com/
ASUSTeK Computer, Inc.	http://www.asus.com.tw/
ATI Technologies, Inc.	http://www.ati.com
A-Trend Technology Corporation	http://www.atrend.com/
Aztech	http://www.aztech.com.sg/
Best Data	http://www.bestdata.com/
Biostar Group	http://www.biostar.com.tw/
Britek International	http://www.viewtop.com/ html/brititle.htm
California Graphics USA	http://www.california graphicsusa.com/
Canopus Corporation	http://www.canopuscorp.com/voodoo.htm
ChainTech	http://www.chaintech.com.tw/
Colorgraphic Communications	http://www.colorgfx.com/
Creative Labs	http://www.americas.creative.com
DataExpert	http://www.dataexpert.com.tw/
EONtronics	http://www.eontronics.com/
ESS Technology, Inc.	http://www.esstech.com
Gallant Computer	http://www.gallantcom.com/
Genius	http://www.geniusnet.com.tw/
Gigabyte Technology	http://www.gigabyte.com.tw/
Hercules	http://www.hercules.com/
InnoVISION	http://www.ivmm.com/
Intergraph Corporation	http://www.intergraph.com/
Jetway Information	http://www.jetway.com.tw/
Joytech Computer Co. Ltd.	http://www.joytech.com/
Magic-Pro	http://www.magic-pro.com/
Matrox	http://www.matrox.com
Mirage Video Solutions	http://www.mirage-mmc.com/

continues

Table 14.1—CONTINUED

Company	Website
Omnicomp Systems, Inc.	`http://www.omnicomp.com/`
Quantum3D	`http://www.quantum3d.com/`
Real 3D	`http://www.real3d.com/`
Sierra	`http://download.sierra.com/`
STB Multimedia	`http://www.stb.com`
Tekram	`http://www.tekram.com/`
Toshiba America, Inc.	`http://www.toshiba.com/`

Listed below are several sites for finding joystick and game pad drivers and information.

Looks good—JERSAITEK	`http://www.saitek.com/pcpindex.htm`
CH PRODUCTS	`http://www.chproducts.com/index.html`
Microsoft Sidewinder Home Page	`http://www.microsoft.com/insider/ sidewinder/default.htm`
Thrustmaster	`http://www.thrustmaster.com/`
Logitech	`http://www.logitech.com`

If you're not having any luck with the manufacturer's site, you might try the following sites.

3D Files	`http://dfiles.com`
WinDrivers.com	`http://www.WinDrivers.com`
DriverHQ	`http://www.driverhq.com`
WinFiles.com	`http://www.winfiles.com`
DriverZone	`http://www.driverzone.com`

Microsoft is the manufacturer of a piece of software by the name of DirectX. DirectX is a set of instructions that is built into Windows to enhance the multimedia experience. This is a piece of software that is updated on a regular basis. To obtain the newest version of DirectX visit the Microsoft site at `http://www.microsoft.com/ directx/homeuser/downloads/default.asp`.

Having the right drivers can make a world of difference when gaming. It can mean the difference between getting to see that video clip, or just wondering what is supposed to happen when you pull the lever in that cave.

Gaming Tips Beyond Your Wildest Imagination

Gaming can be fairly taxing on both the brain and the trigger finger. If you love to win and hate to lose, you might want to find all the helpful tips you can. Fortunately, the online world gives players who've mastered a game an opportunity to boast of their prowess by offering tips to other players. Finding a site that gives good tips on how to play the game can be better than having your own personal coach. Remember that there is a difference between getting a tip and cheating. We'll discuss where to find *those* sites later.

If you want to know a little bit about just about every game, try www.gamecenter.com/tipcheat. Here you can find a few tips on many games and even do a search to find more tips out on the Web.

Looking for a select group of tips? Try gamedudes.infinity.net/tips/. This is a cute site with a whimsical interface. You can find a few tips on select games.

If you want to see a site that is saturated with all types of gaming information, try www.cdgames.com also known as Computer Games online. This site has everything from hints and tips to reviews of the latest and greatest games.

There are entire communities of people that have been in the exact same position you are in now. These people have seen the game, stared it straight in the eye, and beaten it. These are the people from whom you can get the best tips. If you are looking for them, you can find them lurking in the discussions area of www.deja.com in the Computer Games category or they may be traced through a simple search on a search engine for the name of the game plus the word walkthrough or FAQ. All you need to do is Ask Jeeves or any other search engine.

Cheaters Never Win...Except in Computer Games

Okay, so you've looked at some of the tips, tried them, and gotten stuck...again. Are you ready to cheat? Here's a site that has an exhausting amount of cheats for all different games: www.pcgameworld.com/cheats/. If you can't find it here, you can even try their message boards where you can converse with other gamers.

Another great cheater's site is www.gamezone.com/hints/hints.asp. Not only does this site have an amazing amount of games and cheats, but it has links to several other sites, including the following:

Chapter Cheats http://chapter.cheatguide.com

Cheat Index http://www.cheatindex.com/index2.html

Cheater's Guild http://www.cheater-guild.com/index.asp

Some sites try to do everything, like passtheshareware.com. This site has a little something for every computer geek, including a cheater's page for gamers at www.passtheshareware.com/faqs.htm. It isn't exactly the most extensive list in the world, but it might have just the thing for which you are looking.

Note

How to Cheat, the Right Way

If you are going to visit the cheat sites, for goodness's sake take time to savor them. Use the cheats that are given; they can be fun. Cheats come in all different flavors. Some are just a list of key combinations to use to get you into a special type of play, such as being indestructible. In role playing games, cheats may tell you which lever to push, or which room to visit to move you through the game. There are some cheat sites that tell you all of the steps you need to go through to complete the game and reach the end goal.

Cheaters love to have cool names, hence the Cheater's Krypt at www.cheaterskrypt.com. A site devoted to people who don't want to figure out the game, they just want to see all the pretty screens. The Cheater's Krypt has more than 1,400 archived cheats and walkthroughs. The Cheater's Krypt is part of the overall gaming site www.hotmagma.com, which has news, demos, and more.

Looking for even more cheats? Check out www.pcgamers.net. It doesn't support a large number of games, but coverage for the games that are here is extensive. There are also links to fan sites. These are sites that people who really love the game put up and administer. They include hints and tips about the games, cheats, and news. Remember that each fan site is different, so you might want to visit them all.

Gaming News

If you love a game and you are dying to know when the new version will be out, or when there will be updates, you might want to visit a site that has game news. Game news includes all the latest news on which games are being released, demos of new games, reviews of the latest hardware to enhance the gaming experience, and screen shots of games to come. Many of the sites we looked at for cheating and tips also include news of what's new. There are so many sites out there devoted to games that it might get a little overwhelming. There are traditional sites that have been spawned from magazines, Webzine sites that are exclusive to the Web and fan sites that get to the grass roots of things.

We will start with some of the more traditional sites that are based on magazines and popular companies. One of the most reliable sites is the GameSpot site, run by ZDNet at www.gamespot.com.

Gamespot is Ziff-Davis's site for all the latest in gaming. Part of the Gamespot site is based on their magazine, *Computer Gaming World*. The *Computer Gaming World* site is found at www.gamespot.com/cgw/index.html. This site is just part of Gamespot, but it does allow you to order one free issue of the magazine and sign up to receive monthly CD-ROMs that are full of game demos.

Another magazine that you can receive via snail mail or read online is CyberGamer. This magazine specializes in Internet, online, and multiplayer gaming. You can view the latest issue at www.sys-con.com/cybergamer/index2.htm.

Take a look at GamePro World at www.gameproworld.com/, the sister site to the magazine of the same name. Not only can you subscribe to the magazine here, but you also can read choice articles from the issue online. To get the daily news, just log in to this site and you will be updated with the latest and greatest in gaming news. There's something a magazine can't do once a month.

If you are looking for what's new in terms of patches and new versions of software, you might want to try Game Depot. It has all the latest patches and game updates in chronological order. It also has console gaming updates, if using your PC simply isn't enough for you. You can visit Game Depot at www.gamedepot.com.

For a cool-looking, well-designed site with some good content, try GamePen at www.gamepen.com. This easy-to-navigate site has the latest news on PC games and console games. This one is on the Web only; there's no magazine associated with it.

There is even a site for those that want to develop games to get all the news of the industry. You can do so at www.gameslice.com. This is not your typical gaming news site with release dates and patch updates. Instead, it's a behind-the-scenes look at how games are made and developed. It is quite interesting for those that want to know the story behind the story.

Gaming is a popular pastime all over the world. To get the latest gaming news straight from the UK, visit GamesDomain at www.gamesdomain.co.uk. This site has lots of great PC gaming news from across the sea. If the UK isn't your thing, how about checking out what's up with games Down Under? Visit Australia's #1 gaming site at www.hyperactive.com. Here you can find the latest in gaming in Australia. You can also subscribe to the *PC Power Play* magazine.

Daily Radar is a fun site that has 24-hour PC gaming news and a list of the most recent releases. Visit Daily Radar at www.dailyradar.com. This site is the online brother of *PC Gamer* magazine.

You might find a comprehensive PC gaming site at www.electricgames.com. This site not only has news about PC Games, but it has Macintosh information as well. It also has several links to online gaming sites.

If you're a person that faces your addictions head-on, you can get your news at www.gameaholic.com. This site has an abundance of Quake information, but it also has some news about other games such as Kingpin and Hexen II.

Take a look at the Gamers Link site and you'll find a database that is filled to the brim with information. The database is heavy on links to action games and role playing games. This site can lead you to multiple fan sites. Visit Gamers Link at gamers.sclegacy.com/dirs/.

Another site you might find interesting is the Games Planet; this site was designed by gamers for gamers and concentrates on news for a few specific games. Visit Games Planet at `3dgames.simplenet.com`.

Below is a list of other news sites for various online games and genres:

Blue's News	`http://www.bluesnews.com`
CPR Extreme Gaming News and Add Ons	`http://www.cprextreme.com/news/news.html`
GameAddict.net	`http://www.gameaddict.net/`
GameDaily	`http://www.gamedaily.com/`
GameSpot News	`http://headline.gamespot.com/news/index.html`
GibWorld	`http://www.gibworld.com`
Happy Puppy	`http://www.happypuppy.com`
IGamer.net	`http://www.igamer.net/`
MPOG.com	`http://www.mpog.com`
Online Games Library	`http://www.oglibrary.com`
Phatgames.com	`http://phatgames.com`
QuakeWorld	`http://quakeworld.net`
WebRPG	`http://www.webrpg.com.index.phtml`
WONnet	`http://www.won.net/today/`

In addition to the sites mentioned in the news section, you can visit any of the other sites listed in this chapter and find an abundance of gaming news including patches, release, dates, and rumors. If you're looking for the latest scoop, believe me, the truth is out there.

The Planets Network

I have discovered that there is life on other planets. There's a network of sites out there that you can reach through Gamespy.com that is, in effect, the only resource you might need for some games. Some games have such a following that there has been a site with their name that is its planet. The sites have names such as `http://www.planetquake.com` and `http://www.heriticii.com`. These sites are the be-all, end-all authorities on the games. These planets are administered by extreme fans of the game who have devoted themselves to everything about that particular game. These people live and breathe this stuff. This devotion is evident from the Quake site shown in Figure 14.4.

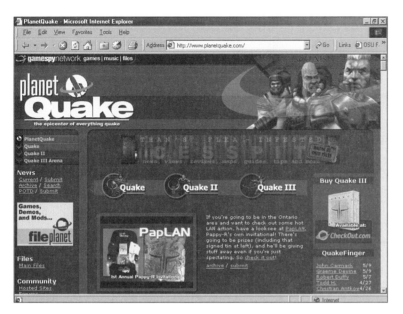

Figure 14.4

Here's a doorway into the world of Quake gamers.

Following is a list of some of the planets in the solar system.

Planet Quake	http://www.planetquake.com
Planet Deerhunter	http://www.planetdeerhunter.com
Planet Descent	http://www.planetdescent.com
Planet Duke	http://www.planetduke.com
Planet AvP Alien vs. Predator	http://www.planetavp.com
Planet Blood	http://www.planetblood.com
Planet Daikatana	http://www.planetdaikatana.com
Planet Fortress	http://www.planetfortress.com
Planet Half-Life	http://www.planethalflife.com
Planet KingPin	http://www.planetkingpin.com
Planet Shogo	http://www.planetshogo.com
Planet StarSiege	http://www.planetstarsiege.com
Planet Unreal	http://www.planetunreal.com
Planet Wheel of Time	http://www.planetwheeloftime.com
Planet Age of Empires	http://www.planetageofempires.com
Planet Annihilation	http://www.planetannihilation.com
Planet Battlezone	http://www.planetbattlezone.com
Planet Vampire	http://www.planetvampire.com

You get the idea. If you think there is a planet out there, give it a try at `www.plan-`
`etgamename.com`. If you would like a listing of even more planet sites, check out
`www.gamespy.com`.

Other Sites of Interest

For all those Macintosh fans out there, never fear; games are not dead on the Mac,
just a little more obscure. If you're looking to take them out of their corner and play
with them, check out `www.macgamer.com`. This site is devoted to using your Mac to
entertain yourself for hours with games. The site contains reviews, announcements,
tips, and forums. The site is not exactly in depth, but it's nice to have something
devoted to the Mac.

The 3d Gamers site is a good overall site that also supports Mac games. It doesn't
have the prettiest interface in the world, but it is chock full of information. There are
news, updates, games, and even tips. You can visit 3d Gamers at `www.3dgamers.com`.

This chapter listed some of the best game sites to give you a start on your gaming
adventure. But there are too many sites to list in just a few pages of this book. New
sites are being added every day. Each day, a new gamer is born and a new fan site
goes up so, if you don't find what you want today, try tomorrow and chances are it
will be there. Maybe by this time next month, you'll have your own site for online
gaming.

The Least You Need to Know

➤ There are many types of video cards and sound cards that will make your
gaming even more realistic. If you are in the market to upgrade a card or
curious as to which is the best, you should visit one of several sites that
review computer hardware.

➤ Having the right drivers can make a world of difference when gaming. The
best place to find a driver for your graphics card, sound card, or input device
is at the manufacturer's site.

➤ Finding a site that gives good tips on how to play the game can be better
than having your own personal coach. Remember that there is a difference
between getting a tip and cheating.

Chapter 15

Online Competition

In This Chapter

➤ Pro computer gamers

➤ The problem of spectators

➤ You are the competitor

➤ What are you waiting for?

Professional computer gaming almost sounds like an oxymoron, but a few gamers have managed to parlay their skills into a decent living. However, the era of NFL-like leagues are still a long way off, but there are now tournaments that offer serious prize money, and there are even endorsements to be won by hotshot players. Let's examine the world of competitive gaming, and check out the early stages.

Pro Computer Gamers

There was a cartoon penned by Gary Larsen (of *The Far Side* fame) which showed proud parents watching their son play video games. They dreamed of a high-paying, professional gaming career for their son, much as a Little League parent might dream of baseball glory for their kid.

The point of the cartoon, of course, was that computer game savvy isn't exactly a marketable skill. But the day when it is may not be far off.

There have been several attempts to start professional gamers' leagues. One of the most high-profile leagues, called, not surprisingly, the Professional Gamer's League, has faded by the wayside, but not before launching the career of at least one Internet success story, Dennis Fong. AKA "Thresh", Fong went on to start several highly regarded and successful gaming-oriented Web sites that attracted serious venture capital.

Another victim of being a little ahead of its time was the NASCAR Racing Online Series (www.nros.com). This league offered occasional prize money from sponsors, and the racers and fans were devoted and serious about their virtual sport. The league eventually folded for both technological and business reasons. On the technology side, the league was highly dependent on Sierra's NASCAR Racing 2. When NASCAR 3 shipped, it didn't support some of the options used by NROS. Secondly, the league also depended on support from TEN (Total Entertainment Network), an online, subscription-based matchmaking service. When TEN evolved into the pogo.net free gaming service, NASCAR 2 players fell by the wayside. There have been local attempts to restart an NROS-style league, but they haven't had the widespread appeal of NROS.

On the positive side, there's the Cyberathlete Professional League (www.cyberathlete.com). NewWorld.com, which is the founding company of CPL, has been quite successful in attracting sponsorship for the league, including some serious prize money. The downside is that it's heavily focused on First-Person Shooters, such as Quake III: Arena. There's no provision for flight sim buffs, and only an occasional nod toward real-time strategy game players.

It should be noted, however, that CPL isn't an online league. Instead, you have to go to the tournament location and play on systems that are connected to a local area network. This adds to the real sports feel of the tournament, but you can't simply join the league and play online.

In a related issue, NetGames USA (www.netgamesusa.com) has developed software that can globally rank players in sponsored online arenas. Their software is used by the CPL. However, the coolest thing about NetGames USA is ngWorldStats, shown in Figure 15.1. This is software that can be built into a game, which then monitors and keeps track of your score in a variety of online arenas. The first game to fully implement ngWorldStats is Unreal Tournament.

Another moderately successful league is the Virtual Golfing Association, started by Access Software and continued by Microsoft when it acquired Access. Also, the PGA (Professional Golfer's Association), the real golfer's pro league, is a cosponsor, which doesn't hurt. The top ranked players in VGA can actually win some fairly serious money, with total prize packages of $100,000 available in the latest tour. The VGA is centered around a single game, Links LS 2000. Unlike the CPL, the VGA is a truly online league.

There are other, smaller associations, clubs and leagues that occasionally offer prizes and money, but these are the largest to date. There's a problem with the idea of a Pro Gamer's League, however.

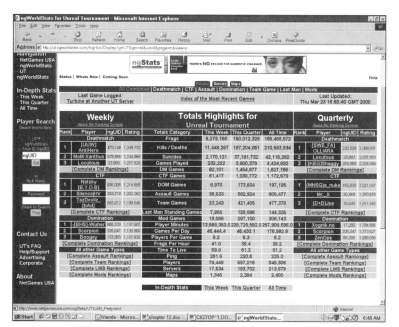

Figure 15.1

The ngWorldStats ranking page for Unreal Tournament. Do you have what it takes to make it to the top of the list?

The Problem of Spectators

Computer gaming is a participant-oriented activity. In many ways, it's similar in scope to solo sports, such as long-distance running (without the aerobic benefit) and bicycling. It also shares a problem with those types of sports: spectators.

That's not to say you can't watch a tournament game in progress. Many games now ship with a passive camera mode, which allows a limited number of spectators to observe the action. It's not perfect, though, because each connection affects the performance of the server—and that directly affects gameplay.

In LAN-based tournaments, like CPL-sponsored events, you can watch the action on slaved computer monitors. In either case, you run into something more fundamental than technology: Watching an online game is dull. If you've ever watched a 10,000-meter race on the track on TV, you'll note that you watch the start and the finish, with the camera occasionally returning in the middle of the race. You almost never see the entire 27 or so minutes of the race, because unless you're a competitor yourself, it's just not very interesting.

So in a similar fashion, pro computer gaming leagues may simply be restricted to a rarified few, in sponsored tournaments. It's uncertain you'll ever see the scale of money and spectator interest of the high-dollar sports such as football or basketball. It's even doubtful that it will achieve the status of, say, World Cup ski racing.

But, if you think about it, that's beside the point.

You Are the Competitor

As we've traversed the chapters in this book, we've talked about how the various gaming matchmaking services offer tournaments, scoring services, ladders, and tournaments. NetGaming USA's ngWorldStats is another kind of subversive service that tracks scores from all around the Internet.

What computer gaming has always brought to the player is the ability to play a role that he or she has only dreamed of. Be the hero in a role-playing game, prove yourself in a 3,000-pound stock car or strut your chops in a virtual golf league. Computer gaming—even online gaming —isn't about *watching*. It's about *doing*.

Whatever your gaming druthers, there's an online version of your favorite genre that can track your results. Even a role-playing game such as Everquest keeps track of your levels and accomplishments, which you can share with the community. Matchmaking sites such as Mplayer, Jane's Combat.Net, or won.net can, if you desire, keep ongoing results of your gameplay.

What Are You Waiting For

So if you're into PC gaming, and love online gaming, find a like minded group of people. If you like, participate in one of the matchmaking sites that can track your progress. You do need to avoid taking your scores too seriously—this is all good fun. But, as you play, you'll meet good players online who can show you how to improve your game—something that's a trial-and-error process in single-player games. In the end, even casual competition can become a rewarding form of entertainment. So, what are you waiting for?

The Least You Need to Know

➤ The era of pro computer gaming, with leagues and serious money, isn't quite here yet.

➤ However, some very good players can make some fairly serious money in gaming.

➤ The amount of effort required to become really good outweighs the financial gain.

➤ Attracting spectators is difficult at best.

Chapter 16

The Phenomenon of LAN Parties

In This Chapter

➤ The phenomenon of LAN Parties

➤ What is a LAN Party and what goes on there?

➤ How to prepare your computer for travelling to a LAN Party

➤ What sites list postings of LAN Parties in all areas of the U.S. and around the world?

➤ What are some popular specific LAN Parties that are run throughout the year?

LAN Parties are a fairly new thing to online gaming. Well, that's not totally true. LAN Parties have been around since the release of Doom in 1993 but no one called them that back then. Back then it was just a bunch of friends getting together in someone's living room or basement with their computers to play Doom for hours on end. No one really dreamed that network gaming would take off to the degree it has and spawn dozens of large-scale events that draw 20, 40, 100, or even 200 plus people for entire weekends of fun playing around the country and indeed around the world.

Online gaming over the Internet, over a company network, or over a one-on-one dial-up connection is fun, but something is missing. While these forms of connectivity keep online gaming alive and prospering, gamers have come to desire a more intimate level of exposure to their fellow gamers. People want to see whom they're blowing up or being blown up by. They want to talk face to face with other gamers, hear what they have to say about the best strategies, learn what everyone else plays the most, compare hardware that everyone uses, and more.

Many games lend themselves to competitive or cooperative play. Flight simulators such as Falcon 3.0 and Air Warrior have spawned virtual squadrons of pilots, and First-Person Shooters such as Doom and Quake were shipped with the ability to connect to a locally networked computer. Certain computers on the Internet were set up as designated hosts for competitive online play. This concept of a *dedicated server* was a major advancement in the multiplayer world. No longer did players have to work out a schedule when they could connect to play. All you had to do was jump out to a computer that you knew was always running a server and you could play at any time.

After this switch was thrown and players began networking with people they didn't know, it was only a matter of time before they wanted to expand their gaming efforts and actually get together at a central place to enjoy gaming without the perils that are inherent with gaming over the Internet. Hence the LAN Party was born.

What Is a LAN Party?

Simply put, a LAN Party is a gathering of computer gamers. They bring their computers along and hook them into a central network. (Don't forget: Many hardcore gamers are skilled at setting up their computers and probably have already heavily customized their machines.) They then compete against each other, enjoying the thrill of going head-to-head with an unpredictable human opponent.

Many large-scale LAN Parties can be found through the U.S. and many more are popping up on a seemingly daily basis. Unlike science fiction conventions that only take place once a year, LAN Parties generally happen more frequently. Some events happen monthly, quarterly, or twice a year. Some are yearly events but gamers normally like to get together more frequently than that.

LAN Parties can happen anywhere. Smaller events are typically held in someone's basement or living room while larger events are held in places like hotel conference rooms, university event halls, or nearly any place that has enough space for dozens of gamers and their equipment. Some groups even use places like the nearest American Legion hall, an Elks Lodge, the local church basement, or any place that rents out its meeting space to the public. Figure 16.1 shows an event occurring using a local hotel as a venue.

Different types of groups sponsor LAN Parties. Most are run by people who are just avid gamers and some events are run on a more professional level, as official events by gaming companies. Finding a LAN Party to attend can be pretty easy because there are several commonly used Web sites on the Internet that allow people to post notices about events, and players can easily browse these postings to find one near them.

Figure 16.1

One of the first Battle Cons in Indianapolis held at a local hotel.

Many large-scale LAN Parties are struggling for success. It's a tough thing to run. It requires a lot of support hardware (network hubs and switches, computers to act as servers, display hardware, and so on), more power requirements than your average convention (100+ computers can draw a lot of amps), and a fair amount of organizational efforts (laying out space for 100+ computers with extension cords and such can be a pain). Many groups that try to run a large event underestimate the logistics of the effort and overestimate their drawing power. Although there might be thousands of computer gamers in an area, getting word out to them is a harder chore than most organizers think. Convincing people who have never been to a LAN Party to take a chance and attend one is also a tough thing to do. A lot of people have reservations about taking their $2,000+ computer to an event for fear of what might happen to it. That's a reasonable concern and one I hope to lay to rest in this chapter.

This chapter isn't really a guide on how to run a LAN Party. It's a guide on attending a LAN Party as a player. If anyone is interested in running an event and would like advice, your best bet is to contact someone who is experienced at it. Most of the events covered here are run by friendly people who are more than willing to talk to anyone interested in running an event and are always willing to dish out all the advice they can from the well of experience they have gained by running their own events. Our group is always willing to help with advice. Just check out our event site at www.battlecon.com.

What Goes On at a LAN Party?

This is a pretty common question. What does go on at a LAN Party? Most people, even avid online gamers, don't have a very good idea about what goes on at a LAN Party if they haven't been to one. Does everyone play the same game at the same time? Is there an official schedule of games that are played or does everyone just play what they want? Does it go straight through day and night (if it's a multiday event)? Does the event provide network cards for those attending? All these questions are common ones asked by nearly everyone who hasn't been to an event.

Setting Up the Infrastructure

Most events require that everyone bring their own computer. Providing computers for attendees would be a little expensive. This means that everyone packs up their own system and brings it along with them. Every computer should have network connectivity. Many events will have spare network cards for sale but most do not provide them for attendees. This means that all computers should have a network card and be ready to plug in to the event LAN. Arriving at a LAN Party without a network-ready computer could mean that you spend the entire event trying to install a network card and getting it to work correctly. Not a good idea.

The majority of LAN Parties are Saturday and Sunday events. Some go all weekend (Friday, Saturday, Sunday) and others are single day events only (usually Saturday). Most events will charge a reasonable fee of about $20 to $30 for a two-day event, which helps cover the cost of the space and helps reduce the cost of the equipment that has been purchased. Most events have a Web site that allows players to register online prior to showing up. This helps the organizers estimate the attendance level of the event and make plans accordingly. If at all possible, you should register online for an event if you plan on attending. It helps the organizers set things up correctly.

Most LAN Parties are held in a hall or conference room that is large enough for the estimated attendance level. If you're going with a group, it's a good idea to travel together and arrive early so that everyone gets to sit in the same area. Late arrivals generally have to sit where they can. Some events have reserved seating for those who have pre-registered online. It's a good idea to find out the seating policy prior arrival. Figure 16.2 shows people pitching in to set up.

What to Do When You Arrive

Upon arrival, it's time to set up. Lugging your computer in and getting it set up is the toughest thing to do mainly because many other people are doing the same thing at the same time and the logistics can be a little hairy. But, patience helps out a lot. After getting set up, it's time to plug into the network.

Most events ask that you bring your own twisted-pair network cable (a.k.a. RJ45). Some provide the cabling but most expect players to bring their own. A cable of at least 20 feet is best. Even though you might be closer than that to the nearest network hub, you sometimes can't take the most direct route to the hub especially if other people between you and the hub are already set up and you don't want to disturb them. A longer cable can help out a lot.

Figure 16.2

Everyone setting up at Lanwar 5 (photo provided by C.L.A.N.G.U.M.P— www.clangump.com*).*

One important word of advice here. Mark your cable uniquely on both ends! This can help in more ways than one. First, if there are network problems and the organizers need to trace down lines, having your cable marked will help immensely. Second, when it's time to leave and you want to unplug from the hub you will be able to quickly locate your cable. Let me tell you, if you can't remember which port your cable is plugged into and it's time for you to leave, randomly unplugging cables to find yours will result in many people not looking very kindly in your direction. Colored cables are also a good idea, but don't just rely on a different colored cable to identify yours. Colored cables aren't as unique as you might think—the photo in Figure 16.3 may be in black and white, but trust me, most of those cables are red.

This brings up another point. Make sure you use "snagless" LAN cables. Snagless LAN cables are cables that have rounded flanges that stick up above the locking clip that enable you to pull the cable out of a wiring mess and prevent the locking clip from snagging on anything else. This quickly can help you extract your cable from a mess of other LAN cables just by pulling it out. If the cable isn't snagless, you might have to go deep sea diving and crawl under tables to get your cable back.

Assuming that your computer is all ready to go network-wise and is plugged in you should be able to power up your computer and see if you can see the rest of the network. A valuable tool to this end is `winipcfg.exe`, a program that comes with Windows 9x. Running this application will tell you if you have been issued an address by the event network. If you have, you'll be ready to start gaming. You should know ahead of time what address range to expect an address in so you can see if you have been successfully hooked up to the network. Unfortunately, it's beyond the scope of this book to explain all the factors involved in configuring your computer correctly for networking purposes. If you're having problems, just let the event organizers know and they should be glad to lend a hand.

Figure 16.3

"Hey, I thought I was the only person with a red cable..." (photo provided by C.L.A.N.G.U.M.P).

Many smaller events require that a player's computer be set up with a static address or, in other words, an address that is configured manually before hooking up to the LAN Party network. It is best to find out the network requirements of the event and have things ready to go ahead of time. The event Web site is usually the best place to get this information.

How the Gaming Is Organized

All right, now that you're at an event, hooked up to the network, and ready to play, just what do you play? How does the gaming proceed? This is the toughest part of any event and one that many organizers leave out of the equation. Many LAN Parties have official tournament games that are ladder-climbing type matches. Attendees can sign up to play these games and try to survive the early rounds but this often is only a small part of the entire event. Plus, many new attendees might be reserved about joining in the official tournament games either because they aren't very good or the competition just isn't their cup of tea.

The question becomes how do you link up with other players at the event? This is the one main point most event planners fail to consider. Most event planners expect players to just connect with each other through their own means. This works for some games like Quake, Unreal, or Descent, which can have perpetual games running at all times. It doesn't help games that support only synchronous joining or, in other words, requires that all players be ready to go at the same time and then enter the game all together (games like Red Alert, Tiberian Sun, Battle Zone, and so on).

It might sound like a simple thing. You have a hall or conference room filled with 100 or 200 gamers and you would imagine that it's a simple matter to find other people to game with. This doesn't always work out too easily though. Most people find it hard to talk to folks they don't already know and what ends up happening is that you end up gaming with the people you came with, something you could have done at home.

So, what's the answer? Well, better event planning for one. Event organizers need to have an easy way for people to notify everyone else of the games they would like to play. A white board or two to provide a sign up or game posting area would help most events tremendously. Another option is a Web server on the LAN Party network that allows people to post games or sign up for games, but this is a little high end, and a dry-mark board is usually all it takes to help players link up with each other. Sometimes an overhead projector provided by the hotel or event location to project available games helps out a great deal as well. Many events also have the luxury of a public address system that the organizers use to notify the event crowd of what is happening. This can be used to announce that certain players are hosting a game that is open for others to join. All you need to do is go up to the control table and ask the nearest event organizer if he or she can announce a game for you.

Failing all these possibilities, how can you notify the rest of the gaming population of the games you are willing to play or are planning on hosting? Well, the best bet is a sign of some kind. I know that it's a basic concept but it's one that works very well. Before you arrive at an event, you should make a sign that you can use to note the games that you will be hosting and indicate the address people can connect to to play. A simple piece of cardboard on a dowel rod and base makes a great display piece that does the job nicely (ahh! I've been possessed by Martha Stewart! Someone kill me now!). You can obviously get fancier and go to someplace like Office Max or Office Depot and buy some inexpensive display devices if you would like.

One thing to keep in mind is that many LAN Parties turn the lights down real low after the majority of the attendees have arrived and are set up. This means that an unlit sign is not going to do you much good in a dark gaming hall. You'll need to make sure to fashion a small light to shine one your sign to illuminate the message. Don't go overboard on the lighting. A battery-operated light might be best because many event organizers prefer to only allow the bare essentials to be plugged into the electrical grid to prevent overloading the circuits. Plus, you only need to illuminate your sign when you're looking for players. Most of the time it can be turned off. Excessive light also tends to irritate the players around you.

The name of the game is getting your message out about what you want to play and link up with others who want to play the same thing. Communication is the goal. A piece of paper on a helium balloon, a scrolling marquee sign if you have a lot of extra scratch, or just a chunk of cardboard on a stick will go a long way to putting you in touch with the rest of the people at a LAN Party.

Another big aspect of going to a LAN Party is the possibility of coming back home with a little extra loot. Larger LAN events can attract the attention of game publishers who can sometimes be rather generous with free copies of some of their games (although most of the time not the absolute latest releases) and hardware companies are known to donate some of their wares in return for a sponsorship note. If you're planning on running an event, it's possible to get sponsors who are willing to cough up some goodies but don't always count on it. People coming to LAN Parties like to get stuff but sometimes a small plague or trophy as a prize for winning a tournament goes further than a free joystick. As we can see in Figure 16.4, organizing a LAN Party is definitely a team effort.

Figure 16.4

Left to right: Norwell9 (David Cwikowski), Red Shivan (John Maggio), Cleatus (Brian Minrath) making sure all goes well at Lanwar 5. John and Brian are official Lanwar organizers and David is everyone's favorite LAN Party Coalition grand-poobah. (photo provided by C.L.A.N.G.U.M.P— www.clangump.com).

So, there you are playing your favorite game against eight other people and having a blast. The event has been going well all day long but it's starting to get late. Because this is a two-day event, you're wondering if the gaming area is going to shut down or if it's going to go all night. Most two or three day events do run 24 hours, nonstop. If the event is held at a hotel, you have the luxury of being able to get a room with your buddies to catch a little shut-eye before returning to the battlefield. Of course, even if the event is held someplace without attached room accommodations, you can still leave to sack out at the nearest Red Roof Inn or Hampton Inn if you want. That means leaving your computer or packing it up. I'll get to this in a moment.

You could, of course, stick it out all night long and bash with the best until dawn. This doesn't leave you in very good shape to drive home the next day but it does let you see the late-night side of a LAN Party. Many LAN Parties do thin out a bit late at night but a few diehards usually stick it out 24 hours straight. Late-night LAN Party games usually take the form of everyone who is in the gaming area deciding on one popular game like Half-Life or Quake 3 and everyone joining in the same session for an awesome 30+ player smash-fest. It can be a lot of fun to participate in or just watch.

The next day comes and the play continues until the event shuts down. The final rounds of the event tournaments are usually held on day two and the ultimate winners are decided upon in a clash of the titans. Then everyone breaks down their computer and packs up, says their goodbyes and heads back up so they can check the LAN Party Web site to see if anyone snapped a digital picture of them and posted it to the party wrap up page.

Attending a LAN Party is a lot less painful than some people think. Many folks are hesitant to travel with their computer (as I was before I first gave it a shot) but after the first time, it comes as second nature to pack up the computer and travel with it. And, you just can't beat the fun of gaming face to face with 150 or more gamers in the same area and getting to personally know some of the people you only know as a game name on the Internet.

Gamer Comment

Red Shivan (a.k.a. John Maggio of Lanwar in Louisville, KY)

"Most of the time what you'll see at Lanwar late on Saturday night is about 30 people who decide to stay all night and end up playing Team Fortress Half-Life or Counter Strike for several hours. I usually get a chance to play at this point (if I'm not asleep) because it's the only time when I'm not busy with something else."

Travelling with Your Computer

Travelling with your computer is easier than you might think. You do have to take a few extra steps to make the task of breaking down and moving your computer easier. This section will give you some insight from people who have done it dozens, if not hundreds of times over the past few years. We'll also take a look at how to keep your computer and your other stuff safe while at a LAN Party.

First off, let's talk about tearing your system down. If you plan on becoming an avid LAN Party rover, you're going to want to look at spending a few shekels on getting some extra cables and cords and an extra keyboard and mouse if you can afford it. What you're striving for is being able to just detach your power cords and cables from your CPU and monitor and leaving them in place at home rather than trying to fish them out and taking them with you all the time. Creating a travel kit of spare cables, a spare keyboard, and a spare mouse or trackball can make breakdown and setup 100% easier. If you don't want to go for the extra stuff, make sure that you have space enough behind your desk or work area at home so that you can easily get behind it and remove your computer cables. This will help you from succumbing to Tourette's Syndrome when trying to find out what that damn monitor power cord is stuck on! Arrggggg!!

Packing up and travelling...Let's read a quote from Norwell9, a man who travels to more LAN Parties than nearly any other five gamers put together:

Gamer Comment

Norwell9 (a.k.a. David Cwikowski—www.lanpartycoalition.com**)**

"When tearing down your rig at home, the first and most important advice I use is to keep my original boxes. If you have seen me around the circuit you know that I still pack up my monitor in the original ViewSonic box I bought it in. It doesn't take much time and it keeps it safer than Fort Knox."

He does, too. I have in fact seen him and his ViewSonic box buddy. I don't know if I wholeheartedly agree with Nor, but you can't go wrong with what he says. Better safe than sorry. I tend to operate on the maxim that a good thick towel around a monitor is plenty. And don't skimp on the travel arrangements of your stuff in your car. Make sure you have it all snugly packed so that it doesn't bounce around. Hard drives have moving parts and read/write heads that can scratch the surface of the disk if bounced too hard. Getting to a LAN Party and not having your machine boot up tends to give you a sinking feeling. But, if that does happen, opening up your case and making sure all your internal cables are seated firmly usually helps bring a non-booting machine back to life. Cables tend to shift some and work loose during transport.

Gamer Comment

Grimlock (a.k.a. Rolf Crozier)

"Don't use a 2-wheeled hand-truck to move your things. They aren't meant for computer equipment and they don't deal well with parking lot potholes or ice ruts in winter. My friends have a new term for dropping your monitor three times—"Rolf'ed" now equates to a cracked monitor case and a dead CD-ROM drive."

Here's my personal rule of thumb when travelling to a LAN Party: "If you're carrying more than your CPU, your monitor, and one tote box, you're travelling too heavy." There really shouldn't be anything else you need to bring other than those three things. Another good bit of advice is invest in a small, foldable flatbed cart that you can fit all your things on (which shouldn't be too hard if you just have those three items). Small flatbed carts can be purchased at Office Depot or nearly any hardware store for about $60 and are an invaluable travelling aid. Some LAN Parties will have an extra cart that attendees can use but you might end up waiting for a while before it is your turn to use it. Having your own cart will put you ahead of the crowd.

Some people like to travel with their peripherals in a gym bag or a backpack but I like using a hard plastic tote box. The main reason is security. If you buy the right type of tote box for about $10, you can lock it up securely with a cable lock that can also link your CPU and monitor together with a lock at each end (or the cable looped back to itself if it's long enough). A soft-sided bag doesn't offer the same amount of security that a hard plastic tote does. You can keep all your smaller items in the tote and not have to worry about them.

That leads to the next point. Buy a nice long security cable and attach lock loops to the back of your CPU and monitor with high strength epoxy glue (the kind that will not come off for any reason). That will allow you to string a security cable through the loops and through the legs of the table so you can lock down your belongings. Theft problems have never been an issue at any of the LAN Parties I have attended but it does give you peace of mind to know that your computer is secure. A large white sheet to drape over your system when you're not with it will also give you added peace of mind especially when you leave for the night and leave your computer behind.

To further give you peace of mind, turn on your BIOS password feature so that your system will not boot up without it. This will make sure that no one can start your system and do harm to it when you're not there. Again, this has never been an issue at any event I have attended but being safe can go a long way to making you sleep better at night.

If you follow those few guidelines, travelling to LAN Parties for some face-to-face online gaming will be a breeze. Here are a few other pointers to keep in mind when travelling:

➤ Always take your driver disks and operating system disks. You never know when you will need them.

➤ Take a small toolkit with you. Even the simplest of tools can be the difference between a weekend of fun and a weekend of watching others have fun.

➤ Take a pair of headphones. Most LAN Parties don't permit speakers due to the excessive noise and power drain they create. Subwoofers are out.

➤ Don't forget your game CDs. You'd be surprised how often this happens.

➤ Don't forget these essential pieces of hardware: computer, monitor, keyboard, mouse/trackball, cables, and joystick.

➤ Don't forget a flashlight that can stand on its own. A snake light is best. As I said previously, most LAN Parties turn down the lights after the majority of people get set up. If you need to work on something or if you arrive late, a flashlight will be a godsend.

Another suggestion is to take a small cooler of snacks/food with you. Some coldcuts, bread, and pretzels make a great dinner at a LAN Party. Some events are held in areas where finding a fast food joint is hard to do (like in a downtown area or by an airport). Having a little grub with you will make sure you don't lose a couple hours looking for some sustenance. A large number of LAN Parties take place in hotels and have some food catered in for the event. And others will order out for everyone and ask for a buck or two from everyone. Just check the event Web site for details on the food arrangements and be prepared ahead of time.

LAN Party Organization Sites

Well, now that you know what a LAN Party really is and how to best lug your computer around to them, the next logical question is "Where can I find one to attend?" I'm glad you asked!

There are a handful of sites dedicated to expanding the LAN Party universe and way of life. Many of these sites list parties from all over the country and there are a few sites that are regional in nature and cater to one specific area of the country. LAN Parties are not just an American item. Countries from all over the world have their fair share. Australia, Germany, Canada, and many others have dozens of LAN Parties each year and the numbers are increasing rapidly. Each area of the U.S. has its own set of events and the numbers here are expanding faster than anywhere else in the world. Admittedly, the Midwest and the West Coast tend to have the most for some reason. You don't see a large number in the plains or the East Coast but that will change shortly as recognition grows.

LAN Party (`www.lanparty.com`)

Lan Party is probably the best known Web site for LAN Party announcements, postings, and new items from around the world. LAN Party is the one definitive place that most of the gaming world uses to inform everyone else about its events. The site is easy to understand and the submission process is easy to use. Any event organizer can post a notice about his event to LAN Party and it will be displayed on their home page beginning about a week prior to actual event date. After the event date has passed, the event notice will go back into the database and redisplayed at the event date if it has been listed as a reoccurring event. If it has been listed as a one time only event it will be removed from the database. Event postings can include any information you would like about the event, not just the bare facts of where and when. The LAN Party database allows events to have a wide range of information tagged to them. Figure 16.5 shows a list of parties you can find on lanparty.com.

The LAN Party database can be searched by region or by date, so if you're looking for one in your area, it's easy to do. The site features a message board and a review section so you can see or give player comments about LAN events.

If you're looking for an event to attend, LAN Party will be the place you can find one.

Blues News (`www.bluesnews.com`)

Blues News is a general FPS (First-Person Shooter) gaming information site that has a very expansive LAN Party listing section. Blues News is almost as good a LAN Party information site as LAN Party itself. The list is very complete but can only be viewed by region. Finding out which ones are coming up soon is up to you to figure out which isn't too tough a chore if you're just looking for an event in your area. Figure 16.6 shows the Blues News LAN Party page.

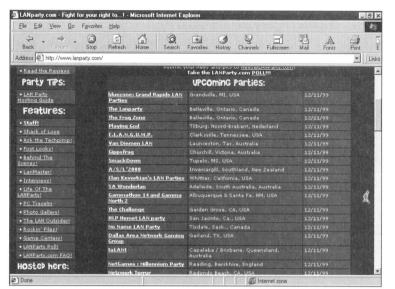

Figure 16.5

The LAN Party Upcoming Parties listing on the main page.

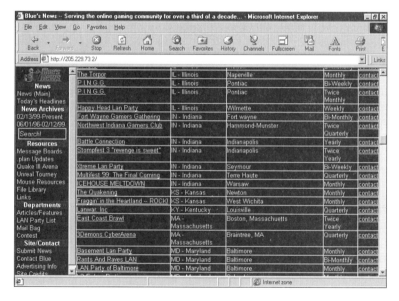

Figure 16.6

The Blues News LAN Party listing.

Blues News has a great reputation for being on the cutting edge of information distribution as far as FPS games go. Many people check this site regularly to stay informed of events and happenings in the gaming world so it's a good idea to check this site for the best LAN Parties to attend.

265

Gaming Events (www.gamingevents.com)

Gaming Events is part of the HearMe family of services and Web sites. HearMe is the company that runs MPlayer and several other prominent gaming sites. While Gaming Events doesn't have the expansive LAN Party lists that LAN Party or Blues News has, it does have a LAN Party posting section and is another place to check when looking for an event to attend or to get word out about your own event. The gamingevents.com LAN Party listing is shown in Figure 16.7.

Figure 16.7

The Gaming Events LAN Party listing.

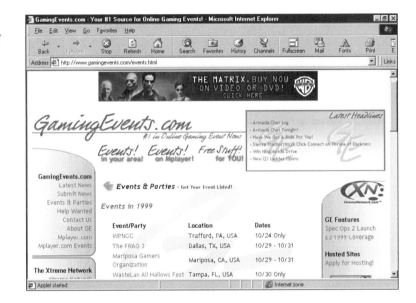

Unfortunately, Gaming Events suffers from lack of overall direction and the site has undergone several rebirths recently, leading people to think that perhaps no one knows where the site is really headed. Plus the fact that it's a HearMe site and spam ads pop up sporadically in their own windows over the top of whatever you might be looking at makes it sometimes irritating to visit. It is a corporate speak site that typically only parrots press releases about gaming events and software releases but it does have a LAN Party posting area that any can add to.

The LAN Party Ring (www.bangg.org/lanring)

There are many *rings* available for Web sites that share a common theme. There are rings for Java developer sites, rings for literary Web sites, and rings for many other commonly themed Web sites. The concept is simple to understand. All members of the ring add a link area to the bottom of their Web page that allows visitors to jump to another member of the ring quickly. One main site maintains the ring database and ensures that there are no broken links.

There are currently about 225 sites participating in the LAN Party Ring and the database is maintained by The Bay Area Networks Gaming Group (BANGG), a group that also operates LAN Parties in the northern California area. You can hit any member Web site of the ring and check out the bottom of their main page and see the ring logo. Figure 16.8 shows the LAN Party Ring home page.

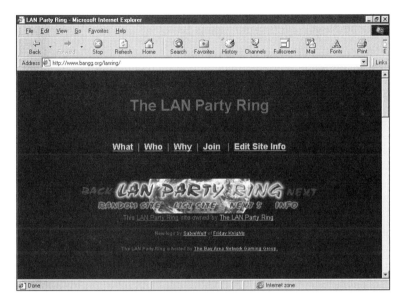

Figure 16.8

The LAN Party Ring Home Page (with member logo displayed).

The logo will allow you to hit a random site, get info about the site you are currently on, start browsing through the sites on the ring, or view a list of the members of the ring. This is a great way to check out the LAN Parties on the ring and see if there are any in your area. Unfortunately there is no way to view the list by location or event date but it is entertaining to browse the ring and check out all the member sites.

The LAN Party Coalition (www.lanpartycoalition.com)

The LAN Party Coalition is an organization started by David Cwikowski and its purpose is to help organize the many LAN Party events that are developing in the Midwest and to offer organizational assistance to those events. Many times people jump into running a LAN Party without realizing all the things that have to be done to make it work on a large scale. David hits nearly every regional LAN Party and is a cornerstone of the Midwest LAN Party community. His efforts and his Web site help to give a sense of community to the local sites and David's excellent commentary on the developing nature of these events helps give everyone some direction on how to make their event better.

The LAN Party Coalition site lists many of the member sites and gives users a jumping-off point from which to browse for a party to attend. By being focused main on

Midwest LAN Parties, the LAN Party Coalition site is better able to help direct the growth of the LAN Party community and ensure that it doesn't deteriorate into a chaotic mess of overlapping and competing events. Figure 16.9 shows the home page for the LAN Party Coalition.

Figure 16.9

The LAN Party Coalition Web Site and Mission Statement.

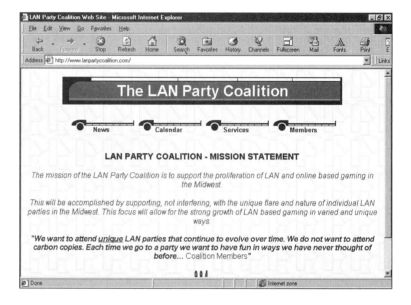

The site is very new and the design is likely to change but not the intent. If you're looking for a Midwest LAN Party event to attend, there is no better place to check out than this one. You'll find all the serious ones listed here and you'll be able to read a review of the event by Norwell9 himself most likely. If you're thinking about starting a Midwest event, this is the place to check out to see how others are doing it.

Gamer Comment

HangMan (a.k.a. Tom Hanagan)

"It's easy to lose track of time at a LAN Party because you are having so much fun. But, be careful because you could also lose your wife, your job, and possibly your head."

Specific LAN Parties and Their Web Sites

To conclude this chapter I'm going to look at a few specific LAN Parties and give you some idea of what is available. I'll admit that I live smack-dab in the middle of Hoosier-ville (Indiana) and my experience is mainly with Midwest events. There are events from all over the country and it doesn't take much to uncover them if you live in a different region.

LANWAR—Louisville, Kentucky (www.lanwar.com)

LANWAR is probably the largest event in the Midwest and the best run. It has an average attendance of 150+ gamers and its attendance rate is increasing with each event, which takes place once every quarter. The LANWAR home page, as seen in Figure 16.10, is a good example of a single event page.

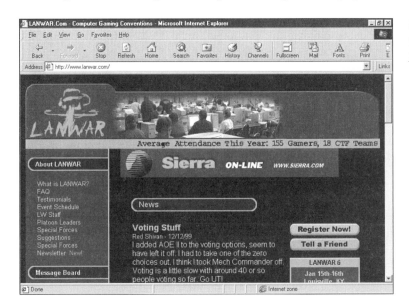

Figure 16.10

The LANWAR Home Page.

LANWAR is normally a Saturday and Sunday event held on the campus of the University of Louisville. It is professionally run by gamers rather than corporate sponsors and continues to gain momentum in the Midwest as more and more people learn about it.

If you're looking for an event to attend, LANWAR should be high on your list. The organizers have been running it for quite a while now and they have it down to a smooth art form. It's unlikely that you'll find a more eloquently administered event.

Battle Con—Indianapolis, Indiana (www.battlecon.com)

Okay, okay, so I'm going to indulge in a little self-promotion here. Battle Con is the event that my fellow gaming cohorts and I run in Indianapolis and one that we are trying to open up to the Midwest and indeed the rest of the country. In the spring of 2,000, we'll be running Battle Con 3—our third running of the event. Our home page can be seen in Figure 16.11.

Figure 16.11

The Battle Con Home Page.

Battle Con is an expansive attempt at running a LAN Party for everyone. We don't focus on FPS games and we don't focus on RTS games. We run an event for everyone, experienced and newbies alike. We're the friendliest bunch of people you could hope to meet and we're looking forward to turning Battle Con into one of the premiere LAN Parties in the area.

Our event is always held at a hotel that can provide sleeping accommodations for attendees and we often have a movie room for taking breaks from the gaming action. If you're in our area, check out our Web site for the latest details on our event.

FragStock—Virginia Beach, Virginia (www.fragstock.com)

An event on the East Coast, FragStock is a medium-sized event that is working hard at becoming a large East Coast nexus for LAN Party gaming. FragStock has the desire and the will to grow into an outstanding large-scale event. If you're an east coaster and are looking for an event to attend, check out their Web site for all the information you need.

QuakeCon—Mesquite, Texas (www.quakecon.com)

QuakeCon is an event held in Texas that mainly focuses on Quake and has official sponsorship from Id Software themselves. QuakeCon 99 was held between August 5th and 8th of 1999 and had a strong turnout. Admittedly this event does cater to the Quake community quite a bit but if Quake and First-Person Shooters are your bag and you're a Texan, this event might be just what you're looking for. It has the name recognition that every LAN event wants and it is bound to grow as it evolves over the years.

*Lanaholics—Elmhurst, Illinois (*www.lanaholics.com*)*

Lanaholics is a group of gamers in Illinois who run a small event that they are trying to open up to the public. They maintain a very well detailed mail-list group and their attendees are always kept well informed of the event happenings and news items. If you're curious about this group, visit their site and sign up for their mailing list.

*Stompfest—Indianapolis, Indiana (*www.stompfest.com*)*

Indianapolis is graced with two large-scale LAN Party events. Our own event, Battle Con, and Stompfest, the first large-scale LAN event in Indianapolis. Gamers in our city have the choice of one or the other or both. Stompfest and Battle Con try not to step on each other's toes and create scheduling conflicts. Both Battle Con and Stompfest participate in the LAN Party Coalition in an attempt to avoid conflicting event dates and such.

*Bay Area Network Gaming Group—Northern California (*www.bangg.com*)*

BANGG is a West Coast event that has been around for a while now. Their claim to fame is of course that they administer the LAN Party Ring. Check out their site and see what they have to offer. If you're on the West Coast you might just want to stop in and say hello.

Other Events

There are obviously other events out there that you can attend. You just need to find them. Checking out LANParty.com, Bluesnews.com, or Lanpartycoalition.com should be your first step to find the right event for you and your friends.

The Least You Need to Know

➤ Large-scale LAN Parties are a fairly new occurrence in the work of multi-player gaming. They are growing in popularity and many of them have attendance levels of 200+!

➤ LAN Parties are gatherings of gamers who are there to play in officially run tournaments and just to have fun. Getting the word out to the rest of the gamers in attendance about what you would like to play is sometimes hard unless you go prepared.

➤ Packing up your computer and taking it to a LAN Party is a little intimidating the first time you do it. But, by following some guidelines it can be an easy process and one that you quickly grow accustomed to. Security is rarely an issue but there are things you can do to make your computer as safe as can be.

➤ Blues News, LAN Party, and the LAN Party Coalition are excellent resources for locating a LAN Party in your area if you are interested in attending an event.

➤ LANWAR, Battle Con, FragStock, Stompfest and other events range from small, medium, to large events. It's easy to find one that right for you and your gaming group.

MAMA NEEDS A NEW PAIR OF SHOES!!

RATTLE

Chapter 17

Online Gaming Utilities

In This Chapter

➤ GameSpy

➤ Kali

➤ ICQ

➤ AOL Instant Messenger

➤ BattleCom

➤ Roger Wilco

Online gaming is great, but several shortcomings exist for gaming as a whole. Games can only know about themselves. For example, although Quake and Unreal can search for games to join, they can only search for themselves. What if there is a nice big Quake tournament going on, but you're searching through the listings in Unreal? You're not going to find it. Even if you did find it, how are you going to get your friends together to play? Email can be slow, phone calls are expensive (and your computer might not like sharing), and online chat rooms are a big pain. Fortunately, a number of utilities—many of them home-brew creations—help to fill these gaps. In this chapter, you'll learn what these utilities do and where to get 'em.

Game Finders

Gaming companies are in business to promote themselves, not games of other manufacturers. While this exclusivity might work for them, as a gamer, it isn't convenient for you—especially if you're new to the arena. Because of this deficiency, there's a need for utilities that can locate multiple online games and provide a common ground for finding whatever it is that you want to play. This chapter will cover two such utilities that can make your life much easier. Rather than manually searching for a great online game, you can run a program to find what's available to be played and immediately start the game.

Instant Messaging

The next type of utility that we'll look at is the instant messenger. Instant Messages are threatening to displace email in many cases—and for very good reasons. Email can take quite a while to reach its destination. Furthermore, just because you get a piece of email from someone, it doesn't mean that that person will still be around when you reply. Although email revolutionized the speed of communication, for today's plugged-in game jockey, it isn't instant enough anymore. Instant Messages are. When you send an instant message, the recipient is immediately notified and can respond in real-time.

Another benefit of instant-messaging programs is that they let you determine if someone is online at any given point in time. Instead of guessing when your friends are available, you can tell if they're busy, offline, or ready and available for a chat or a game.

Voice Messaging

After spending a few hours pushing keys to place your games, typing a few emails, and sending instant messages, your hands are likely to be a bit tired. Luckily, there are utilities that you can use to actually talk to your friends (and enemies) while they are online. Several games already include voice communications, but they are game-specific. The utilities discussed in this chapter will enable you to chat with anyone else who has the utility—regardless of the game you intend to play.

Sounds exciting, doesn't it? Well, let's get started!

GameSpy 3D

GameSpy Industries: www.gamespy3D.com/

Registration Cost: $20.00

The first program we'll look at is the GameSpy 3D software from GameSpy Industries. GameSpy 3D is a great program for finding whatever servers you might want to play on. Rather than starting up each individual game and checking to see what games are available, GameSpy does the job for you. To see how this is done, first download and install the software on your computer using the program's easy-to-follow instructions. Once installed, start the GameSpy 3D application.

The first time you run GameSpy, it opens the option configuration screen shown in Figure 17.1. There really isn't anything you need to set here, but you might want to look at a few of these options. If you are located behind a firewall, you can tell the software now. You can also speed up the time it takes GameSpy to run by turning off DNS and ping time lookups while it queries game servers. The Sounds and Chat tabs enable you to configure feedback options and settings for GameSpy's online chat areas. These options are well documented in the software's online help.

Lingo

What are DNS lookups and ping times?

A Domain Name Server (DNS) takes a numeric computer address such as 192.168.0.12 and translates it into a human readable name. This lets you connect to easy-to-remember names, such as www.planetquake.com rather than a number. When GameSpy returns a list of servers, it attempts to look up the name of the server.

This process takes a while and if you're mainly interested in jumping into a game, you probably don't need this information.

Ping time is a measure of the length of time it takes to send and receive data to a remote computer. The lower the ping time, the faster the connection. Most servers are run on fast connections, so you might not want to waste time checking the speed of all the servers.

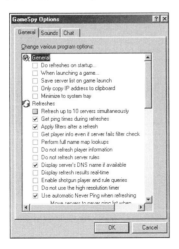

Figure 17.1

GameSpy has a variety of configuration options.

Once you've set the options for the program, it will search your drive for any installed games it supports. When the search is completed, you are given the option of turning support for these games (and any others that it may not have found) on and off. Be sure you check to make sure it found everything you have. If it didn't it will ask to you to help it locate the executables manually.

As a final step before you get to start searching for games, GameSpy will have you set up a player profile for your games. You can actually create different profiles that configure in-game options, like player color and control configuration for the same game. This ability lets you switch between game personas without having to reconfigure the game manually.

When you finally reach the GameSpy server screen, you should see something similar to Figure 17.2. Here you can see the different games that you've chosen to monitor (the ones which GameSpy found on your drive), and the servers that are tracking online games. Choose one of these servers, then sit back for a second. The list of available games will appear in the upper pane of the window. Selecting a game will show the players that are connected on the lower left, and server variables on the lower right.

Figure 17.2

Choose a game, check its stats, and start playing!

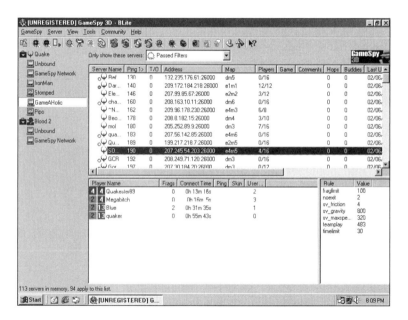

When you've found the server you want, just double-click; the game will be launched and you'll join. It's as simple as that. There are many other features that you'll really appreciate—such as the ability to search for gamers by name on any of the listed servers. This is a good way to find your enemy, and bring him or her down!

Kali

Kali Inc.: www.kali.net/

Registration Cost: $20.00

GameSpy is a great program, but some people might like a more streamlined approach at finding their game servers. Kali is an excellent alternative to GameSpy that has a distinct advantage—it supports multiple operating systems. Using Kali, Mac OS, Windows, Linux, and OS/2 users can find each other and engage in cross-platform warfare.

After downloading and running the Kali installer, start the Kali application. Since it's the first time you've run Kali, you'll be asked to enter information about yourself, as shown in Figure 17.3. This information is visible to all members of the Kali network, so don't enter your primary email address unless you want to make it known!

Figure 17.3

Kali has a streamlined setup—just enter your user info!

Once you've entered your information, Kali searches your system for installed games. This search may take a few minutes, so be patient. When completed, you should be ready to use the Kali system. Figure 17.4 shows a typical Kali session, searching for Quake 3 servers. The right side of your screen is a list of Kali resources—here you can find chat servers and game servers for almost any type of game. Each category can be expanded to further refine your search.

The upper right side of the screen shows the available games for the category you've selected, along with their associated ping times and the number of players connected. Highlighting a game shows information about the individual players as well as the status of the server.

Like GameSpy, you can use Kali to find players that are online and sort servers by a number of criteria. I prefer Kali because of its user interface. If cross-platform gaming is a necessity, then Kali is your only choice. Overall, both GameSpy and Kali are excellent programs that perform a much needed task.

Figure 17.4

The easy-to-use hierarchical resource list makes finding the perfect game simple.

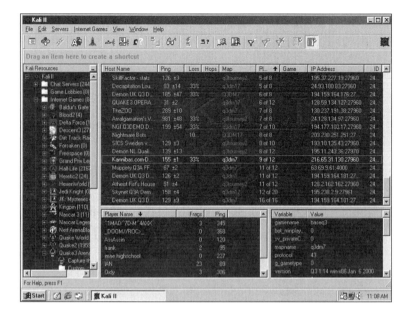

ICQ

Mirabilis: www.icq.com/

Registration Cost: Free

The leader in the world of instant messaging is the fantastic product *ICQ* (*I-Seek-You*). ICQ opened the world's eyes to instant messaging by covering almost every computing platform with an instant messaging client. You've almost certainly seen people giving out their ICQ numbers along with their email addresses—it's popular in both business and personal computing circles.

ICQ can be used to host chat sessions, send messages to friends instantly, and transfer files directly between users. Unlike email, there is little to no delay before messages appear on the receiving end. Residing in your System Tray, ICQ is always available to send a quick note to a friend or check their online status.

The first thing that you'll need to do is create a user profile for yourself. This profile enables you to connect to the ICQ network and provides information about you so that other users can find you. Figure 17.5 shows a portion of the signup process. There are many optional fields that provide detail information about you and your location—only fill these fields in if you feel comfortable doing so.

Once you've registered, the ICQ program starts. Figure 17.6 is a typical display of ICQ in use. You can add users to your system by clicking the **Add** button and supplying the program with all the information you know about the user—email address, real name, nickname, and so. Added users are placed in the main ICQ window, where you can check their online status at any given time. You can send messages to users by double-clicking their name in the list. You can also perform a variety of other actions on the listed users (send them chat requests, transfer files, and so on) by single-clicking their name and choosing the action from the popup menu that appears.

Figure 17.5

Create your ICQ account by filling in the information that the setup wizard requests.

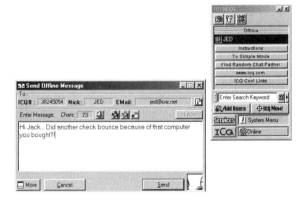

Figure 17.6

It's simple to send messages to your friends—just double-click their name!

ICQ has a wide variety of different options—including multiple sound sets and a *skinnable* appearance. There are literally hundreds of different controls that govern how the software works. You'll want to spend some time getting used to the software, because it can definitely be intimidating to the first-time user.

AIM: America Online Instant Messenger

America Online: www.aol.com

Registration Cost: Free

Before you start thrashing around wildly at the name of the company that produces this software, there are a few things you should know. First, AIM is an excellent piece of software that cuts through the complexity of ICQ's interface and has most of the same functionality. Second, America Online acquired ICQ's parent company Mirabilis several years ago, so, technically, ICQ is actually an America Online product as well. The decision you need to make is which one will best work for you. Usually this can be decided for you after determining which messaging package is being used by your friends! Indeed, there's no reason you couldn't use both. You have two choices for installing AIM—either by downloading the executable from America Online, or by installing Netscape. Because Netscape is owned by AOL, the popular browser installs AIM automatically.

Lingo

What is a "skin"?

Skins refer to the outside appearance of a piece of software. If the software is *skinnable*, you can change the way it looks. Many people are sick of the same old windows day in and day out, so they add variation to their system by changing skins on pieces of software. You can find information on ICQ skins at `www.icqplus.org/`.

After installing AIM, you'll be asked to register a new screen name. This process is similar to that of creating a new ICQ account, but carried out in a slightly different manner. The software takes you to America Online's Web site, as seen in Figure 17.7, and will let you register via the Web, rather than through the software itself. After completing the simple registration, you can enter your login information into the AIM client and click the **Sign On** button to join the network. Don't worry, this doesn't enroll you in the AOL service—it just signs you up for the AIM service, which is entirely free.

The first thing you'll notice about the AIM interface, shown in Figure 17.8, is that it is far cleaner than ICQ. The Online tab shows any users that are currently logged in and added to your buddy list. The List Setup tab lets you configure groups of users and add new users to your buddy list. To send an instant message, just double-click the person you want to send a message to. You can also highlight the name of a user, then choose one of the other available options, such as chat from the People menu.

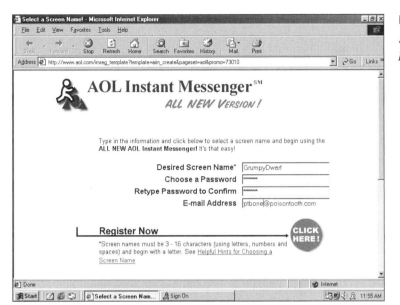

Figure 17.7

Signup for AIM is accomplished through the AOL Web site.

Figure 17.8

The AIM interface is much less cluttered than ICQ.

The ICQ software offers far more customizable features than AIM, but over the years has become increasingly complex. AIM's interface is simple enough for anyone to use, and has most of the same functionality. Unfortunately, members of one service are invisible to users of the other. Most people tend to use ICQ, so if your friends are already on the ICQ network, you're going to have a difficult time getting them to switch. If, on the other hand, you and your friends are just starting with instant messaging, you might find that AIM is the more refined of your choices.

281

BattleCom

Shadow Factor: `www.battlecom.com`

Registration Cost: $5.00

So you don't like typing? You don't have to! The BattleCom system is a very inexpensive means by which you can talk directly with your friends over the Internet. For $5, you can avoid the phone charges of organizing games with your friends from around the country, or around the world. The installation process is very quick and simple. You'll be asked a few questions about your network and how you are connecting, as well as a name that you'll use to identify yourself. This process is shown in Figure 17.9.

Figure 17.9

It's simple to set up BattleCom—just step through the easy-to-use wizard.

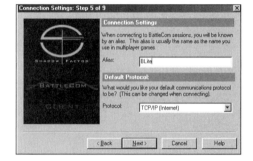

The BattleCom interface is relatively simple. The buttons at the top of the screen allow you to host a chat session, join an existing session, test the BattleCom configuration, and find sessions related to a particular topic. The tabs on the screen let you check your connection parameters, view your current chat session, and adjust the volume and cutoff levels of the sound input and output. Figure 17.10 shows the main BattleCom screen.

Figure 17.10

BattleCom offers high functionality with a simple interface.

The best feature of BattleCom is that it doesn't just let you form a little chat group to talk about games—it lets you take the chat *into* whatever game you're playing—even if the software doesn't support voice communications. Use the Hotkeys option under Settings to configure which keys you need to press to speak during your game. For example, you might press the F5 key to send the message, "Another victory for me!" when you score a simulated kill.

You can also set the system to have a threshold for the microphone input—anything over this threshold is automatically transmitted to the other BattleCom participants.

BattleCom is a great piece of software that makes gameplay much more personal. The program uses very little bandwidth and works well with your existing software. In fact, BattleCom is so good that it will be included as a future feature of DirectX.

Note

What is DirectX?

DirectX is an abstract graphics, sound, and controller layer developed by Microsoft that programmers can use to write games. By writing games for DirectX, the programmer doesn't need to know anything about the user's hardware—the game takes advantage of anything on the system that is recognized by the DirectX system. BattleCom will be included in an upcoming release of DirectX—this means that if you have Windows, a microphone, and speakers you'll immediately be able to use BattleCom without installing additional software.

Roger Wilco

Mpath Interactive, Inc.: www.rogerwilco.com

Registration Cost: Free

An alternative to the BattleCom software is a free program called Roger Wilco. Roger Wilco is another voice communications system that allows you to interact with other players while you're gaming. The software is even simpler than BattleCom, but does not offer as many options for controlling the levels and quality of sound. Luckily, this isn't much of a detraction from the software, because it offers excellent sound quality as-is. Additionally, Roger Wilco is available for Macintosh users—offering gamers the chance to have cross-platform verbal battles!

As you can see in Figure 17.11, Roger Wilco has a rather utilitarian interface. The Channel tab lets you create new channels for your friends to join, or enables you to enter existing channels. You can use the Kick button to forcibly remove people from a channel you are hosting, or the Leave button to exit a channel and join another.

The other tabs on the Roger Wilco screen are for adjusting the way the program works from within your game. The Transmit tab lets you pick how you will transmit messages—via pressing a hotkey, or voice-activated mode. Adjust enables you to set your speaker level and microphone input level. There is a wizard located under this tab to help you if you have any problems with your sound settings.

Figure 17.11

Roger Wilco offers many of the features of BattleCom, but with none of the price!

After you've installed Roger Wilco, be sure to check out the available free add-ons that are offered on their Web site. One of the add-ons, for example, let's you talk with people who are viewing the same Web site as you while you surf the Web. Pretty neat stuff, huh?

These utilities can greatly enhance your gaming experience by letting you find and communicate with other gamers far easier and faster than in the past.

The future for gaming is quite secure as long as companies continue to create innovative applications that bring people together. Since these utilities are popular, the cracks for these programs are also popular. Don't be drawn in by the thought of saving $20. Support these companies and other programmers as much as you can—they're building a better world for gamers.

The Least You Need to Know

➤ Finding online games is one of the most difficult things to do if you're a connected gamer. Kali and GameSpy simplify the search experience by locating servers and allowing you to connect from a straightforward interface.

➤ Once you've developed a gaming group, you'll want to be able to contact them quickly when they log on to the Internet. ICQ and AIM provide instant messaging services and let you organize games with ease.

➤ If you'd like to talk to your friends (and enemies) directly, Roger Wilco and BattleCom offer walkie-talkie like communications if you have a microphone and speakers.

➤ Gaming utilities often are offered as shareware applications with a very low fee. To encourage further development of the Internet gaming community, be sure to support the developers of the software you choose to run.

The Future of Online Gaming

In This Chapter

➤ Demographic Shifts

➤ Offline Versus Online

➤ Media Marvels and Bandwidth

Online gaming is here to stay. But will it be simply a small niche, or is it the wave of the future? It's unlikely that single-player games will vanish, because they fill a variety of needs. But one need—wanting to play when you can find another person to play—is no longer relevant. The online world now has thousands of players, ready to engage you, compete with you, and challenge you.

The future of online gaming is a rich one, as the children of today's gamers grow up in an online world. We'll see virtual worlds in the not-too-distant future which seem like the stuff of science fiction.

Demographic Shifts

We're in the middle of a huge, generational demographic shift. The baby boom of the '50s and '60s had an enormous impact on society and societal trends. The upcoming *baby boom echo*, a.k.a. Generation Y, is poised to do much the same. (It's also an unfortunate truth that Generation X is sandwiched between the two). Generation Y is even bigger than the baby boom, and is a mix of kids of Gen X'ers and the late-blooming baby boomers finally having children.

Generation Y will be more computer savvy, more media aware, and more technology oriented than any generation in history. It will be a digital generation in many ways.

I can see it here, in a very personal way, in my two daughters. My oldest daughter is nine years old, and is quite comfortable with computers. She has no problems with installing game titles, dealing with arcane dialog boxes and other necessities of living with a PC. While she does play CD-ROM based games, I often see her logged on to sites like ZoogDisney and the Nickelodeon site playing Java or Shockwave games. I asked her once why she liked the rather simplistic games offered on those sites. "Because it's so easy."

She didn't mean easy to play. Rather, all she had to do was run the Web browser, go to the site, and play. There was no installation process, no CD-ROM to search for, and less opportunity for system crashes. We're lucky in that we have a fairly high-speed DSL connection, so bandwidth isn't a large issue. (In other words, our connection is plenty fast.) But watching her gives me a little bit of insight into online gaming's future. You can also see it in the popularity of the card games, which has a completely different demographic, consisting of older people. Like the kids, the older generation appreciates the ease of play. While card games are also a comfortable and familiar metaphor for that generation, the fact is you only need to have a recent browser. Even a $500 PC can play those titles credibly.

But it's the next generation that will define the future of online gaming. And my prediction is that it will split. There will be a large component who want to play games that are easy—that is, have modest system requirements and only need a browser. Then there will be the hard-core, and for those players, there's no limit. The level of realism in the graphics and the depth of gameplay will only increase over time. Already, Verant has announced a massively multiplayer game based on the *Star Wars* universe that will likely dwarf Everquest in technology and scale. Imagine a hundred worlds like Everquest, all different...

Offline Versus Online

Every now and then, you see various pundits talk about the death of single-player games. After all, with lots of bandwidth and human opponents, why would anyone want to play single-player games any more?

Those people haven't seen the huge numbers of people playing solitaire online.

Single-player games have a role above and beyond providing training for multiplayer games. Take the Tomb Raider series, for example. The designers were asked on more than one occasion why there wasn't a multiplayer component. But Tomb Raider is a *story driven* game that follows a single character. I suppose you could have a death-match between multiple Lara Crofts, but that would be rather silly. It's the story that drives Tomb Raider, and stories are often linear. If a game designer wants to tell a carefully crafted story, about the best multiplayer experience they can offer is some form of co-op play. Even then, that won't be viable in all types of stories.

Single-player games are great when you can't find someone to play your game. Wargames are a good example of this. Most turn-based wargames are two-player affairs, and often very personal. Playing against the computer opponent through the campaign can be quite satisfying.

It is true, however, that most games in the future will have some type of multiplayer or online component. In fact, an excellent precursor to the future of both online and offline gaming is Bioware's *Neverwinter Nights*. Set in the world of Advanced Dungeons and Dragons™, Neverwinter Nights, shown in Figure A.1, tells a story that allows up to six players to participate in. But the engine can support up to 64 players, and there will be tools to allow players to create and gamemaster their own stories. Bioware envisions hundreds of game servers, running either the story that ships with the game or user-created stories. There's even the potential for a competitive element, where several parties may be trying to reach the same goals.

Figure A.1

Neverwinter Nights represents one future for online gaming.

Bandwidth and the Blurring of Media

Over the next decade or so, the amount of bandwidth available to the average American home will skyrocket. Not only will users have high-speed Internet connections, but the advent of HDTV (high-definition television) will allow for two different high-speed data pipes into the home.

HDTV is a digital medium with limited interactive capability. It's unlikely you'll see high-performance, 3D-accelerated virtual reality games on an HDTV. But imagine being able to actually participate in Jeopardy or Who Wants to Be a Millionaire?

287

On the gaming side, the emergence of both high-performance consoles and serious PC horsepower, coupled with high-speed net connections, means a much higher level of interactivity, with voice and video communication becoming part of the mix.

It's even likely that games and other types of media will blur together. Imagine watching a TV show, which then launches a game. As thousands of users play it, the show producers might be watching the outcome of the games being played, and design the plot around that. Now *that's* interactivity!

Cheaters: How to Spot and Avoid Them

In This Chapter

➤ The Symptoms

➤ What You Can Do

➤ It's Not Cheating If...

The Symptoms

You're playing a hot and heavy session of Mechwarrior 3. As you play, you notice something odd: One player always seems to be winning fights—and no one has been able to kill his mech! It's as if...as if his mech is invincible.

Maybe it is. You might have found a cheater.

Cheaters in online games take a variety of forms, some subtle and some blatant. The invulnerable mech is a pretty blatant and well-known cheat, but there are more subtle cheats, too. For example, there's the player that plays on his own server. In some cases, this can't be helped—not everyone has multiple computers. But perhaps he could just as easily log on to another server. Playing on your own server, particularly in a First-Person Shooter, gives you a slight edge in reaction time.

The most opportunities for cheating comes with games that weren't designed to catch cheaters, or games that don't have a strong server side to the game. For example, when Diablo first emerged, there was a rash of cheaters who would actually edit their character files and create *munchkin* (all-powerful) characters. This is reduced in other similar games, by client-side file encryption and checksums to make sure that the data sent by the player's computers isn't something not usually possible in the game.

Note that not all seemingly implausible behavior is cheating. For example, in Quake 3: Arena, you can do some very exotic things with key bindings. So, when you see someone jump into the air, spin, and fire impossibly fast, they may have a single key bound to that action. If you want to compete at that level, you need to learn about specific game capabilities, such as key binding.

What You Can Do

If you're playing on a casual, user-managed server, there's not a lot you can do if someone is cheating. However, if you're playing a massively multiplayer game, you should report any potential cheating incidents.

Take Everquest, for example. A clever programmer can write a program that sends keyboard and mouse messages to the game. This allows, for example, automated behavior. In Everquest, these "trainers" allow repetitive action to occur, so that you don't need to be present. Not all of it is necessarily bad, but if you see something truly odd, you should report it to the game publisher.

This is really critical in a massively multiplayer game, where you may be shelling out a subscription fee. One bad apple can create an unpleasant situation for all players. After the word spreads, a company might find itself with a roomful of game servers and no subscriptions. So they want to hear about cheaters.

And whatever you do, don't you cheat.

It's Not Cheating If...

Note that clever game behavior can often be interpreted as cheating.

Take camping, for example. In a First-Person Shooter, *camping* usually means hanging around a valuable spawn point (say, where the big keg o' health respawns in Unreal Tournament) and shooting anyone who approaches that point. If you can hang around in shadows and be harder to spot, so much the better.

Is it cheating? Not really, although it's not always fair. However, on large games, campers usually pay a pretty stiff price after they're spotted.

We talked earlier about key bindings, which is another example of simply exploiting a game feature. In Mechwarrior 3, you can design your own mech, and there are some interesting features that allow you to design a mech that delivers a devastating amount of damage with very little heat generated.

A well-designed game will let you minimize this kind of behavior. Mechwarrior 3, for example, has an option that lets a player select only standard designs. Similarly, the Baldur's Gate role-playing game lets online players bring their own characters. But the game host has the option of restricting objects and experience points that are brought along.

In the end, cheating is a fairly serious problem that detracts from most people's gameplay. If you run across it in a subscription game, you should definitely report it. If you see it in a multiplayer game such as Warcraft II, simply find a different server. There's just not enough time to play good games as it is, much less having to deal with munchkins.

Gaming Related Magazines Worth Reading

> **In This Chapter**
>
> ➤ Hard Copy Publications
>
> ➤ Online Magazines

Gaming publications come in two forms: hard copy and online. Online publications generally offer more timely news, but print publications are more portable and have deeper analysis of individual titles or the industry.

Hard Copy Publications

Despite the timeliness of the Web, print magazines still have a place. It's tough to read a Web browser when lounging by the pool or riding a train. And there's a visceral pleasure in simply curling up on a couch with a good read. Here's a rundown of the top game mags. Many boast an online presence as well.

Computer Gaming World

This is the granddaddy of all computer gaming magazines. It has evolved over time, and is somewhat edgier now, but the goal is the same: to bring good reviews, previews, and strategy tips to gamers everywhere. CGW covers the range of gaming activities, from online to single-player, and has a pretty good hardware section. Best of all, as one of the most popular and reputable magazines, you can find it at almost any newsstand. You can find its online version at www.computergaming.com.

PC Gamer

Computer Gaming World's archrival is *PC Gamer*. It began as a brash upstart, but has matured over the years into a solid publication. Its strength has been its preview coverage and extensive interviews and industry coverage.

PC Gamer has a somewhat more irreverent style, but the reviews are often spotty and inconsistent. However, its interviews with industry insiders are often superb and thorough. Find it online at www.pcgamer.com.

Computer Games

The magazine formerly known as *Strategy Plus* had hit on some lean years, but new owners and a new editor-in-chief (Denny Atkin, formerly of CGW) have worked wonders, turning the once-moribund publication into a serious contender. As in prior years, preview coverage is good, and the hardware section is getting better all the time.

Web Magazines

Web-based magazines can be much more timely with reviews and previews, than print magazines, but the downside is that they are often wrong. There's also a tendency to call a series of screenshots a preview. Still, if you want timely news and information on PC gaming, then there are some very good Webzines out there.

ZDNet's Gamespot (www.gamespot.com)

Gamespot is strong on coverage of the industry, has good previews, and often has playable demos ahead of the competition. Still, its game reviews are sometimes a little spotty, possibly because the authors are often working to very tight deadlines, especially for hot titles. Gamespot overall has a strong affinity with game players and a loyal following. Gamespot also tries hard to get readers involved, allowing readers to post or rebut game reviews right on the reviews page.

CNet's Gamecenter (www.gamecenter.com)

Gamecenter is the online publication that tries harder. However, many of the previews feel rushed, and the pub sometimes tries too hard. Still, someone needs to be a gadfly in this industry where often shoddy practices go unquestioned.

Daily Radar (www.dailyradar.com)

Imagination Publishing has consolidated its various gaming Web sites for its print publication into a single clean, edgy, online publication. Like its print counterparts, Daily Radar is often brash and too quick off the mark, but it's rarely dull. Still, you may find yourself disagreeing more than agreeing with some of their observations.

VoodooExtreme (www.voodooextreme.com)

VoodooExtreme began life as a fan site for a particular brand of 3D hardware, but the focus has evolved to 3D and other types of gaming. VE, as it's fondly called, has a distinctly Gen-X feel to it, and the personalities of the editors often shine through. It specializes in scouring the Net for other sources of news and directing readers there, acting more as a gaming news portal than a source of original content.

Gone Gold (www.gonegold.com)

Gone Gold is a labor of love by former New York City policeman Rich LaPorte and a terrific supporting cast of volunteer editors. This is the site to hit if you want information on what games have shipped, are about to ship, or their shipping dates. The highlight, though, is Rich's daily columns on his gaming experiences and his take on the gaming scene as a veteran gamer.

Inside Macintosh Gaming (www.insidemacgames.com/)

This is the publication for Mac gamers. It has up-to-date news on Macintosh games, and even covers PC games as they might relate to Mac gamers. It's superbly laid out, written, and designed.

Women Gamers (www.womengamers.com)

This is gaming news told from the perspective of the majority of the human race. Often witty, occasionally dark, the writing is generally high caliber and the content is thought provoking. Drop by if you want to learn about how women really feel about Lara Croft. But make sure to bring an open mind.

Macs in the Online Gaming World

In This Chapter

➤ Popular Games

➤ Massive Blues

➤ Browser-based Games

➤ The Impact of the iMac

Apple's Macintosh has a long history in gaming, sometimes despite Apple's own efforts. The first Macs even eschewed game ports due to Steve Jobs's insistence that serious computers don't need games. However, games rapidly began appearing on the Mac, including early breakthrough titles like Maze Wars and Glider.

Popular Games

The Apple Macintosh is easy to use, easy to set up, and offers increasingly better performance. This is certainly true for the G4-based systems, which rival (or even surpass) higher clock-rate Intel compatible systems in certain applications that make use of the G4 CPU's Altivec instruction set. In general, though, the Macintosh lags behind PCs in game performance, particularly 3D game performance. Part of this discrepancy is due to the lack of high performance 3D accelerators for the Macintosh, though that is changing quickly. But part of it is due to the Windows game developers who use the advanced 3DNOW! and SSE instructions available on AMD and Intel processors, respectively. When those games are ported to the Mac, not enough time is paid to performance tuning.

A more serious issue for dedicated Mac gamers is the fact that the hottest PC games either never get ported to the Mac, or they are ported much later. This is particularly ironic since some of the first network playable games ever shipped on personal computers were shipped on the Mac first (Maze Wars, anyone?). There are bright spots on the horizon, though. The Mac version of Unreal Tournament shipped nearly at the same time as the PC version. And game developers Blizzard and Bungie both try to ship Macintosh products at roughly the same time as the PC version. (In fact, Bungie started out as a Mac-only game developer.)

However, there are some good, current titles available for the Mac. Bungie's Myth and Myth 2, both superb real-time tactical combat games set in a fantasy world, are quite popular on both PC and the Mac. In fact, Bungie has done an excellent job of designing the game so that players who use Bungie.net, Bungie's matchmaking service, can play together without knowing which computer they're on. The same is true for Blizzard.net, Blizzard's own matchmaking service. Warcraft II and Diablo players can play together whatever the platform. Quake III: Arena was simultaneously developed for Macintosh, PC, and Linux.

Some recent, hot PC games have been ported as well, including Unreal Tournament and Falcon 4.0.

However, other popular gaming portals such as Mplayer and the Zone don't cater to the needs of Macintosh gamers. Surprisingly though, Microsoft has catered to Mac gamers on occasion, with the latest being the Mac edition of Age of Empires.

Massive Blues

One glaring downside for Macintosh gamers is the inability to play the popular massively multiplayer titles. Games like EverQuest, Asheron's Call, Allegience, Ultima Online, and 10Six all lack Macintosh versions. I know of a number of Macintosh adherents who have reluctantly bought PCs only to play these games. Unfortunately, with the possible exception of Ultima Online, emulators and CPU cards don't work well with the 3D accelerated titles.

Browser-based Games

The good news is that browser-based games play no favorites. If you have a Web browser capable of handling Java applets and running Shockwave, then you're in luck. You can fully participate in online card games and any other browser-based title.

While the browser-based games today are fairly simplistic, that will change over time. Companies like Metacreations, with the Metastream streaming 3D technology, simply need a browser and an OpenGL compatible graphics card. As bandwidth increases, the game companies themselves are seriously looking at Java-enabled games using advanced Web technologies to deliver serious gaming content over the Web. While the bleeding edge of gaming will still be CD- or DVD-based, Web gaming will evolve in the next several years to something more sophisticated than card and board games. And that's good news for *all* users.

The Impact of the iMac

Apple's compact, all-in-one iMac has been a huge hit, particularly among teenagers. With a good processor, modest 3D capabilities, and decent audio, the iMac makes an excellent system for Web gaming.

More importantly, it is very much an information appliance that has penetrated a generation of new users. Most particularly, the iMac has been extremely popular among young girls. Several game companies that cater to girls are actively investigating how to take advantage of this demographic phenomenon. Although it's not terribly high powered, it does raise the bar for the lowest common denominator, and that may prove to be the iMac's lasting legacy.

Index

309